(S)electing the President

Selecting political leaders by popular election is an unquestioned hall-mark of representative democracies—the institutional manifestation of Lincoln's promise of a government of the people and by the people. But in 2016, Lincoln's promise seems to have given way to Hamilton's nightmare—with his worries that popular elections would produce dema-gogues who paid an "obsequious court to the people," appealing to their passions and prejudices rather than to their reason. This book examines the commitment to the widest level of participation among the largest number of citizens in the selection of the president. It looks at two sali-ent characteristics of our current presidential election environment that bring the wisdom of this commitment into question: the declining influ-ence of political parties and the communication revolution in the forms of the internet, social media, and cable television. Ultimately, Mezey asks whether our now fully democratized presidential selection process has in fact diminished the quality of our presidential candidates and the cam-paigns they run, whether the turn to demagoguery that the Founders feared has materialized, what the consequences of our presidential selec-tion process have been for American government, and whether or not it would be valuable to rethink our wholehearted commitment to popular election of the president. His answers do not topple our commitment to popular elections but rather point the way toward improving the quality of both participation and democracy.

Michael L. Mezey is Professor Emeritus of Political Science at DePaul Uni-versity. He earned his B.A. from the The City College of New York, and his M.A. and Ph.D. from Syracuse University. He served on the faculties of the University of Virginia and the University of Hawaii before joining DePaul University in 1977 as chair of the Political Science Department. From 1993 through 2005, Dr. Mezey served as Dean of DePaul's College of Liberal Arts and Sciences. He is the author of four books: *Comparative Legislatures* (Duke University Press, 1979), *Congress, the President, and Public Policy* (Westview Press, 1989), *Representative Democracy: Legis-lators and their Constituents* (Rowman and Littlefield, 2008), and *Presi-dentialism: Power in Comparative Perspective* (Lynne Rienner, 2013).

(S)electing the President
The Perils of Democracy

Michael L. Mezey

Routledge
Taylor & Francis Group

NEW YORK AND LONDON

First published 2018
by Routledge
711 Third Avenue, New York, NY 10017

and by Routledge
2 Park Square, Milton Park, Abingdon, Oxon, OX14 4RN

*Routledge is an imprint of the Taylor & Francis Group, an
informa business*

© 2018 Taylor & Francis

Library of Congress Cataloging-in-Publication Data
A catalog record for this book has been requested.

ISBN: 978-1-138-21225-1 (hbk)
ISBN: 978-1-138-21226-8 (pbk)
ISBN: 978-1-315-45085-8 (ebk)

Typeset in Sabon
by Apex CoVantage, LLC

Contents

Preface

I developed the proposal for this book in January 2016, a few weeks before the Iowa caucuses. Like most political observers, I was fascinated and often appalled by Donald Trump's candidacy for the Republican Party's presidential nomination and convinced that his campaign would at some point collapse. And on the off chance that he was nominated, I thought that it was impossible for him to win the general election. As I write these words, however, the country is in week three of Donald Trump's presidency, so make of that what you will.

Even though I did not think that Trump would win, his candidacy, as well as Bernie Sanders' insurgent challenge to Hillary Clinton, interested me for what it said about the process by which we in democratic republics select our political leaders. Although popular election of our political leaders is now a given in the United States, it was not always so. The Founders worried about the techniques that candidates would need to adopt in order to get elected and about the quality of the candidates who would be selected. In response, they designed a political system that they hoped would minimize the role of the voters in deciding who would govern them. They especially wished to remove the selection of the president from the people.

But things have changed. Now, not only do the people elect the president, but they also determine who the nominees of the major political parties will be through a chaotic process of caucuses, primaries, and debates stretching over a nearly two-year period. This democratized process coexists with a democratized media environment, featuring multiple sources of news and information, some more reliable than others, and all competing for viewers and, in the case of the internet, clicks. Through social media platforms such as Twitter and Facebook, candidates are able to make direct contact with the voters, bypassing mediating institutions such as newspapers, broadcast news sources, or political parties.

Other political scientists are certain to provide excellent blow-by-blow data-filled accounts of the 2016 presidential election, as will many journalists. That is not my goal. Rather, the message of this book is that a democratized selection process and a democratized media environment has opened the door to exactly the type of presidential candidates about whom the Founders worried the most. Donald Trump's ascension to the presidency is the major case in point, but his victory was foreshadowed by earlier presidents and presidential candidates. In this sense, Trump's victory may not be, as many observers have suggested, a one-off occurrence arising from a unique political environment and a unique candidate, but a new normal for presidential elections and the types of candidates who participate in them.

I first considered the question of presidential selection and how it affected presidencies in my 2013 book *Presidentialism*. In that volume, I looked at popularly elected presidencies around the world, and, among other topics, how they tended to justify their expansive view of their own power by referring to their democratic legitimacy. I am grateful to my publisher, Lynne Rienner, for permission to include some of the materials from that book in this discussion.

I have some other people to thank for their support as this project has gone forward. Although I am retired from DePaul University and no longer reside in Chicago, Valerie Johnson, the chair of the Political Science Department, and Wilma Kwit, the department's administrative assistant, printed and mailed hard copies of various drafts of the manuscript. Jennifer Schwartz in DePaul's library arranged for me to have borrowing privileges at American University, here in Washington, DC, and the staff at that library were helpful to me as well. Jennifer Knerr at Routledge arranged for my book proposal, as well as the final draft, to be assessed by outside reviewers, read and commented on a draft, and in her typically expeditious manner, handled all the administrative work necessary to bring this book out. I am also grateful to Sarah Binder, Alan Gitelson, Sandy Maisel, Thomas Mann, and James Thurber for their helpful comments on the book proposal and the manuscript itself. As always, all errors of omission, commission, and interpretation are mine.

I no longer have the opportunity to discuss politics with my friends and colleagues at DePaul except via emails, and this perhaps is the greatest loss of my decision to retire. But I am in nearly constant dialogue with my wife Susan, a gifted political scientist, about the political events going on around us, and her insights are apparent at various points in the manuscript. I also have benefitted from several panel discussions at the Brookings Institute and the American Enterprise Institute.

As always, I am grateful to Susan not just for her political acumen but for her love and companionship. Our children Jennifer and Jason, their spouses, and our five truly remarkable grandchildren—Rebecca, Norah, Paul, Benjamin, and Daniel—are the joys of my life, even sufficient on most days to dispel the gloom that contemporary American politics more than occasionally generates.

Michael L. Mezey
Friendship Heights, Maryland

1 Candidate Quality and the Presidential Election of 2016

The 2016 presidential election was unlike any that this nation has seen. The Republican Party, with a field of nearly twenty presidential aspirants to choose from, nominated Donald Trump, a real estate tycoon and reality television personality with no political or governmental experience and with little to no knowledge about, or even interest in, the particulars of domestic and international affairs. In addition, as recently as 2009, he was a registered Democrat; two years later, he switched his registration to Independent and a year later re-registered as a Republican. Given this somewhat checkered history, it was not surprising that several of his stated policy positions substantially deviated from Republican Party orthodoxy. In addition, he ran a campaign that was characterized by racism, misogyny, xenophobia, and personal insults directed at his opponents for the nomination, at the Democratic candidates vying for their party's nomination, at members of the media, at leading members of his own party, and at anyone else who criticized him. And in the final weeks of the general election campaign, tape recordings of conversations emerged in which, using the most crude language, he seemed to boast of his ability to make unwelcome sexual advances on women. In the following days, several women who had been his victims appeared to confirm these stories.

In a normal election, any one of Trump's outrageous statements or actions would have been disqualifying, and the demise of his candidacy was regularly predicted by journalists and other political commentators. But in Trump's case, his apostasies seemed to have no effect on the allegiance of his supporters, and in some instances, it seemed that the more extreme his comments, the more support he generated. Although some members of his party indicated from the outset that they could never support him and others parted ways with him after the tape recorded conversations became public, most Republican leaders and candidates ultimately indicated that they would be voting for him, albeit with various qualifiers designed to distance themselves from Trump's more heinous statements and actions. And even though many voters who identified themselves as Republicans told pollsters that they worried that Trump had neither the qualifications nor the temperament to be president, most voted for him in November 2016. These voters, combined with a plurality of independents and some Democrats, proved to be sufficient for Trump to win the majority of the electoral votes, although his Democratic opponent received nearly three million more popular votes.

The contest for the Democratic nomination, although relatively tame by the standards set by the Republican Party, had strange moments as well. Ultimately, the party selected Hillary Clinton, making her the first woman to be nominated for president by a major political party. Clinton was a seasoned politician who had a demonstrated mastery of public policy, which was gained through eight years as an active First Lady during her husband's presidency, another eight years as a member of the Senate, and four years as secretary of state. Despite these obvious qualifications, she experienced a long and hard-fought nomination contest against an opponent, Vermont Senator Bernie Sanders, who had variously identified himself as an Independent and as a democratic socialist, but never before his presidential candidacy as a Democrat. Sanders had a long career in Congress—sixteen years as a member of the House and ten years as a member of the Senate—but no one in either of those bodies would refer to him as a productive colleague with a strong legislative record. Nonetheless, Sanders' fiery commitment to a progressive policy agenda, including free college education for all, generated a great deal of support among younger people, and his fervent opposition to international trade treaties gained him supporters among blue collar workers who felt that these agreements had a history of costing them jobs. Sanders depicted Clinton as the ultimate insider in an economic and political system that he claimed was controlled by the rich and rigged against ordinary Americans.

After Clinton prevailed in the nomination contest, most of Sanders' supporters came around to supporting her, but without much enthusiasm, and more because of their contempt for Donald Trump than their affection for Clinton. Throughout the campaign, Clinton was dogged by criticisms of the way she had handled sensitive information while secretary of state, by allegations of improper conflicts between her family's charity operation and her responsibilities at the State Department, by some embarrassing emails hacked from the account of her campaign director, and by a perception that she could not be trusted, that her policy statements were driven by electoral considerations rather than political convictions. In July 2016, the director of the FBI had seemed to put the issue of her handling of classified information to rest when he announced that the agency's investigation had concluded that, although Clinton had been careless in the way she handled this information, she had not committed an indictable offense. But in the final days of the general election campaign, the director reopened the investigation, announcing that a trove of emails had been discovered on her assistant's computer. Then, three days before the election, he announced that a review of these emails did not warrant any change in his original position that she should not be charged with a crime. Nonetheless, all this occurred in the middle of the early voting period, and the story gained traction among a large number of voters, many of whom had developed an unflattering image of Clinton and her husband in part because of their actions and in part because of more than two decades of relentless attacks on them by Republicans and their allies. Added to this was the not unexpected sexism that Clinton encountered as the first woman who had a real shot at winning the presidency.

When the nomination process concluded, both major party candidates were viewed unfavorably by the majority of the electorate. Nothing occurred during the general election campaign to change these views. The campaigns were characterized by high levels of vocal anger from the candidates and their followers and more than a few occasions of actual violence. Trump spoke in apocalyptic tones about the state of the nation and the dire consequences for the country if he lost the election. He even implied that violence might ensue if he lost, and that if he did lose, it would have had to be the result of cheating on the part of the Democrats. During the second presidential debate, he said that if he was elected, he would order his Attorney General to pursue criminal charges against Clinton, and at his rallies, the crowd, with the candidate acting as cheer leader, chanted "lock her up." Although Clinton did not use the same inflammatory language, she frequently characterized Trump as unstable and dangerous for the country and emphasized at every turn his comments demeaning women, Latinos, Muslims, and the disabled.

In the weeks prior to the election, virtually all the forecasting models and available polling data predicted a Clinton victory. The national polls were not far off in terms of the popular vote, where she did in fact prevail by about a 2% margin. But Trump won a majority of the electoral votes by scoring narrow pluralities in Pennsylvania, Michigan, and Wisconsin, states that had reliably voted Democrat in the recent past. In the end, the election reflected the high level of polarization between the two political parties, with exit polls indicating that 90% of Republicans voted for Trump and 89% of Democrats for Clinton. When questioned, about one-quarter of these partisan voters said that they were casting their ballots against the other party's candidate rather than for their party's candidate. Those voters who said that they were politically independent split their votes, with Trump winning 48%, Clinton winning 42%, and the remainder voting for minor party candidates. In total, 12% of the people who voted for Clinton said that they had an unfavorable opinion of her, and 20% of those who voted for Trump said that they had an unfavorable opinion of him.[1]

It is easy to view the presidential election of 2016 as *sui generis*— a one-off event resulting from a unique presidential candidacy on the

Republican side, a much criticized presumptive nominee on the Democratic side, and a political culture poisoned by eight years of relentless hostility toward President Obama by the Republican opposition, particularly the most conservative wing of the party that had come to dominate its congressional delegation. Added to this was a growing sense of economic insecurity, particularly among less educated voters, many of whom believed that their jobs had been put at risk, and in many cases lost, because of the rapid technological changes overtaking American industry, the forces of globalization that had moved so many businesses overseas, and the large number of immigrants, many undocumented, who were coming into the country. Finally, the combination of an African American president, a woman running to succeed him, the increasingly diversifying American population, the Supreme Court's decision legitimizing gay marriage, and a spike in violent confrontations between black citizens and the police appeared to stimulate cultural insecurities among a portion of the population, particularly less educated white males. Some of these people worried that their vision of America and its culture was being undermined by the advances and demands of women and people of color, by rapidly evolving norms on gay and transgender rights, and by increasing immigration from Latin American, African, and Muslim countries. For these people, Trump's promise to "make America great again" meant rejecting these economic and cultural changes and returning to an era when immigrants came from Europe and therefore looked the way "real Americans" looked, marriage was between a man and a woman, and people did not demand special treatment based on their gender, race, ethnicity, or sexual orientation.

There will be many scholarly and journalistic books published on the 2016 presidential election, and they can be depended upon to provide a comprehensive analysis of what happened and why. The thesis of this book is that this presidential campaign represented the culmination and combination of two larger, long-term phenomena: the democratization of the presidential selection process—particularly the changes in the party nomination procedures that began after 1968—and the communication revolution that began in the second half of the 20th century and continues unabated today. The first change turned the presidency, an office that the Founders had envisioned as insulated from the influence of the American people with no mandate other than to pursue the public interest, into a purely democratic office, with party nominees selected by the people, the president selected by popular vote, and a continuing and intimate connection between the president and the people during his term in office.

The latter change saw the rise of radio and then television as the primary vehicle for popular entertainment as well as political communication between voters and candidates. This was followed in the last quarter of the 20th century by the dramatic expansion in the number of television channels that took place with the arrival of cable and then by the birth of the internet as a source of information and entertainment for voters and as a way for citizens to communicate with each other. These changes in communication were also a manifestation of democratization. Rather than news being controlled by a few network executives and newspaper editors, information can now be broadly disseminated by anyone with an internet connection. Multiple cable channels provide room for broadcasts aimed at niche audiences with particular entertainment and political interests. Just as people living in a democracy can choose whom they wish to place in office, they can now choose among multiple sources for what they want to watch and hear. And the democratic freedom to influence the views and votes of ones fellow citizens, previously restricted to those with access to established media, is now available to anyone with a blog, web site, Twitter account, or Facebook page.

It is difficult to argue against more democracy. The idea of government by the people is firmly entrenched in the minds of not just Americans but of individuals around the world, and an assertion that "the people should decide" stops most conversations. But moving the responsibility to select the president directly to the citizens places a heavy bet on the rationality and civic competence of the American voter, a bet that generations of political thinkers have warned was risky and probably unwise. These risks have been confirmed by decades of empirical research demonstrating how little most citizens know about politics, public policy, and the processes of government. Given this data, it is clear that the democratization of the media and the presidential selection process have opened the door to candidates who in the past would not ordinarily have been considered for the presidency and invited a mode of campaigning for the office that seems to privilege entertainment over policy, image over competence, and rhetoric over action. And, as 2016 so painfully demonstrated, these changes have lowered the level of political discourse and reduced the likelihood that a person of quality and competence would succeed to the office.

Obviously, this critique raises some serious questions about representative democracy and the electoral process. In Chapter 2, I will explore the meaning of democracy both in its pure form, one in which citizens decide public policy questions directly, and in its more modern form, in which citizens elect representatives who make public policy decisions. Direct democracy has always had its critics, some arguing against any role for average citizens in government while others argue that direct democracy is not practical in a modern nation-state and that in any event, representative systems provide a satisfactory safeguard against the dangers of direct citizen involvement. Elections, which are at the procedural heart of a representative democracy, have also been criticized from a number of perspectives. Some have argued that they provide citizens with too much influence on their political leaders, others that they are symbolic exercises that make no difference to political leaders, and still others that citizens are as ill-equipped to choose competent leaders as they are to choose among competing policy alternatives. There is also a cultural dimension to democracy that privileges equality over elitism and that has the potential, fully on display in 2016, to de-emphasize expertise and experience as requirements for both public office and media commentary.

The men who wrote the Constitution of the United States of America were well aware of the problems and promises of pure as well as representative democracy, and in many respects, they foresaw the spectacle of 2016. As we will see in Chapter 3, they had harsh words for the very concept of democracy, and they took great pains to insulate their new political system from the influence of voters. This was especially the case for the presidential selection process. They had little faith in the political intelligence of their fellow citizens, and because of that, they feared for the quality of presidents that a democratic selection process would produce. A broad electorate, they believed, would be vulnerable to demagogues who appealed to the passions of the voters rather than to their reason. Elections would invite disorder and corruption as candidates did whatever they thought necessary to win popular support. And, it is well to remember that they voiced these concerns at a time when the electorate was restricted to a small number of white, male, property holders and nothing remotely like our modern communication system existed or could even be envisioned. Their concerns are simply magnified in our contemporary environment of nearly universal suffrage and a world of instant unregulated communication among people across the nation as well as around the globe.

The Founders also worried about the rise of political parties, or factions as they called them, because they thought that such groups would pursue the narrow self-interest of those who formed them at the expense of the public good. They also thought that a faction that appealed to the class interests of those with fewer resources would always prevail over a faction based on the interests of elites like themselves. Nonetheless, political parties arose soon after the ratification of the new constitution, parties based on both regional economic interests and philosophical differences among elites about the role of the national government and the rights of the states. But for our purpose, the most crucial role that the new parties played was modifying the presidential selection process, first by removing the role of the Electoral College as an independent decision-maker and second by providing an institutional means to identify and nominate candidates for office. In Chapter 4, we will discuss the role parties played in deciding who the candidates would be and how that role was altered, especially during the last half of the 20th century, to the point where today, ordinary citizens have as much say about who the nominees will be as the party leadership itself. This has meant a decline in the party's ability to vet the credentials and qualifications of prospective candidates, a change that can have adverse consequences for candidates and, ultimately, presidential quality.

Chapter 5 provides a full discussion of the current wide-open system by which the nominees of the two major political parties are selected. Today, it is a nearly fully democratized process and therefore vulnerable to a number of criticisms. Several issues are discussed: the grueling nature of the new nomination process, the types of candidates it favors, the factors that determine who emerges with the nomination, the pivotal role of the media, and the capacity of the new system to produce candidates who are capable of being president as well as capable of winning the nomination of their parties. It is here that we will talk specifically about the factors that led to Donald Trump's emergence as the Republican Party's presidential nominee and that allowed Bernie Sanders to persevere until the last moment in his ultimately failed quest for the Democratic Party's nomination.

Chapter 6 discusses the democratization of the mass media that accompanied the democratization of the presidential nomination process. From 1948, when the television networks first broadcast the national conventions of the two parties, to the present, the nomination process has evolved into an increasingly intimate partnership between the media and the candidates. Television has used the nomination process as a way to attract viewers by turning the enterprise into a drama that emphasizes personalities, scandals, and the horse race rather than any differences among the candidates in terms of policy positions or ability. Candidates, in turn, have used the media as a way to circumvent the leaders of their parties and go directly to voters, particularly the most ideological voters in the primaries, in their quest for the nomination. Although more citizens are aware of the different candidates for their party's nomination, it is not at all clear that more citizens are knowledgeable about the competence and capabilities of the candidates. Along the way, the distinction between politics and entertainment has become increasingly vague. Television almost inevitably emphasizes style over substance, rhetoric over ability, scandals over integrity, and short-term events over long-term considerations. And the proliferation of media sources with the advent of cable television, the further eclipse of newspapers, and the rise of the internet and social media has meant that political gatekeepers who used to provide some level of quality control for the news no longer exist. In the fully democratized media world, facts often take a secondary position to opinions. For many, a blog post of dubious provenance about climate change has the same authority as a peer-reviewed scientific study, and a 140-character tweet has the same impact as a 1000-word analysis by a seasoned political reporter. And the "likes" that friends post on their Facebook page or the fake news stories that they forward may have more influence on their political opinions and voting decisions than a careful study of the candidates and their records.

In Chapter 7, we discuss the ways in which the combination of a democratized nomination process and a democratized media environment can encourage a particular type of presidential candidate and campaign. Distinguishing among terms such as charisma, demagoguery, populism, and celebrity, the discussion will make the point that each of these styles fits well with the open and democratized system of presidential selection under which we now operate. Each of these styles can also have a deleterious effect on the political system, with some more dangerous than others. In the case of Donald Trump, we find an amalgamation of these styles culminating in the least qualified major party presidential candidate, and now president, in history. Trump represents the worst nightmare of those who wrote the Constitution of the United States of America and the philosophers upon whose insights they based so many of their decisions. Although it may turn out that 2016 is a unique election that will not be repeated, the argument of this book is that there is no reason to expect that the next presidential race will be any different from this one, in terms of how the nomination is contested and the capabilities of the candidates ultimately selected.

The changes in the presidential selection process have taken place in the context of an increasingly "presidentialized" political system. By that I mean, first, that over the course of American history, the presidency has been transformed from a relatively constrained office with limited power to the dominant office in the land, equipped with a wide array of unilateral powers. Second, citizens focus most of their political attention on the presidency; many vote only in presidential elections, and for a large number of citizens, the president is the only public official they can name. For almost two years, the presidential selection process dominates the news media. Even before the general election votes were cast in November 2016, there was speculation about which Republican would emerge as the party's 2020 nominee, assuming Trump lost. With Trump's victory, that speculation shifted to the Democrats. Not three weeks after the election, *The Washington Post* ran a column assessing the likely Democratic candidates for 2020.[2] This high level of public visibility, combined with the heroic narratives that have described our past presidents and the augmented powers that the president now possesses, have inflated the public's expectations for what a president can accomplish well beyond the president's capacity to meet these expectations. The very nature of the campaign for office required by the new environment encourages candidates to over promise what they can deliver and emphasize their own singular abilities to govern, an emphasis at odds with the collective decision-making process dictated by our constitutional arrangement of separate institutions sharing power. When a successful candidate's campaign claim of virtual omnipotence collides with the reality of actually governing, two things can happen. The first is that people will become even more disappointed with and alienated from their government institutions. Having been promised the world by the winning candidate and then receiving a good deal less, they will come to the conclusion that their votes do not matter and that the system as a whole is rigged against them. The result can be widespread alienation from the political system. The second possible outcome (not necessarily incompatible with the first) is that the president, so frustrated by an inability to deliver on his promises, will turn to unilateral and arguably extra-constitutional actions to achieve policy goals. Claiming that he has been chosen by the people, he or she will justify such actions in democratic terms, arguing that he is simply responding to the will of the people who elected him. In this scenario, foreseen by Plato and Hamilton, democratization can lead to tyranny and despotism. These are the themes that we will seek to develop in Chapter 8.

Finally, in Chapter 9 we will ask what, if anything, can be done. Obviously, it is too late to rethink the idea of elections; eliminating elections to solve the problems that they create would be viewed by most as a case where the cure is worse than the disease. But can the inherent tension between democratic selection and presidential quality be reduced? Can the current problems of our presidential selection process be remedied? Can the role that the political parties played in vetting presidential candidates be restored without compromising the democratic legitimacy of the selection process? Can the atomized media environment be convinced to take the selection of the president more seriously than they take the need for viewers, ratings, and clicks? Can our presidential candidates be convinced to speak realistically to voters, explaining the impediments that our constitutional system places in the way of unilateral presidential power during the campaign? Or, does our current situation support the predictions of democracy's critics, from Plato to the Founders—that as political systems become more democratized, the possibility of good government and good leaders declines?

Notes

1 American Enterprise Political Report, "Assessing the 2016 Candidates." 12:10, November, 2016.
2 Chris Cillizza, "Early Leads in '20 Race, But No Clear Democratic Heir." *The Washington Post*, 11/28/16.

2 Democracy, Representation, and Elections

Democracy is a nearly universal aspiration woven into the rhetoric and culture of people and nations around the world. A recent World Values Survey of the thirty-four most populous countries, including many which would not ordinarily be classified as democratic, found that huge majorities of citizens said that it was important to them that they live in a democracy.[1] Here in the United States, the speeches of our public officials, as well as the everyday conversations of our citizens, are filled with references to our democratic heritage, to self-government, to the will of the people, and even to our goal of fostering democracy around the world. Although it contains several distinctly undemocratic features, our Constitution nonetheless begins with the phrase, "We the people." The Declaration of Independence, the nation's other founding document, articulates the central characteristics of democracy in its first paragraph: all men are created equal, they enjoy the right to liberty, their rights are not bestowed upon them by their rulers but by virtue of their humanity, and the right of leaders to govern is based on popular consent. Democracy even permeates the micro politics of our personal and communal lives—the Parent–Teacher Association, the Student Government Association, the neighborhood bridge club—where phrases such as "let's vote on that" or "the majority rules" are regularly heard. Today, although many Americans believe that their country falls short of its democratic aspirations, few question the legitimacy of those aspirations or their centrality to the nation's political history.

Democracies and Republics

A literal definition of democracy begins with the Greek words from which the term is derived—*demos*, referring to the people, and *kratos*, referring to political power. Democracy means that the people hold political power, and democracies are characterized by "popular sovereignty"; that is, the people have the final say about the policies that govern their lives. There are two ways the people can exercise their power to govern: they can do so directly, by voting on the laws that will govern them, or indirectly, by electing representatives who vote on laws. The latter arrangement is commonly referred to either as a republican form of government or as a representative democracy.

Both democracies and republics share a commitment to individual liberty and equality. Procedurally, this means that both systems require a citizenry that is free to engage in political discussion and action, such as advocating for one policy position or another, and voting either for their policy preferences in the case of direct democracy, or for those who will make those policy decisions in the case of republics. In terms of equality, it means that each vote, whether for a policy alternative or for a candidate for office, counts the same, and every citizen is eligible to participate in the political realm, as a voter, as an advocate, and/or as a candidate. Democracies and republics also share a commitment to democratic legitimacy, which means that if a decision is taken by the people or by their representatives, it is legitimate on its face.

In direct democracies, epitomized by the New England town meeting or the Athenian city-state, citizens gather together, consider policy alternatives, and choose among them by majority vote. But direct democracy, with very limited exceptions, does not exist in the modern nation-state. Rather, those nations that we usually classify as democracies are really republics, political systems in which citizens affect political decisions indirectly by electing and influencing the behavior of the government officials who actually make public policy and control its implementation.

Some republics have elements of direct democracy in the forms of referenda and initiatives. A referendum asks citizens to vote either yes or no on a policy question. These exercises usually require the agreement of the legislature and/or the executive before they can be put before voters, and in many cases, the referendum results are advisory to elected officials rather than binding. Some American states also have provisions for citizen-inspired initiatives that can be placed on the ballot without the consent of government officials by gathering a certain number of signatures from voters. But initiatives and referenda are relatively rare; in nearly all cases, public policy is determined by elected government officials and the bureaucrats whom they supervise.

Democracy is not just about procedures; it also has a cultural dimension. Tocqueville observed that the democratic commitment to equality permeated American society and had the potential to devalue merit and sometimes demonize assertions of cultural superiority or high-mindedness. He noted "a depraved taste for equality, which impels the weak to attempt to lower the powerful to their own level" and argued that a "middling standard is fixed in America for human knowledge."[2] Plato made the same point, observing that equality could mean that all opinions must be honored on an equal basis, thus putting truth and falsehood on equal footing.[3] This strain of anti-intellectualism and marginalization of merit has been a recurrent theme in American history. Tocqueville would recognize it today in populist attacks on intellectual elites, the denial of scientific facts by those who find them to be politically or economically inconvenient, the success of candidates whose primary virtue is their ability to connect with the common man, and a media environment in which every voice and view can gain credibility, no matter how uninformed or detached from reality it might be.

Direct Democracy and Its Critics

The most obvious reason why direct democracy gave way to republican government is its impracticality in a modern nation-state. All the citizens of a small New England town can assemble to debate policy options and decide by majority rule which one is preferable. But it would not be possible for all citizens of a modern nation-state to assemble, discuss, and decide among competing policy options. Committed democrats might reply that referenda avoid the problem of physically assembling citizens, and technology has the potential to eliminate it entirely. Imagine all citizens sitting at a computer participating in a giant electronic chat room to discuss policy options and then clicking on a box to cast their vote for one policy alternative or another. But even if technology could solve the problem of assembling citizens, skeptics question the extent to which the discussion that took place would be of sufficient quality to enable an informed assessment of the various policy alternatives.

Democracy, such skeptics would argue, assumes not just popular participation but, more importantly, an informed and politically competent citizenry able to make wise choices. There has always been ample reason to question this assumption. Plato, presaging modern empirical findings about the policy knowledge of voters, believed that citizens were incapable of making good public policy decisions because they knew so little, and had no desire to educate themselves, about the great issues of the day. He concluded that this lack of citizen information was the major reason why democratic systems would fail. Some people, he argued, are more intelligent and more moral than others. If one wanted good government, those people ought to govern; this position led him to a discussion of rule by philosopher-kings. If citizens ruled, poor public policy would result; worse yet, the decisions of ill-informed citizens would be vulnerable to manipulation by demagogues who appealed to their emotions and prejudices and who sought power for their own aggrandizement. Democracy could then be a precursor to despotism.

In Plato's time, citizenship was the privilege of the few, but in modern societies, all have the title of "citizen," no matter what their station in society might be. Today's citizens, even more so than the limited citizenry of which Plato spoke, are consumed with the challenges and joys of their everyday life, pay little attention to politics and government, know very little about public policy, and often have difficulty identifying their political leaders and the issues with which they are grappling. As Walter Lippman put it, citizens "are not equipped to deal with so much subtlety, so much variety, so many permutations and combinations."[4] This is especially the case in our contemporary world, where governments legislate on a wide variety of matters, and each policy area requires decision makers to obtain and understand detailed information if they are to choose wisely among competing alternatives. Understanding a nation's system for delivering health care to its citizens is an infinitely more complicated task than assessing the need for a new school in a small town. Deciding among competing plans for revising health care requires a great deal more information than deciding who will build the new school and where it will be located. On such local matters, citizens may be well equipped to make decisions, but in the case of complex public policy issues, citizens are unlikely to have the time, the interest, or the education to gather the necessary information, to understand the costs and benefits of the various alternatives, and to choose wisely among them. This would especially be the case if the policy domain under consideration was not one that citizens thought would affect them in some direct way, as compared, for example, with the siting of a new school in their community.

The other question that arises is what factors would influence the policy decisions of citizens in an environment in which they had relatively little information. Would their choices be manipulated by those who spoke the loudest and played to their emotions? Would their vote be guided only by their self-interest, or would they consider the public interest as they decided? Would they be willing to vote, let us say, to pay higher taxes in order to support the less fortunate members of the society, or would they look first and foremost to their own economic interests? The referenda and plebiscites that have been used in republics are not particularly encouraging on these points; often, these exercises have been less an expression of the considered view of the population, and more the product of media manipulation, the financial resources that interested parties pour into these campaigns, and the hyperbolic claims that advocates make on behalf of their preferred outcome.

One example of the defects of these episodes of direct democracy is provided by the June 2016 referendum in which the citizens of Great Britain decided by a very narrow margin to leave the European Union (EU). Although there were undoubtedly many voters who had well thought out and informed positions on the EU, it was also the case that many others—likely a majority of those who participated—had little or no understanding of the issue itself. Some decided to cast a protest vote based on general discomfort with the governing Conservative Party, and still others were moved by xenophobic attacks on immigrants whose presence the leaders of the leave movement attributed to EU membership. It also seemed clear that a portion of the electorate had no understanding of what the EU was and what the specific connections were between their lives and the governing structures and actions of the EU. It was reported that in the hours following the vote, the number of Google searches for "what is the EU" and "what is Brexit" (the term used by the press for a decision to leave the EU) spiked.[5] Leaving the EU may or may not have been a wise decision for Great Britain, but for those who worry about direct democracy, the vote demonstrated all the problems with turning complex policy decisions over to a mass vote. In addition to information deficiencies, many voters were moved by emotional and hyperbolic appeals from elements of the "leave" group concerning the alleged corrosive impact of immigration. The "remain" group engaged in its own hyperbole, prophesizing the almost immediate collapse of the nation's economy if the leave side prevailed. As one political scientist put it in a general discussion of referenda, "a vote that is supposed to be about an important public issue ends up instead being about the popularity or unpopularity of a particular party or leader, the record of the government, or some set of issues or events that are not related to the subject of the referendum."[6]

The critique then of direct democracy is aimed at the fundamental assumption of popular rule—an informed citizenry. Direct democracy cannot work if one has a population with too little information, too little interest in or ability to become better informed, few avenues for rational discussion that would allow people to form or re-form their opinions, and vulnerable to having their opinions manipulated through hyperbole, demagoguery, or their attitudes toward the advocates of the proposal rather than the proposal itself.

Republican systems offer themselves as an institutional response to these concerns about popular decision-making. Rather than citizens making policy decisions, they vote for representatives who are empowered to make decisions on their behalf. These representatives are likely to be more educated than the average citizen, and because they devote their time and efforts to public service, they will be able to deal with the subtlety and variety about which Lippman wrote and, therefore, more likely than the electorate at large to make wise policy decisions. In the case of the Brexit decision, although views on the issue in the British House of Commons were divided, it seemed clear that there was majority support for remaining and a greater understanding of the implications of the decision among Members of Parliament on both sides of the issue than among the people at large.

The practical argument for representative government then is one of division of labor. Just as it makes sense that the work necessary to complete a complex task should be divided among different people, each with the skills to understand and master his or her part of the project, it makes just as much sense for a small number of citizens to take responsibility for learning about and deciding among policy alternatives. The republican argument is that those to whom policymaking responsibilities are assigned will be more likely to rely on reason and information rather than emotion, and out of their deliberations, a decision more closely reflecting the national interest will emerge. And even though citizens themselves are not directly involved in the decision-making process, popular sovereignty is preserved because those who are involved are elected for this task and are accountable to the citizenry for their decisions when the next election comes around.

Republican Government and Its Critics

Elections are at the procedural heart of republics. Although conducting an election is not the sole requirement for classifying a nation as a representative democracy, a nation that does not conduct regular elections cannot be so designated. In republics, elections legitimize the right of office holders to govern. Advocates of republican government argue that elections link citizens with their leaders, provide opportunities for voters to express their views on public policy issues, and ensure that elected leaders will be responsive to these views. Elections are also instruments for holding government leaders accountable for their actions. When citizens are displeased with the state of the nation or with the policies that their leaders are pursuing, elections provide them with an opportunity to remove incumbents from office and select new leaders in whom they have greater faith. Election campaigns are occasions for citizens to take the measure of prospective candidates, assess their character as well as their policy positions, and then, by popular vote, empower the winning candidate to govern.

One venerable critique of representative government is that elections do not in fact deliver on the promise of popular sovereignty. Karl Marx suggested that as long as all candidates subscribed to essentially the same economic paradigm, elections were simply occasions when "the oppressed are allowed once every few years to decide which particular representatives of the oppressing class are to represent and repress them."[7] From this perspective, elections are held primarily for symbolic reasons; they give citizens the impression that they are in control of their politicians when they really are not, and no matter what the election results are, public policy remains essentially unchanged. In this sense, elections serve as little more than a safety valve—an opportunity for those with grievances to blow off steam without threatening the basic structure of the state. They provide political leaders with a democratic fig leaf, allowing them to say that the election means that they are acting with the consent of the people. Elections also provide those in power with a defense to use against those who are aggrieved by the policies in force; they are told that they have only themselves to blame for bad public policy because, after all, they voted for these leaders, or they chose not to vote, thereby enabling the leaders and the policies that they condemn.

This idea that the results of elections do not really make any difference has been articulated in the United States by those who have argued that the two major political parties are essentially a duopoly that constitutes a political establishment bound to maintain the power of existing political and economic elites. From this perspective, it doesn't matter whether a Democratic or Republican candidate wins; the essentials of public policy remain unchanged. Candidates of both parties, it is argued, depend on campaign contributions from rich donors and lobbyists for established economic interests, and this nexus between money and elections will determine the policy decisions that will be made, no matter who is elected. Thus, American elections at all levels have been characterized by some as choices between the lesser of two evils, or in a frequently stated meme, a choice between "tweedle dum and tweedle dumber." In 1964, Barry Goldwater, the Republican candidate for president, presented himself as providing voters with "a choice rather than an echo" of the Democratic Party's position. In 1968, George Wallace ran for president, asserting that "there ain't a dimes worth of difference" between the Democratic and Republican Parties. In 2016, Ted Cruz, Donald Trump, and Bernie Sanders argued that the political leadership of both parties had lost contact with the American people, that the system was rigged to benefit the status quo no matter which party wins, and that the conventional choices offered by the two parties would not produce the real changes that, in their view, citizens wanted.

Some more serious political thinkers have made the point that the apparatus of elections and representative institutions are poor substitutes for real democracy. Rousseau famously argued that the entire notion of representation was at odds with democracy, because the general will of the people cannot be represented by someone else, but has to be expressed by the people themselves. He advocated for constant attention to public affairs by citizens and suggested that once citizens abdicated that responsibility, freedom disappeared.[8] The sociologist Robert Michels observed that all organizations inevitably become oligarchical as leaders drift away from, and become less responsive to, their followers.[9] Applied to representative institutions, this means that a gap between the views and interests of elected officials and those who elect them is inevitable, and as politicians spend more time in office, that gap gets wider. Political scientists have found empirical support for this position, concluding that with certain exceptions, there is a relatively poor fit between the attitudes of citizens and the actions of their representatives.

The philosopher Hannah Arendt[10] concluded that "representative government has become oligarchic government. . . . once more the people are not admitted to the public realm, once more the business of government has become the privilege of the few." Echoing this theme, the political theorist Benjamin Barber[11] has written that reliance on elections and the representatives that they produce is a form of "thin democracy" that reduces citizens to mere political spectators whose only role in the process of self-government is the episodic casting of votes. As the political scientist Nadia Urbinati put it in her treatise on representation, "a government that relies only on electoral participation resembles an authorized oligarchy."[12] In such an arrangement, the people, in effect, are told that once they have voted, they have fully discharged their duties as citizens, that politics and government are no longer their business, and that their opinions have no meaningful role in shaping public policy.

Republics and Their Defenders

Defenders of republics argue that in the modern world, the alternative to representative democracy is not direct democracy, but rather the more authoritarian leaders that representative institutions were designed to resist. Among their virtues, republics are characterized by legislatures that are capable of restraining the authoritarian tendencies of executives, tendencies that they may exhibit both in attempts to unilaterally control public policy and to restrain the political and personal liberties of citizens. The political theorist Machiavelli argued for a powerful "prince" in whose hands the right to govern would be concentrated. The idea of the modern republic originated in the notion that such a "prince" needed to be tamed and his absolute power checked, if liberty was to be preserved. Independent legislative institutions, along with independent judiciaries, were the instruments for imposing such restraints. The French political thinker Montesquieu wrote about the dangers of concentrating power in the hands of the executive. Liberty, he said, is preserved in a political system characterized by "moderation" in its leaders, and moderation can be achieved only through limitations and constraints placed on executive power. Such a political system requires the rule of law and a limited government whose various components would have an egalitarian, rather than a hierarchical, relationship with each other. The best constitution, for this purpose, is a system of interlocking and mutually checking interests and powers.[13]

In addition to their capacity to check executive power, legislatures are arenas for the open debate of public policy issues. Although these debates can be occasions for sharp rhetorical conflict, defenders of republics argue that democratic politics is always messy, and that it is better to have conflicting views on public display rather than suppressing them in the name of order and forced consensus. They also argue that better public policy will emerge from an open discussion of competing views and that, at a minimum, the decisions taken will be accepted as legitimate by those who lose the debate because they had the freedom to articulate their views. Elections are valuable, even though they may not guarantee congruence between public opinion and parliamentary decisions or produce the best policy decisions. As Urbinati puts it, the elections that representative democracies engage in are "in the service of political liberty" since they presume and claim "the equal right and opportunity citizens have to participate in the formation of the majority view with their individual votes and opinions." Elections make "inclusion and control by the included" possible.[14] Holding regular elections can also contribute to political stability by conferring a degree of legitimacy on the political system. Although such legitimacy may maintain the power of existing elites, stability itself has virtues for citizens, compared with the disorder and violence that often plagues political systems that are viewed as illegitimate.

The Problem with Elections

In contrast to the view that republican systems marginalize citizens, others claim that they give too much power and place too much faith in the people, and because of that do not, as their advocates suggest, produce wiser leaders and more informed public policy outcomes. If the argument against direct democracy is that citizens do not have the interest or intellectual wherewithal to make wise decisions with regard to public policy, critics of republican government ask why we should assume that citizens have the ability to make wise choices when they select their representatives? If citizens make poor choices when they cast their votes, are representative systems really much of an improvement over direct democracy? One response to that critique is that choosing among various candidates for office is a less challenging task than choosing among various policy alternatives. Rather than studying complex policy issues, in order to choose among candidates, the voter must simply identify the policy positions of the candidates and assess the proximity of those positions to his own. In addition, (or instead) the voter may try to evaluate the personal qualities of the candidate, such as his or her moral character or trustworthiness, or the candidate's ability to understand citizens and empathize with their concerns. Although this task involves a certain degree of complexity and requires some commitment of time, it is a more manageable undertaking for the average citizen who generally devotes relatively little of his or her time or attention to the political arena.

The problem with this rationale for elections is that it tends to ignore a number of factors that influence voting decisions. First, it assumes that voters have positions on major policy issues that they can try to match with the views of the candidates. But modern survey research in the United States has consistently demonstrated that many citizens "do not have meaningful beliefs, even on issues that have formed the basis for intense political controversy among elites for substantial periods of time."[15]

Citizens are also poorly informed, a condition that has shown no signs of abating, even though we have had rising education levels for decades.[16]

It can be argued that because potential voters have no reason to believe that their vote will make a difference, they have no incentive to inform themselves about the candidates or their positions. In such instances, a voter may make the rational decision to abstain from voting, or she may decide to ignore facts and cast a vote that simply makes her feel better, attracted perhaps by the image or the personality of a candidate rather than by the candidate's experience or policy positions.[17] Frank Luntz, a leading American pollster, argues that "Americans, by and large, decide who to vote for based on the candidates' attributes—personality, image, authenticity, vibe."[18] One recent discussion has even taken this view to its logical platonic extreme, criticizing the principle that citizens have a responsibility to vote, even if they have no information, and recommending limiting the franchise and political power to those who are knowledgeable. Democratic principles may be sacrificed, but policies that promote the general welfare are enabled.[19]

This perspective slights the fact that citizens may have clear and often well-reasoned positions on relatively straightforward, binary issues— abortion rights, same sex marriage, and gun control, for example. And because candidates may also have fairly clear positions on these issues, voters, if they wish, can successfully compare their views with the views of candidates. Citizens may also have informed positions on issues that affect them directly. Farmers will have a keen understanding of agricultural price support policies, and coal miners will understand the personal consequences of efforts to reduce the nation's dependence on fossil fuels. But on most of the more complex issues, such as trade, defense policy, health care, and public spending, the views of individual voters are less clear, less informed, and often contradictory. American voters, for example, have often voiced support for a limited role for the national government and lower taxes, while simultaneously supporting (and often advocating the expansion of) most of the programs that the national government pursues.[20] On issues like these, candidates often develop complex and arcane policy proposals that few read, while publicly retreating to general platitudes or abstract philosophical principles, such as lower taxes, or living within our means, or compassionate conservatism, or the need for a strong military, or a defense of the skill and productivity of the American worker.

At best, voters bring to their decisions a sense of how well government and their leaders are performing. From this perspective, citizens cast their votes retrospectively, changing leaders and their political parties when they think that the country is on the wrong track or when they are dissatisfied with some significant initiative pursued by the incumbent. But these decisions often have little to do with specific public policies, or even with the candidates themselves. Rather, they are a response to the political environment. And even more important, such retrospective decisions are usually myopic, focusing on the short term rather than the long term.

As Achen and Bartels observe, a voter's sense of how well the economy is growing and therefore, how well the incumbent president is performing, is more likely to be influenced by income growth in the months immediately prior to an election than by the performance of the economy over a president's full term in office. There is also evidence that voters punish incumbents for events that are beyond their control, even natural disasters such as floods or droughts. This sort of "blind retrospection" follows from an environment in which voters are generally ignorant of whether and how the actions of their leaders' affect their own welfare, or alternatively wish to vent their anger and frustration about events that they cannot understand and the president may not be able to control.[21]

If understanding a candidate's position on the issues or the level of his responsibility for the state of the nation is difficult, it may be equally difficult to assess the personal qualities of candidates. Modern campaigns spend a great deal of money on efforts to market their candidate to voters with media ads and public appearances that are designed to present the candidate in the most attractive way. And they spend perhaps more money attacking the character and qualities of their opponents, defining them in the most extreme and most negative manner. Voters, of course, have no personal contact with the candidates, so their opinions are influenced by these marketing efforts as well as by short snippets of the candidate's speeches and statements that they may read about in the newspaper or on their Twitter feed or see on television. Given the proven ability of advertising to create demand for a variety of consumer products, many of dubious necessity or quality, it is not difficult to appreciate their capacity for creating a warm and empathic image for a candidate who may be characterized by neither of these virtues, or, on the other hand, producing an image of a candidate that makes him or her evil personified. And just as advertising can sell a product that does not actually do what it claims to do by emphasizing packaging, it can sell a candidate who may have little in the way of qualifications by education, experience, or competence for the position that he is seeking.

Finally, in order to gain votes, candidates may appeal to the emotions of voters. To some extent, this is understandable. Winning the support of the people requires skills that are different from the skills necessary to govern. Voters want to "connect" on a personal level with their leaders, and if the candidate is able to invoke themes or experiences from their personal histories that touch the emotions of the voter, that connection is facilitated. Ronald Reagan drew upon the skills that he developed as an actor to form a bond with voters, many of whom did not share his policy positions. Bill Clinton had a remarkable capacity to project empathy and understanding to diverse audiences. But the darker side to this appears when aspiring or incumbent leaders rely on the tools of emotional manipulation to the exclusion of appeals to reason and experience in order to gain public support.

The risks of unqualified office holders and candidates are endemic to a system that depends on popular selection of its political leaders. In *The Republic*, Plato noted that the two hallmarks of democracy—freedom and equality—each had dangers for the political system. If freedom was interpreted as people doing whatever they wanted to do, the result would be anarchy. And if equality led to the belief that every citizen has the same ability to rule, all sorts of power-seeking individuals would enter the political arena, including not just those without the intellectual capacity to govern, but also people motivated simply by personal gain and a lust for power, rather than a passion for the public good. The vulnerability of democracies to anarchy as well as demagoguery, either of which could lead to tyranny, was, in Plato's view, a fatal flaw of democracy as he understood it.

These are the problems with elections for those who are skeptical of them, not because they are imperfect substitutes for true democracy, but rather because they suffer from the same problems as democracy. The entire project of representative democracy is built on the concept of an interested, informed, and politically active electorate conveying their views on public policy to elected officials who have strong incentives to be responsive to these views. But if citizens bring the same lack of information to the voting booth that they typically bring to a discussion of public policy alternatives, their voting decisions will be manipulated by designing politicians and the marketers they hire. Just as the democratic critics of representative systems argue, in effect, they will be ceding political decision-making to these leaders and will even further marginalize the notion of popular sovereignty. More worrisome will be the vulnerability of citizens to those who offer simple solutions to complex problems and excel at persuading voters through rhetoric and personality rather than their qualifications or experience or specific public policy positions.

Mediating Between Citizens and the State

Democratic theory presumes a direct relationship between the people and those who govern them, and that is the reason why the informational deficits of so many voters are such a threat to the viability of the democratic project. But such a perspective ignores the role that other institutions can play as mediators between citizens and the state. Political parties, interest groups, and mass media can facilitate the interaction between citizens and their political leaders and at least in theory, ameliorate some of the problems associated with an uninformed and inactive electorate.

Political parties, for example, can identify and simplify policy options for voters. If parties are characterized by established and coherent ideologies, they can provide an intellectual shortcut for citizens who identify with the party's philosophical beliefs and are willing to leave the details to the officeholders. Then, a vote for a particular candidate is not necessarily a vote for that person as much as it is a vote for the party that he represents. Rather than voting on the basis of issues or specific policy alternatives, the decisions of voters are heavily motivated by a psychological commitment to the ideology, policies, and history of a political party—what political scientists call party identification.

In the United States, a large percentage of the American voting public either identifies with one of the two major political parties or habitually votes for one of the parties, even while verbally maintaining their independence. In the late 20th century and the beginning of the 21st, these party allegiances appear to have hardened to the point where those who identify with a party vote for that party's presidential candidate (and often the party's congressional candidates) regardless of how they assess the qualities and qualifications of the candidate. And while at one time, there was some overlap between the views and policy positions of the two major parties, in recent years the parties have become more ideologically distinct. Perhaps as a result of this, we have also witnessed the emergence of what has been called negative partisanship, a condition of extreme partisanship where citizens vote for their party's candidate not so much out of affection, but because of their contempt for the opposition party.[22]

No matter what the basis for party identification might be, decades of research has demonstrated that it remains the strongest explanatory factor for citizens' voting decisions. If that is the case, parties and their leaders have a responsibility to provide a level of quality control for candidates for higher office, weeding out the incompetent, the inexperienced, the amoral, and the demagogue, so that voters will have a choice among vetted and qualified candidates rather than relying solely on the impressions gained from the efforts of the candidates and those who market them. For much of American history, the parties have proved to be relatively effective institutions for selecting candidates for the presidency. Even though the quality of presidential candidates has varied and less qualified candidates have sometimes prevailed over more qualified ones, no party conferred its nomination on a person demonstrably unqualified for the position.

But beginning in the last part of the 20th century, party organizations began to lose control over their presidential nomination processes. Rather than its leaders and office holders determining the party's nominee for president, the party now simply organizes a wide-open process of primaries and caucuses and serves as a sort of referee, while candidates for the nomination establish their own campaign organization and fight it out with each other. So while American political parties now serve as an ideological reference point for many voters, they no longer serve the function of candidate quality control. The result in 2016 was the designation of a demonstrably unqualified and potentially dangerous person as the Republican Party's presidential nominee.

Interest groups are another mediating institution between citizens the state. In this role, interest groups can serve a number of functio For example, they can amplify the voice of the individual. One worker in a steel plant may have little influence on a politician, but as members of the United Steel Workers union, workers have a great deal of influence on what political leaders do. An individual who believes that the planet is in danger from global warming may have few ways to advance that cause, but as a member of the Sierra Club, her cause can be more powerfully advocated. And an individual gun owner, worried that proposed legislation might infringe upon what he believes to be his Second Amendment rights, can find a voice for his concerns when he joins with others who have the same concerns in the National Rifle Association.

Interest groups, like political parties, can serve as reference points for individual citizens. They can provide short cuts to political information for their members or for people who have the same concerns but aren't members. Such groups and their leaders can identify candidates who share their views and then announce their support for those candidates. They can organize letter writing campaigns to influence the decisions of representatives, pay for television ads to support or oppose particular candidates, and organize voter turnout operations on behalf of preferred candidates.

But it is not clear that in performing this mediating role, the interest group system is conducive to public policies that pursue the national interest. The social scientists who first articulated the idea of interest groups as a central and saving mechanism for democratic politics argued that all citizens were represented in some group or other, or at least had the potential for such representation. Their argument was that the public policy that emerged from conflicts and negotiations among these interest groups would reflect the public interest. This view has been roundly criticized by others who maintain that the interest group system is biased in favor of established interests, does little to represent the interests of those with little in the way of economic resources, and ultimately protects the status quo from the forces of change. Rather than public policy in pursuit of the public interest, the system produces policies that satisfy and protect the interests of the most powerful groups but may do little to solve problems. And, of course, the groups that have the most influence on representatives and the policy outcomes that they pursue are those with access to large amounts of cash that they use to lobby legislators and bureaucrats to influence elections. This shuts out unorganized interests, such as poor people or groups with few financial resources. So rather than acting as a saving grace for representative democracy, the argument goes, the interest group system provides support for the critique that elections have no impact on the basic economic and political structures of the nation.[23]

The contemporary *mass media* environment has created multiple opportunities and techniques for direct contact between the people and

:s. This has proven to be something of a mixed bag
:presentative democracy. On the one hand, there is
ion and more political discourse available and acces-
ı ever before. Citizens have many more opportunities
ly aware. But as we shall see in Chapter 6, although
ɔrmation has gone up, the quality has not increased
ts, has degraded.

The other concern is that the new media environment increases the
vulnerability of the system to candidates who play to the emotions and
prejudices of voters. Rather than mediating between the people and
their politicians, portions of the new media provide a direct connection
between citizens and those who seek to lead them. The candidates best
able to exploit this connection have been referred to variously as charis-
matics, populists, demagogues, and, more recently, as celebrities. These
terms are quite distinct, but they share something in common. They all
refer to the ability of a candidate to gather the support of voters based
not on the policy positions that he is advocating or his experience or
fitness for office, but on his ability to evoke a personal bond with those
whom he is proposing to lead. The decline of the party's control over its
nomination process and the rise of the electronic mass media has meant
that these qualities are much more important today to the presidential
selection process than they were in the past. It also means that the presidency is open to a much wider array of candidates, many of whom would
not (and should not) have been considered viable or qualified under our
previous, party controlled process.

Conclusion

The idea of democracy is contested terrain for political theorists as well
as political practitioners. On the one hand, the principle of popular sovereignty and the right of the people to decide their own destiny through
their voices and their votes is by now a universally accepted ideal. On the
other, there has always been well-founded skepticism about the capacity
of citizens to make wise decisions about the policies under which they
will live. Republics seek a middle ground by removing policy decisions
from the hands of the people and placing the power to govern in the
hands of representatives elected by the people.

Such an arrangement has been criticized by advocates of pure democracy who argue that representative systems do not deliver on the promise of popular sovereignty, that elections are imperfect instruments for
reflecting the views of the people, and that the ability of citizens to
control the actions of their elected representatives is at best tenuous.
From their perspective, either the people govern or they don't; there is
no middle ground. But republics do not completely satisfy the concerns
of democratic skeptics who argue that citizens are no more capable of
making wise choices about who their elected officials will be than they

are capable of choosing wise public policies. Because citizens have so little information about government and politics, their electoral choices are vulnerable to manipulation by those who market candidates and by demagogues who appeal to the emotions of the voters rather than to their reason. Although political parties and interest groups may have the potential to inform and empower citizens and to enhance the likelihood of better leaders and good public policy, they do not always succeed in doing this. Their efforts are, to some extent, undermined by the new mass media that allows candidates for office to circumvent these institutions and establish a direct connection with the people.

The cultural and political forces unleashed by changes in the mass media combined with the eroding influence of other mediating institutions has the potential to fulfill the platonic prophecy that democracy, even in its indirect republican form, will ultimately yield to demagoguery and despotism. The men who wrote the Constitution of the United States shared Plato's concerns, even in an era with a much more restricted view of democracy and, of course, nothing like the modern media. Those concerns are reflected in the document that they wrote, one that limited the franchise to a small percentage of the citizens, only allowed them to vote for the House of Representatives, and provided the people with little to no role in selecting the president.

Notes

1 Christopher H. Achen and Larry M. Bartels, *Democracy for Realists: Why Elections Do Not Produce Responsive Government* (Princeton: Princeton University Press, 2016), 4–5.
2 Alexis De Tocqueville, *Democracy in America* (New York: The Modern Library, 1981), 44–5.
3 David Lay Williams, "Shadow Boxing and Pizzerias: Plato's Cave and Fake News." *Washington Post*, December 13, 2016.
4 Walter Lippman, *Public Opinion* (New York: Penguin, 1946), 16.
5 Barry Fung, "The British Are Frantically Googling What the EU Is, Hours After Voting to Leave It." *Washington Post*, June 24, 2016.
6 Lawrence LeDuc, "Referendums and Deliberative Democracy." *Electoral Studies* 38 (2015), 141. See also Amanda Taub and Max Fisher, "Why Referendums Aren't As Democratic as They Seem." *New York Times*, October 4, 2016.
7 In V. I. Lenin, *The State and Revolution*. https://www.marxists.org/ebooks/lenin/state-and-revolution.pdf, 51
8 J. J. Rousseau, *The Social Contract* (New York: Penguin, 1968), 140–1.
9 Robert Michels, *Political Parties: A Sociological Study of the Oligarchical Tendencies of Modern Democracy* (New York: Simon and Schuster, 1968).
10 Hannah Arendt, *On Revolution* (New York: Viking Press, 1965), 240.
11 Benjamin R. Barber, *Strong Democracy: Participatory Politics for a New Age* (Berkeley: University of California Press, 1984).
12 Nadia Urbinati, *Representative Democracy: Principles and Genealogy* (Chicago: University of Chicago Press, 2006), 15.
13 See Judith N. Shklar, *Montesquieu* (New York: Oxford University Press, 1987); Harvey G. Mansfield, Jr. *Taming the Prince: The Ambivalence of Modern Executive Power* (Baltimore: Johns Hopkins University Press, 1993).

14 Nadia Urbinati, *Democracy Disfigured* (Cambridge: Harvard University Press, 2014).
15 Philip E. Converse, "The Nature of Belief Systems in Mass Publics." In David Apter, ed. *Ideology and Discontents* (Glencoe, IL: Free Press, 1964), 245. Also see Achen and Bartels, *Democracy for Realists*, chapter 2.
16 Ilya Somin, *Democracy and Political Ignorance* (Stanford: Stanford University Press, 2013).
17 Bryan Caplan, *The Myth of the Rational Voter: Why Democracies Choose Bad Policies* (Princeton: Princeton University Press, 2007).
18 In Kenneth T. Walsh, *Celebrity in Chief: A History of the Presidents and the Culture of Stardom* (Boulder, CO: Paradigm Publishers, 2015), 8.
19 Jason Brennan, *Against Democracy* (Princeton: Princeton University Press, 2016).
20 Joel Aberbach, *Understanding Contemporary American Conservatism* (New York: Routledge, 2017), chapter 4.
21 Achen and Bartels, *Democracy for Realists*, 16, 143.
22 Alan I. Abramowitz and Steven Webster, "The Rise of Negative Partisanship and the Nationalization of US Elections in the 21st Century." *Electoral Studies* 41 (2016): 12–22.
23 See David Truman, *The Governmental Process* (New York: Alfred Knopf, 1951); E.E. Schattschneider, *The Semisovereign People* (New York: Holt Reinhart, 1960); Theodore J. Lowi, *The End of Liberalism: The Second Republic of the United States*. 2nd Edition (New York: W.W. Norton, 1979).

3 The Founders and Presidential Selection

The attitudes of the men who wrote the Constitution of the United States toward democracy in either its pure or republican form ranged from skeptical to hostile.[1] Elbridge Gerry, a delegate to the Constitutional Convention from Massachusetts, asserted that "the evils we experience flow from an excess of democracy."[2] John Adams wrote that "democracy never lasts long. It soon wastes, exhausts, and murders itself. There never was a democracy yet that did not commit suicide."[3] Roger Sherman, a convention delegate from Connecticut, said that the people "should have as little to do as may be about the government. They want information and are constantly liable to be misled."[4] And in the first *Federalist Paper*, Alexander Hamilton warned that "of those men who have overturned the liberties of republics, the greatest number have begun their career by paying an obsequious court to the people; commencing demagogues, and ending tyrants."[5]

These misgivings about democracy led the Founders toward representative government, but they were ambivalent about that model as well. On the one hand, they were committed to the republican notion that the legitimacy of government rested on the consent of the governed. That commitment meant that the process for selecting government leaders needed to involve the citizens, for clearly, if leaders were to claim legitimacy for their actions based on their connection with the people, the people needed to have a voice in deciding who these leaders would be. On the other hand, if one of their reasons for rejecting pure democracy was the belief that citizens could not make wise choices about the policies under which they would be governed, how, they worried, could citizens be expected to make wise decisions about who their leaders would be? They also feared that elections would provoke conflict and instability. James Madison lamented "the vicious arts by which elections are too often carried"[6] and Hamilton referred to elections as occasions for "tumult and disorder."[7] And, finally, they were concerned that elections would create an overly intimate relationship between political leaders and voters, thus encouraging politicians to do what was popular rather than what was necessary.

It should be noted that the Founders voiced these concerns about elections at a time when relatively few people were permitted to vote, rather than in our modern era of near universal suffrage. These men were products of their time, so when they thought about the composition of the electorate, they excluded women and slaves. John Adams wrote that women should not be allowed to vote because "nature has made them fittest for domestic cares" and unfit for "the great business of life, and the hardy enterprises of war, as well as the arduous cares of state."[8] They also had little confidence in the ability of the poor and uneducated, whom some of them referred to as "the mob," to participate in politics.[9] Servants and those without property, Adams said, were "too little acquainted with public affairs to form a right judgment, and too dependent upon other men to have a will of their own."[10] And certainly, in much of the country, African Americans could not be considered for the franchise because they were defined as property rather than as people. Finally, the Founders believed that voters would be motivated by their narrow economic interests. If all citizens, regardless of their station in life, were eligible to vote, this could result in the election of candidates who would pursue the majority interests of those lower on the economic scale at the expense of the minority interests of the economic elite.

These class biases of the Founders were always near, and often at the surface, of their deliberations about the electoral process. They were from the educated and economic elite of the new nation, and they wanted a government structure that would provide as much protection as possible for their interests. Elbridge Gerry thought that elections would imperil these interests, that they were a concession to a "leveling spirit" that would empower the masses at the expense of the elite.[11] Based on the experience of the state legislatures under the Articles of Confederation, Adams warned that a democratic legislature would "vote all property out of the hands of you aristocrats."[12] Although Madison acknowledged the possibility that the economic minorities of the well-off might undermine the rights of economic majorities of the less well-off, he thought that there was a much greater danger from majorities: ". . . the danger to the holders of property cannot be disguised, if they be undefended against a majority without property. . . . Hence the liability of the rights of property, and of the impartiality of laws affecting it, to be violated by legislative majorities having an interest real or supposed in the injustice. Hence agrarian laws, and other leveling schemes. Hence the cancelling or evading of debts, and other violations of contracts. We must not shut our eyes to the nature of man, nor to the light of experience."[13]

If there was to be a republican system, it needed to be one rooted in the concept of public virtue—a term the Founders thought of as a willingness to sacrifice one's own interest for the greater good of the country, or in pursuit of justice. John Adams wrote that "public virtue is the only foundation of republics." His view was that republican government could not survive unless there was "a positive passion for the public good, the public interest . . . established in the minds of the people . . . superior to all private passions."[14] Madison hoped that the people will at least have sufficient "virtue and intelligence to select men of virtue and intelligence"[15] to represent them, but he had his doubts. In *Federalist Paper* No. 10, he wrote that "As long as the reason of man continues fallible, and he is at liberty to exercise it, different opinions will be formed. As long as the connection subsists between his reason and his self-love, his opinions and his passions will have a reciprocal influence on each other; and the former will be objects to which the latter will attach themselves."[16] Hamilton added the patronizing thought that although the "people commonly intended the public good," they did not "always reason right about the means of promoting it."[17]

In endorsing republican government over more democratic systems, Madison noted that the former would "refine and enlarge the public views, by passing them through the medium of a chosen body of citizens, whose wisdom may best discern the true interest of their country, and whose patriotism and love of justice will be least likely to sacrifice it to temporary or partial considerations." The result would be "that the public voice, pronounced by the representatives of the people, will be more consonant to the public good than if pronounced by the people themselves."[18]

Conveniently for their own interests, Madison and his colleagues thought that such virtue, such ability to "reason right," was more likely to reside with the intellectual, social, and economic elite of the country—in other words, men like themselves—than with ordinary citizens, especially those citizens with little in the way of economic resources. George Mason, a delegate to the convention from Virginia, had been the author of that state's Bill of Rights, a document in which those eligible to vote were defined as all men "having sufficient evidence of permanent common interest with and attachment to the community."[19] In practice, such evidence meant holding property. Madison said that "the freeholders of the country would be the safest depositories of republican liberty."[20]

Congressional Elections

The attitude of the Founders toward elections was most clearly reflected in their discussion of the House of Representatives. Although they viewed decision-making by representatives as superior to decision-making by the people themselves, they also were concerned that legislative decision-making might be less than virtuous, because legislators would be responsive to the opinions and short-term demands of the electorate rather than to their real interests, as well as the interest of the nation as a whole. It was the job of the virtuous legislator to discern the difference between the true interest of the people (and the nation) and their more transitory and uninformed opinions and to privilege the former over the latter. But because legislators would wish to maintain their popularity with the electorate, they might be tempted to respond to public opinion rather than to advocate for the public good.

This view was confirmed by what many felt was the irresponsibility of the legislatures in the independent states and by the vulnerability of these bodies to popular and, in their view, dangerous demands. Based on his experience in his home state of Massachusetts, Gerry was not very confident about the quality of the representatives who would be elected by the people. There, he said, "the worst men get into the legislature—men of indigence, ignorance, and baseness." He thought that many were demagogues, or "designing men" who mislead the people "into the most baneful measures and opinions."[21] Madison, after voicing his hope for the quality of representatives compared with citizens, qualified this by suggesting that "men of factious tempers, of local prejudices, or of sinister designs, may, by intrigue, by corruption, or by other means, first obtain the suffrages, and then betray the interests, of the people."[22]

Although it is likely that their colleagues were sympathetic to these concerns, they nonetheless voted for an elected House of Representatives. James Wilson, a delegate from Pennsylvania, argued that popular election of the House was essential if the people were to have confidence in their government, and Madison agreed, calling the election by the people of at least one branch of the legislature "a clear principle of free Government."[23] George Mason said that direct election was necessary so that the House would be "the grand depository of the democratic principle" in the sense that it would "know and sympathize with every part of the community."[24] Madison concluded that it was "indispensable that the mass of citizens should not be without a voice in making the laws which they are to obey, and in choosing the magistrates who are to administer them."[25]

Although the Founders endorsed popular election of the House, with each state allotted representatives in proportion to their population, it is important to note the limitations that they placed on this ostensible commitment to the people. First, they failed to establish a national right to vote, leaving the decision about who would be eligible to vote for the members of the House to each of the states. This meant that the electorate, in most instances, would be white, male, property holders—a very small percentage of "the people," very few of whom would come from the less privileged segments of society. Second, the House would have no unilateral power of its own. It could not act without the consent of the Senate, a body that at one point Madison argued should be elected only by those with a "freehold or equivalent of a certain value."[26] The final document called for senators to be selected by the state legislatures, thus eliminating all voters, even those with property, from the selection process. Senators would serve for six years in office, four years longer than the term of House members, further distancing themselves from popular opinion. Furthermore, states with the smallest population would have equal representation with the states that had the largest population. That provision, agreed to in order to satisfy the concerns of the smaller states that they would be marginalized by the voting power of the larger states in the House, also made it highly unlikely that the Senate would reflect the majority view of the country at large. Finally, even if the House and the Senate were to agree on legislation, their actions could be vetoed by a president who was most assuredly not to be selected by the people.

Creating the Presidency[27]

The decisions of the men who designed the office of the president and the process by which its occupant would be selected were the product of a number of factors: their goals for the new federal government; their hopes for the role that the president would play in this new system; their fears, shared with many of their countrymen, about the dangers of executive power; their skepticism about the wisdom of the voters, as shown by their ambivalence on the question of House elections; and finally, their desire to produce a document that would be approved by the thirteen now independent states.

The primary goal that brought the delegates to Philadelphia was the need to establish a national government that was stronger than the very weak one that existed under the Articles of Confederation, the first post-independence governing arrangement. Under that document, each state had one vote in the Congress, the agreement of nine of the thirteen states was required to act, and states were also able to ignore the actions of the central government. The result was a structural inability to act as a nation. With each state possessing the discretion to conduct its own affairs, there were different forms of currency, individual and independent armed forces in some of the states, boundary disputes between states with no mechanism to resolve them, and significant impediments to commerce between the states and with foreign powers. In addition, many of the Founders were concerned that actions were being taken in some states that threatened the economic interests of the elite, including the nullification of debts, the printing of paper money, and, in the case of Massachusetts, intimidation of state officials by armed citizens. The writer Noah Webster complained of "public invasions of private property" and "wanton abuses of legislative power."[28] Justifying the removal of some powers from the states to the new federal government, Madison, in *Federalist Paper* No. 10, said that the state legislatures were "much more disposed to sacrifice the aggregate interest . . . to the local views of their constituents," and that "measures are too often decided not according to the rules of justice and the rights of the minor party, but by the superior force of an interested and overbearing majority."[29] In the face of all of this, Hamilton wrote of the need for "the firmness and efficiency of government"[30] and in *Federalist Paper* No. 9, he identified the challenge to the convention as ensuring that "the excellence of republican government may be retained and its imperfections lessened or avoided."[31]

Strengthening the national government, in the view of most of the Founders, would require a fortified executive branch. As Hamilton put it, "energy in the executive is a leading character in the definition of good government. It is essential to the protection of the community against foreign attacks; it is not less essential to the steady administration of the laws." He concluded that "a feeble executive implies a feeble execution of the government" and a feebly executed government must be "in practice, a bad government."[32] Although it was clear, at least to Hamilton, that a strong executive was necessary, it was not at all clear what such an executive would look like. There were existing models for the other institutions of the new national government. The British Parliament and the existing state legislatures provided models for the Congress, and the British tradition of common law and the role of judges in interpreting these laws provided an adequate model for an independent judiciary. But when it came to the executive power, there were no good examples.

The prevailing model of executive authority was the hereditary monarchies that dominated European countries. But the Americans had just completed a revolution against the British monarch, and the unilateral and tyrannical power that he wielded, particularly in the colonies, was not something that they remembered fondly. The instruments of monarchial power were the royal governors appointed by the king to enforce British law in each of the colonies. These widely detested men were the more proximate objects of the revolution, and the colonial legislatures that existed prior to the revolution took resistance to these executives as one of their primary functions. Aside from the British experience, where at least the monarch and his appointees were checked to some extent by Parliament, the other examples of executives were the emperors and tyrants who had dominated most of the polities around the world from the Roman Empire forward.

These unsavory models of executive power, along with the esteem in which legislatures were held by the population at large, led the Founders toward a commitment to a form of government in which, as John Locke, the political theorist most admired by the Founders, put it, "the legislative power must dominate." Under the Articles of Confederation, at the national level, there was only a Congress. There was no executive, save for the person who presided at meetings of the Congress; although the term "president" probably originated from this position as "presiding" officer, the responsibilities of the position, which rotated among the representatives of the various states, consisted almost entirely of keeping order at the meetings. In the former colonies, now independent states, where most of the governing in the new nation took place, nearly all power was in the hands of state legislatures. Not wishing to recreate the abusive office of royal governor, the new constitutions of these states, with the exception of New York, were characterized by governors with little in the way of power, in some cases appointed by the legislature, typically serving only a brief term in office, and in some instances, required to act in concert with a council.

The hostility toward executive power abroad in the land was so strong and the commitment to republican government (to which a strong executive was viewed by many as antithetical) so firm that if the new Constitution was to provide for a powerful executive, it might well have torpedoed the entire enterprise. The Founders' dilemma was neatly summed up by Edmund Randolph, a delegate to the convention from Virginia, who acknowledged that while "the turbulence and follies of democracy" that were on full display in the state legislative bodies needed to be checked by the executive, a strong executive was "the fetus of monarchy."[33] Hugh Williamson of North Carolina warned that such an executive would "spare no pains to keep himself in for life and then lay a train for the succession of his children."[34] So, as they thought about a new Constitution, the Founders had to contend with a strong public bias against executive power, the skepticism of some of their own members, and no handy models for an executive that would be stronger than what had existed under the Articles of Confederation, but that would not be so strong that it would threaten to replicate their experiences under the Crown.

It is not surprising then that the first branch of government listed in the new Constitution is the Congress—the elected House and the appointed Senate—a body in which "all legislative powers" are vested. Among the legislative responsibilities for the new Congress were all the key policy areas that would require action by the new government: the power to raise revenue and decide upon what it would be spent, the power to raise and support military forces, the power to declare war, to govern the size of the military, and to determine the rules under which it would operate, along with a whole range of other responsibilities in regard to interstate commerce, the coinage of money, and the building of roads.

Nonetheless, an executive power was necessary if for no other reason than to prevent the new national legislature from engaging in the same abuses that the Founders saw taking place in the state legislatures. When Madison critiqued these state legislatures for "extending the sphere of its activity and drawing all powers into its impetuous vortex"[35] and for its tendency to capitulate to majority power at the expense of the common good and justice for the minority, he was clearly warning against a similar tendency in the new Congress, particularly in the popularly elected House. And so Article II created a potentially strong president that would have the capacity to check the power of the legislature.

This potential for presidential strength was suggested by a number of factors. First, the office would be held by one person rather than by a council, as was the practice in some of the states. Second, although he would serve only a four-year term (Alexander Hamilton argued at one point for a president who would serve for life), the president would be eligible for perpetual reelection. He would also be in a position to check the powers of the legislature by vetoing the legislation that it passed. But the veto was conditional, subject to being overridden by a two-thirds vote in both legislative chambers, a decision contrary to Hamilton's preference for an absolute veto that could not be overridden.[36] But whether conditional or absolute, the veto was a negative power that the president could use to stop Congress from acting; what was much less clear was what, if any, affirmative powers the president would have.

The words of Article II are quite vague on the subject. It vests the "executive power" in the president of the United States, who is instructed to report to the Congress "from time to time" on the State of the Union. He is also permitted to recommend measures for the Congress' consideration. He is empowered to make treaties with foreign nations, although such treaties needed to be approved by a two-thirds vote of the Senate. He also has the power to appoint administrative office holders, ambassadors, and judges, subject again to confirmation by the Senate. And finally, he is the commander in chief of the armed forces, presumably directing their day-to-day activities in the event that the Congress declared war and decided to raise and support an armed force for the president to command.

The ambiguousness of the constitutional provisions that describe the powers of the president has been a subject of puzzlement and debate among scholars, especially when one compares the brevity of Article II with the long and detailed enumeration of congressional power contained in Article I. It is apparent that the most specific portions of Article II deal with comparatively trivial responsibilities—for example, reporting on the State of the Union, requesting information in writing from government officers, and granting reprieves and pardons. At the same time, what turned out to be the most important aspects of presidential power are written so vaguely that they literally cry out for definition. The Constitution vests the "executive power" in the president, but it doesn't define that power. What does it mean to "faithfully execute the laws?" Is this simply an automatic ministerial function—doing exactly what the law instructs—or does it imply a degree of discretionary power in terms of interpreting the meaning of the law and acting accordingly? Does the treaty-making clause, combined with the power of receiving and appointing ambassadors, suggest a leading role for the president in foreign relations? Does the State of the Union requirement, along with the provision allowing him to recommend measures for the consideration of the Congress, amount to an expectation that the president would provide policy leadership to the legislature and to the nation? Does the role of commander in chief confer upon the president a broad unilateral power to commit the military to the protection of the nation against all enemies, foreign and domestic, or is it simply meant to say that at times of war, he is in charge of military decisions? Absent a declaration of war by the Congress, does it mean that he simply has the power to defend the country against a sudden attack, or does this role mean that he can deploy troops even in peace time?

Some argue that the vagueness of the Constitution was attributable to the fact that the Founders, lacking established models for a republican executive, were uncertain about what they wanted from this new office and that they were genuinely worried that extensive executive power posed a threat to liberty. Speaking at the Constitutional Convention, George Mason said that while he accepted the idea that the executive's capacity for secrecy, dispatch, and energy were important attributes for the new government to have, they were also contrary to "the pervading principles of republican government."[37]

It may be that most, if not all the Founders, were prepared to resolve these doubts in favor of a strong executive but the need to convince a nation that was at best skeptical about executive power to ratify the new Constitution militated in favor of the cautious and vague wording that they chose. From this perspective, they wrote in generalities, in the hope that the ambiguities that they created would permit future presidents the latitude to interpret the language in a way that allowed them to meet the new and largely unknown challenges that they knew that the nation would surely confront in the future. Scholars have also noted that the Founders designed the presidency with the certain knowledge that George Washington was going to be the first person to hold the office. They knew that the first decisions of the first president would set a precedent for those who would follow, and they were confident that Washington was both prudent and strong enough to make the right choices.

Selecting the President

The characteristics that the Founders saw in Washington were those that they hoped his successors would display. They wanted the president to be a man with a national reputation and a national point of view, rather than someone who represented a narrow sectional interest. They wanted someone who had a demonstrated capacity for leadership, who was of high moral character, and who had the intellectual ability to deal with the issues that would confront the government. It is also fair to say that they sought a person who was part of the governing and economic elite of the nation—the establishment, as it might be called today. They wanted a person who would pursue the public good, even if it was politically inconvenient to do so, just as Washington himself had suggested when he admonished the delegates at the convention against producing a document they knew to be insufficient, simply "to please the people." And, finally, they were suspicious of ambition. They feared the person who affirmatively sought political power and favored the person who was simply willing, if asked, to serve his fellow citizens.[38]

Their problem was how to arrange a selection process that would produce such a man. Existing executive arrangements faced no such problem; monarchs inherited their positions, royal governors were appointed by the monarch, and the governors of the new states were typically selected by the state legislature. But in a republic, the right to rule did not come from divine sources or through inheritance or appointment, but was derived from the people, from the consent of the governed. In *Federalist Paper* No. 68, Hamilton asserts that republicanism made it "desirable that the sense of the people should operate" in the process of presidential selection. He then laid out four goals for the presidential selection process, as he and his colleagues saw them. It was important that steps be taken to ensure that a person of high quality be selected, that the selection process be free from "tumult and disorder," that it not be tainted by "cabal, intrigue, and corruption," and that it guaranteed that the president would be independent of the legislative branch.[39]

The most obvious way to render the president independent of the Congress was to have him elected directly by the people—the most republican option. However, this would come at the expense of an orderly selection process and make it less likely that a person who matched their criteria would be selected. Consequently, direct election of the president was rejected. When the possibility came up, the Founders reiterated the concerns that they raised about popular election of the House of Representatives, emphasizing their view that the people did not have the capacity to make a wise choice among presidential candidates. Roger Sherman, a delegate to the convention from Connecticut, thought that the people "will never be sufficiently informed of characters," and George Mason suggested that referring the choice of the president to the people was analogous to referring "a trial of colors to a blind man."[40] The smaller states were also opposed to popular election, fearing that their preferences would be overwhelmed by the votes coming from the larger states.

The Founders also worried that in a system with a popular election, candidates for the presidency would have a strong motivation to appeal to the passions and emotions of the voters, rather than to their reason and virtue. Hamilton said that the inability of the people to see what was in the common good was due to the "wiles of parasites and sycophants, by the snares of the ambitious, the avaricious, the desperate, by the artifices of men who possess their confidence more than they deserve it."[41] Elbridge Gerry thought that the people were often "the dupes of pretended patriots."[42] They thought of these politicians as demagogues who would secure the popular vote by flattery, by telling the people that they knew best, and that they would be a vehicle for their interests and demands. The role of political leaders, especially the president, the

Founders believed, was to do what he thought was in the national interest, public opinion to the contrary notwithstanding.[43]

The concerns about the qualities of the president and an orderly process for his selection could be met if the president were to be selected by the Congress, along the lines of the parliamentary model then emerging in England. But that option would imperil the last two goals that Hamilton listed—avoiding corruption in the selection process and guaranteeing executive independence from the legislature. Madison reminded his colleagues at the convention that one of the reasons why an executive was needed was "to control the National Legislature," which, like the state legislatures, could be expected to have a "strong propensity to a variety of pernicious measures."[44] Certainly, a president selected by the Congress would be unlikely to resist such "measures" because Congress would take care to select someone who would do their bidding and depose after one term someone who resisted them. Therefore, a president selected by the Congress who wished to serve another term would have a strong incentive to follow the direction of the legislature. As for the issue of corruption, if the selection of the president was to be in the hands of the Congress, those ambitious for the office might use unscrupulous means to achieve their goal, means that might include bribery, the promise of future office, or partisan considerations. Gouverneur Morris, a delegate from New York, argued that a congressional selection process would "be the work of intrigue, of cabal, and of factions" and compared with such an awful prospect, he was even prepared to support election by the people whom he believed "will never fail to prefer some man of distinguished character or services."[45]

But for nearly all of Morris' colleagues, direct election of the president was the worst option. So as the convention wound down, the document that they sent to the Committee on Detail for refinement provided for the president to be selected by the Congress. However, the document that emerged from the Committee on Detail presented a third option. The Electoral College—something that Hamilton had suggested early in the convention but that did not get much consideration—was proposed, and it would speak to all four of his goals.

Under that arrangement, the president would be selected by a designated group of electors, rather than by the people or by the Congress. Each state would have a number of electors equal to the size of their delegation in the House and the Senate. This provision was aimed at sectional interests; the smallest states would have no fewer than three electoral votes, and the southern states would gain more power because of the size of their congressional delegation by virtue of the 3/5ths provision in Article I, reflecting their nonvoting population of slaves. The electors in each state would be selected in any manner that its state legislatures decided. Each elector would cast two votes, only one of which could be cast for a person from his own state. In order to win the presidency, a candidate would need a majority of the electoral votes. If someone did achieve a majority, the person who came in second would become vice president. If no one received a majority, or if two candidates had the same number of electoral votes, the selection would revert to the House of Representatives, which would choose among the five top Electoral College finishers, with each state delegation casting one vote. The winning candidate under that scenario would be required to get the votes of a majority of the states. The Senate would then select the vice president.

Thus, the "sense of the people would operate" in the presidential selection process, but at some distance from the actual decision. The president would be chosen by a "small number of people selected by their fellow citizens from the general mass" who would, according to Hamilton, "possess the information and discernment requisite to so complicated an investigation" as to the qualities of potential candidates. This process, Hamilton concluded, would avoid the "tumult" of direct election, guarantee to "a moral certainty that the office of president will seldom fall to the lot of any man who is not in an eminent degree endowed with the requisite qualifications" and make it most likely that the person chosen would be characterized by "ability and virtue."[46] Also, the electors would never assemble in one place; rather each state's electors would meet in their home state, thus reducing the danger that the selection process would be tainted by bribes and corruption. Because the Congress would only be involved in the selection of the president if no candidate received a majority of the electoral votes, the winner was likely to be independent of that body.

The Electoral College arrangement reflected the argument that Madison had made in recommending republics over democracies—the idea that although the popular will needed to be a part of the process, it needed to be filtered and refined by removing it from a direct impact on the final decision. In republics, the people would choose legislators who would make policy; in the case of the presidency, there would be two filters: the people would choose state legislators, who would choose electors, who would then choose the president.

A second essential component of the electoral arrangement was the president's eligibility for reelection. This, according to Hamilton, would provide for continuity in office that would ensure stability and encourage good public policy. The four-year term for the president was longer than the terms for governors, but obviously much shorter than the lifetime terms of monarchs, and shorter than the six-year Senate term. On the other hand, the president, unlike many state governors, would be allowed to run for reelection as many times as he wished. This would "enable the people, when they see reason to approve of his conduct, to continue him in the station in order to prolong the utility of his talents and virtues, and to secure to the government the advantages of permanency in a wise system of administration."[47] Unlimited prospects for reelection would encourage presidents to take the long-term view of public policy and act for the public good rather than bowing to public opinion when the two conflicted. It would also encourage honest behavior among those who occupied the office. A limited term in office, in contrast, might tempt presidents to place their own private interests ahead of the public interest against the day when they would be compelled to return to private life.

What stands out from these deliberations is the Founders' fear of popular election by the people, even by an electorate narrowed by 18th century considerations of race, gender, and property. Originally, this fear produced a provision calling for congressional election of the president; so great was their antipathy toward popular election that they were willing to ignore their frequently voiced concerns about the need for an independent president who could check the Congress. In fact, they saw the provision calling for congressional selection in the event that no candidate received a majority of the electoral votes as the typical way in which the president would be selected, rather than what has turned out to be a rarely used fallback mechanism. They assumed that the electoral votes would be divided over many candidates so that the House would usually choose, but at least from a restricted list of the top five vote recipients in the Electoral College. Although not the optimum situation from their point of view, it was certainly preferable to election by the people.

The voters were unlikely to choose the best person for the office, but even more importantly, in order to gain the office, candidates would need to appeal to the people. In doing so, they would be tempted to cater to their viewpoints and incite the worst instincts of the population in order to win votes. Direct election of the president would create an intimate and ultimately unhealthy relationship between the people and the president. On the one hand, the president could exploit the emotions of the population for his own purposes, and on the other, he might be overly sensitive to the transitory wishes of an uninformed, self-interested, and ephemeral public opinion. In either event, popular election would put at risk the Founders' desire for a president of high character who would pursue the public interest.

Limiting the Presidency

Those who wrote the Constitution were about to create the first republican executive and to do so, they had to overcome the view that executive power was antithetical to republican liberty. At every turn, they needed to reassure skeptics that the presidency would not be a danger to liberty and that the office was so structured that its occupant could never indulge in the abuses associated with the king of England.

The primary limitation on presidential power was the system of institutional checks that the Founders placed in the Constitution. Even though they knew that Washington would be the first president, and they had some confidence that the convoluted electoral process that they had designed would produce worthy successors, they also knew that at some point, a less able person might succeed to the office. As Madison famously put it in *Federalist Paper* No. 51, the men who governed were unlikely to be "angels" and, at a later point, writing about the problems of placing the war-making power in the hands of the president, he suggested that future presidents after Washington would not be "such as nature may offer as the prodigy of many centuries" but "such as may be expected in the ordinary successions of magistracy."[48] Therefore "auxiliary precautions" needed to be taken. That meant equipping both the Congress and the president with the ability to defend their own institutional independence against possible incursions by the other, thus ensuring that "ambition would be made to counteract ambition."[49]

In war-making, in treaty-making, in ordinary legislation, and in the appointment of government officials, neither the president nor the Congress could act unilaterally. Each had the capacity to check the other, thereby ensuring that wise decisions would be made, or, put differently, that unwise decisions would be less likely to be made. This system is more accurately characterized as "separate institutions sharing power" rather than the more familiar "separation of powers."[50] This is not simply a matter of semantics. Precisely defined executive powers clearly separated from equally well-defined legislative powers would create the possibility that either institution would abuse those powers exclusively consigned to it. And the beauty of the system was that while it served the purpose of reassuring the population at large that there would be checks on the executive, at the same time it dealt with the concern of many of the Founders, who thought that the real danger to the nation was legislative rather than executive abuse of power.

This last concern of Madison's betrayed the worry of several of the Founders that government action would be taken too hastily, that it would be too responsive to the moods of transitory majorities, that these majorities were likely to be composed in the main of people with more meager resources than the property-holding elites, and that these decisions therefore might not be in the public interest, at least as the Founders viewed that concept. But under their constitutional model, in order for government to act, agreement would have to be secured from separate and independent institutions—the popularly elected House, the appointed Senate, the president, and, arguably, the Supreme Court. Such agreements, the Founders believed, would occur only when action was absolutely necessary, clearly in the public interest, and therefore no threat to the interests of elites, such as them.

Some of the Founders' did prefer very limited power in the hands of the national government, and for them, a system in which policy inertia was a likely outcome was not necessarily a problem. Virtue would be assured, or at a minimum, policies contrary to the public good would be

unlikely, because it would be difficult for such policies to gain appr
from the multiple centers of power that the Founders had created with
the federal government. But others recognized that it was possible that
too many precautions had been taken against abuse, and that the system
could lead to a paralyzed government unable to take necessary action, an
outcome that might not necessarily be in the public interest in a situation
where the needs of the nation demanded action. Hamilton, for one, feared
that they might have gone too far. After completing the exercise of divid-
ing and balancing power, he said, "you must place confidence; you must
give power."[51] He repeated this sentiment in *Federalist Paper* No. 26:
"Confidence must be placed somewhere," he wrote; "it is better to haz-
ard the abuse of that confidence than to embarrass the government and
endanger the public safety by impolitic restrictions on legislative authority."[52] Although Hamilton's last phrase mentioned legislative authority,
it seems clear that the confidence that Hamilton believed needed to be
placed "somewhere" ultimately would be placed in the executive, his
source of government "energy." In the end, it may be that Hamilton was
a bit more optimistic about human nature than Madison. While Madison
lamented the absence of angels to govern men and wrote that "passion
never fails to wrest the scepter from reason,"[53] Hamilton asserts that
"there is a portion of virtue and honour among mankind which may be
a reasonable foundation of confidence."[54]

As Hamilton had hoped, over the course of the nation's history, we
have been more likely to find virtue, at least as the Founders thought of
the term, in the presidency than in the legislature. Although the selection
process for presidents has sometimes been less than elevating, more often
than not, once in office, presidents, because of their national constituency, have been willing to make decisions and take positions that spoke
to the general interest of the nation rather than to their own or their
party's self-interest. And while electoral considerations are never absent
from presidential decision-making, they are more likely to take a back
seat to larger concerns than would be the case in the Congress where,
because every member of the House and one-third of the Senate must
face the voters every two years, virtue often seems in short supply.

Also as Hamilton anticipated, the power of the presidency has
expanded as presidents have interpreted the ambiguous provisions of
Article II in ways that enabled them to meet the challenges that they and
the nation confronted. As we will see in Chapter 8, the increase in presidential power was driven by a much greater role for the national government in policy areas that the Founders intended to be in the purview of
the state governments, and by a much more active role for the nation in
international affairs than would have been imaginable in the late 18th
century. The third factor leading to an increase in presidential power was
the democratization of the presidential selection process, and because
of that, the ability for the president to claim democratic legitimacy for

'e claims to power. Although the Founders could not
he first two developments, they did recognize that a
nocratic connection between the people and the presi-
e presidential power, possibly to an extent that would

Conclusion

It is always a speculative and, in the end, unproductive enterprise to ask
what the Founders would think of our modern day political environment. They were members of an economic and social elite who came
to political consciousness more than 250 years ago when, to state the
obvious, the world was a quite different place. But what may be more
productive is to distill their ideas and ask to what extent they have les-
sons for today.

As the foregoing discussion has demonstrated, they were not fans of
democracy, as they understood that term. They thought that republican
government was a better alternative but that elections, the central procedural component of representative government, were, at best, a necessary
evil. They did not like the idea of empowering mass publics to decide
who their political leaders would be, but at the same time, they recognized that some level of citizen involvement was necessary if the people
were to be confident in their political system.

They had several concerns about elections. First, they viewed them as
unseemly events that featured candidates attacking not just the policies
but the character of their opponents. Second, they feared a symbiotic
relationship between candidates and the voters, with the former evoking
or responding to the passions and prejudices of the latter. This sort of
demagoguery betrayed naked political ambition, and they viewed this
as contrary to republican virtue and ultimately destructive of republican
government. Third, they worried that elections would create an unhealthy
connection between the views of voters and the actions of politicians,
with the latter inclined to do what was popular, rather than what was
necessary or just. Fourth, they feared that a majority composed primarily
of those with less economic resources would undermine the rights of a
minority with greater resources. Finally, they feared that popular elections were unlikely to produce the best person for office, particularly for
the presidency, the highest office in the land.

They addressed these concerns with what might be called a limited
republican system: allowing popular election for only the House of
Representatives, accepting voting qualifications for those elections that
effectively restricted the franchise to white property-holding males, establishing an unelected Senate and thereby denying the House any unilateral
policymaking power, removing the process of presidential selection by
at least two steps from popular influence, and establishing a Supreme

Court whose members would be selected by the unelected president and approved by the unelected Senate.

But today, the American political system is an almost fully democratized representative system. Although the Supreme Court remains beyond the control of the voters, both the House and Senate are popularly elected, and virtually all adult Americans, regardless of race, gender, and economic status, are eligible to vote. As we will see in the next two chapters, the Founders' plan to remove the selection of the president from the people, with the Electoral College as an independent decision-maker, vanished, and direct election of the president by an electorate much broader than the Founders could ever have imagined is a fact in both the United States and in every other presidential system. To be sure, the Electoral College mechanism remains capable of frustrating the will of the majority of the voters, but this results from the sometimes imperfect fit between popular votes and electoral votes, rather than the substitution of the judgment of informed electors for the judgments of ostensibly uninformed citizens, as the Founders had planned.

Thus, in the 2000 presidential election, Al Gore received half a million more votes than his main opponent, George W. Bush, but he lost the election because Bush achieved a majority of electoral votes. And in 2016, Hillary Clinton received nearly three million more votes than Donald Trump, but lost decisively in the Electoral College. The Electoral College also gives disproportionate power to the smaller states. The 230,000 citizens of Wyoming who voted in 2016 elected three electors, which works out to about one elector for every 77,000 voters. The 5,100,000 voters of Illinois elected twenty electors, which works out to about one elector for every 255,000 voters. The vote of a Wyoming resident, from an electoral vote perspective, is worth 3.3 times the vote of an Illinois resident. The split between popular votes and electoral votes was not the way in which the Founders intended to insulate the selection of the president from the voting public, but the disproportionate power to smaller states was certainly part of their plan. So whether intended or not, these remaining aspects of the Electoral College system suggest that the selection system still has some less than democratic vestiges.

The framers hoped that men of national prominence would be drafted for the office by the electors who would recognize them for their stature and talent. People were not expected to "run" for the presidency in the sense of contesting for the office. Rather they were expected to "stand" for office in the sense of volunteering their service. But shortly after the ratification of the Constitution, political parties emerged as instruments that would put forth candidates for the presidency and organize Electoral College support for them. So the selection process evolved into a highly politicized two-phase affair in which candidates for the presidency would first, seek the presidential nomination of their co-partisans and second, vie against the nominees of other parties for the office itself. Today, presidential candidates seek their parties' nomination in a lengthy, chaotic, wide-open, fully democratized process featuring mass participation in primaries and caucuses across the nation. That phase of the selection process, more than any other, epitomizes the tumult and disorder that the Founders feared elections would produce. Clearly, the current presidential selection process is much more democratized than the Founders would have preferred. The question that we will seek to answer is whether or not their concerns about such a process were prescient, particularly in regard to the type of leader that such a process would produce.

Notes

1 My discussion of the Constitutional Convention draws on material I published in Michael L. Mezey, *Congress, the President, and Public Policy* (Boulder, CO: Westview Press, 1989), chapter 2.

2 This and all subsequent quotes from the proceedings of the Constitutional Convention come from Madison's notes, as presented in Max Farrand, ed. *The Records of the Federal Convention of 1787*. Volumes 1 and 2 (New Haven: Yale University Press, 1966). Each citation carries a volume number and a page number. Gerry's opinion of democracy is found on page 48 of volume 1 and is cited as Farrand, 1:48.

3 Richard Hofstadter, *The American Political Tradition* (New York: Vintage Books, 1948), 13.

4 Farrand, 1:48.

5 This and all subsequent quotes from the *Federalist Papers* carry the number of the paper quoted and the page in the 1961 New American Library edition where the quotation can be found. Hamilton's statement is found on page 35 of the first *Federalist Paper* and is cited as *Federalist* 1:35.

6 *Federalist* 10:82.

7 *Federalist* 68:412.

8 Forrest McDonald, *Novos Ordo Seclorum: The Secular Origins of the Constitution* (Lawrence: The University of Kansas Press, 1985), 161.

9 See Hofstadter, *The American Political Tradition*, 45.

10 McDonald, *Novos Ordo Seclorum*, 161.

11 Farrand, 1:48.

12 Hofstadter, *The American Political Tradition*, 13.

13 Philip B. Kurland and Ralph Lerner, eds. *The Founders' Constitution* (Chicago: University of Chicago Press, 1987), 534, 536.

14 Gordon Wood, *The Creation of the American Republic, 1776–1787* (Chapel Hill: University of North Carolina Press, 1969), 570.

15 Ibid., 544.

16 *Federalist* 10:78.

17 Wood, *The Creation of the American Republic*, 508.

18 *Federalist* 10:82.

19 Hofstadter, *The American Political Tradition*, 14.

20 Farrand, 2:203.

21 Farrand, 1:48.

22 *Federalist* 10:82.

23 Farrand, 1:134.

24 Farrand, 1:48.

25 Hofstadter, *The American Political Tradition*, 6.

26 Kurland and Lerner, *The Founders' Constitution*, 650.
27 Much of the material in the following pages is drawn from Michael L. Mezey, *Presidentialism: Power in Comparative Perspective* (Boulder, CO: Lynne Rienner, 2013), 41–53.
28 Wood, *The Creation of the American Republic*, 411.
29 *Federalist* 10:77.
30 *Federalist* 1:35.
31 *Federalist* 9:72–3.
32 *Federalist* 70:423.
33 Farrand, 1:51.
34 Farrand, 2:101.
35 *Federalist* 48:309.
36 Richard Morris, ed., *The Basic Ideas of Alexander Hamilton* (New York: Washington Square Press, 1956), 12.
37 Farrand, 1:112.
38 James W. Ceaser, *Presidential Selection: Theory and Development* (Princeton: Princeton University Press, 1979), 62.
39 *Federalist* 68:412–13.
40 Farrand, 2:29, 31.
41 Wood, *The Creation of the American Republic*, 508.
42 McDonald, *Novos Ordo Seclorum*, 202.
43 See Ceaser, *Presidential Selection*, 52ff.
44 Farrand, 2:110.
45 Farrand, 2:29.
46 *Federalist* 68:414.
47 *Federalist* 72:436.
48 James Madison, *Helvidius Papers #4* (1793). http://oll.libertyfund.org/titles/hamilton-the-pacificus-helvidius-debates-of-1793-1794 84–89.
49 *Federalist* 51:322.
50 Richard Neustadt, *Presidential Power*. 2nd ed. (New York: John Wiley, 1980).
51 Richard Loss, "Alexander Hamilton and the Modern Presidency: Continuity or Discontinuity?" *Presidential Studies Quarterly* 12:1 (Winter, 1982), 10.
52 *Federalist* 26:168.
53 *Federalist* 55:342.
54 *Federalist* 76:458.
55 The factors leading to an increase in presidential power are more fully explored in Mezey, *Presidentialism*.

4   Democratization and Political Parties

The Founders were conflicted about the role that the people should have in selecting their leaders. On the one hand, they were philosophically committed to the principle that government legitimacy was based on the consent of the governed and that, in the words of John Adams, there could be "no free government without a democratical branch to the constitution."[1] On the other, because they wanted voters to have as little to do with governing as possible, they did not want them to be too involved with the selection of those who would govern them, for fear that elected leaders would give too much weight to public opinion when they made decisions. And, as we saw, they had grave doubts about the ability of the voter to choose capable people for office. Ultimately, the system that they designed was more reflective of their fears about election by the people rather than their republican aspirations. Except for members of the House of Representatives, no other national office holders would be selected by the voters, and the gender, race, class, and in some cases religious restrictions on the right to vote that existed in the states were accepted in the new Constitution. As the years passed, however, the political system slowly democratized. The right to vote was extended to previously disenfranchised groups, the Senate evolved from a body whose members were appointed by the state legislatures to one elected by the people, and the presidential selection process was transformed from one controlled by elites to one controlled by the voting public.

Political parties played a crucial role in the democratization of the presidential selection process, first by eliminating the independent role of the Electoral College and then by their efforts to expand and organize the electorate. Parties also assumed the function of winnowing the field of potential presidential candidates by organizing nomination procedures that would identify their party's candidate. And, as we will see in Chapter 5, eventually the nomination process succumbed to the forces of democratization, with voters, rather than party leaders, now possessing the decisive voice in selecting the party's standard bearer.

The Birth of Political Parties

The Constitution makes no reference to political parties, and the men who wrote the document never used the term in their deliberations. Instead, they talked about "factions," which Madison defined in *Federalist Paper No. 10* as "a number of citizens, whether amounting to a majority or a minority of the whole, who are united and actuated by some common impulse of passion, or of interest, adverse to the rights of other citizens, or to the permanent and aggregate interests of the community."[2] Madison's definition of faction seems to describe what we would call today an interest group rather than a political party. He seems to foreclose the possibility of a faction devoted to the task of governing in the public interest, something that modern political parties aspire to do on their best days. From Madison's perspective, the common interest that would unite a group of leaders and/or citizens into a faction would have either an unjust goal—attacks on the rights of other citizens, for example—or a narrow sectional or economic interest that was contrary to the public interest. In either case, factions undermined the goal of establishing a virtuous republic, which to the Founders meant prioritizing justice and the public good over narrow self-interest.

The problem was that despite these concerns, Madison and his colleagues also knew that in a free society where people are allowed to organize and advocate for their interests, factions would naturally arise and could not be suppressed. He turned his attention instead to designing institutional mechanisms that would make it less likely that factions, particularly majority factions, would be able to engage in the "mischief" that he thought would undermine republican virtue. As we saw in the previous chapter, that mechanism consisted of a republican rather than a democratic form of government, a limited role for ordinary citizens who supposedly would be unable or unwilling to discern the public interest, and a political system that dispersed power among the executive, legislative, and judicial institutions of the new national government and between that government and the various state governments. This dispersal of power and the capacity of various national institutions to check each other would make it more difficult for a faction to seize control of the totality of political power.

The factions that began to appear shortly after the Constitution went into effect were more like political parties than interest groups. Although they represented sectional interests, they were also motivated by different views of the proper role of the national government. They were elite organizations in the sense that their adherents were the political leaders of the day at the national and state level—people whom Madison had argued were most likely to prioritize the public good. Simply put, parties emerged as mechanisms for like-minded leaders to advance their view of the public good. Thus, John Adams and Alexander Hamilton, although personal rivals, joined with many others to constitute a Federalist faction that favored a stronger role for the new national government, especially in regard to the financial affairs of the nation, and an aggressive use of executive power. Jefferson and Madison led the Democratic Republicans, a group of leaders more skeptical about centralized power and the role of the executive, and more disposed toward what we would call today states' rights. There was a strong sectional element to the division as well, with the Federalists entrenched in New England and the Democratic Republicans strongest in the South. By 1796, when Washington, who refused to identify with either group (although his positions were strongly influenced by Hamilton and the Federalists) stepped down at the end of his second term, the race to succeed him devolved into a purely partisan affair—a contest between Adams as the Federalist leader and Jefferson as the Democratic Republican leader.

The Evolution of the Electoral College

The Electoral College, as the Founders had imagined it, was the first casualty of this embryonic party system. As emphasized in the previous chapter, the Founders' expectation was that the electors would make an independent decision about which person or persons possessed the character traits and background that they desired for the presidency. The result of such a process, they hoped, would be a president of national stature and unassailable character. But the two political parties had gathered adherents not just among members of Congress, but also in the several state legislatures in which the Constitution had vested the decision about who should be eligible to vote and how the presidential electors should be selected. These legislatures divided along the factional (or partisan) lines that had come to characterize the national government, and so they contrived to select electors whose views reflected the partisan majorities in their states. Thus, in the election of 1796, the electors from the New England states, along with New York, New Jersey, and Delaware, each cast one of their votes for Adams (each elector had two votes and could not cast them both for people from the same state), while nearly all of those from the remaining states cast one of their votes for Jefferson. In a few of these states, there was a single electoral vote for the candidate of the other party, and Maryland had a more significant division of its vote, but for the most part, the electoral votes reflected the party that dominated the state's politics. The result was Adams' election by a margin of three electoral votes. Thus, by this first contested presidential election, the electors were well on their way to becoming what they are today: the agents of their political parties, rather than independent decision makers.

Although the Founders' scheme for independent electors had begun to fall apart by 1796, the plan to insulate the voters from the presidential selection process was still in force, although signs of fraying had begun to appear.[3] The Constitution had allowed each state legislature to decide how its electors would be designated, and the states developed different models with various degrees of citizen participation. In seven states, electors were simply appointed by the state legislature. But in four states, the legislature established "electoral districts" with the voters in each district selecting one elector. In three states, electors were chosen by a statewide ballot. In Massachusetts, the state legislature appointed two electors and selected the rest from among the top two vote recipients in each congressional district. And in the newest state, Tennessee, the state was divided into electoral districts comprised of different counties. The voters in each county in the district elected one delegate, and then these delegates selected electors.

The election of 1800 featured a rematch between Jefferson and Adams. Again, in a majority of the states, the legislatures chose the electors, so the party that held the majority in the state legislature selected electors who would support their party's presidential candidate. Adams' support once again came from Federalist New England, while Jefferson was supported by most of the electors from the remainder of the country. The problem that arose in this election had to do with the constitutional requirement that the candidate who finished second in the Electoral College would become vice president, a provision that in 1796 had the awkward result of making Jefferson, Adams' opponent for the presidency, his vice president.

In 1800, the Democratic Republicans tried to avoid this situation by designating Aaron Burr of New York as their candidate for vice president. The plan was to arrange for all but one of the Democratic Republican electors to cast his two votes for Jefferson and Burr, with the single elector casting his second presidential vote for someone other than Burr. The result would give Jefferson one more electoral vote than Burr and make the latter Jefferson's vice president. But for some reason, the plan did not work; all the Democratic Republican electors cast votes for both Jefferson and Burr, resulting in an electoral vote tie between the two. Under the Constitution, the tie was to be broken by the House, with each state delegation casting one vote. Because there were now sixteen states, the votes of nine states (a majority) would be required to select the president. Although Burr publicly disavowed any intent to take the presidency from Jefferson, there were indications that he was less than sincere about this.

Because Federalists in the House viewed Jefferson as their archenemy, many were prepared to vote for Burr in order to prevent Jefferson from ascending to the presidency. It took seven days and thirty-six ballots for the House to select Jefferson, a result in part attributable to Hamilton's intervention with his Federalist colleagues on behalf of Jefferson and against Burr. Hamilton disliked Jefferson but loathed Burr, an animosity that was to lead to Hamilton's tragic death at the hands of Burr a few years later. This unseemly process led to the Twelfth Amendment to the Constitution that required electors to cast separate ballots for the president and the vice president, thus creating our current arrangement whereby the party's candidates for president and vice president run on the same ticket.

Democratizing the Electoral College

With the parties now in control of the Electoral College, the next step in the democratization process was expanding the role of the voters in deciding which party's slate of electors would be selected in each state. By the election of 1804, although several states had moved to popular election of their presidential electors, more continued to use selection by the state legislature. Of those states that had moved to the election of electors, the most common method was what was called the "general ticket" approach, in which voters cast ballots for a party's full slate of electors. The electors on the winning slate would then cast their votes for the party's candidates for president and vice president. By 1824, electors were selected by the state legislature in only six of the twenty-four states; in the rest, electors were elected by the people, with twelve states using the general ticket approach. By 1832, only South Carolina still used legislatively appointed electors, and by 1836, it was the only state that did not use the general ticket process, other states having abandoned the various schemes of district-based elections.

This is a very truncated history, of course, but the heart of the story is this: less than fifty years after the ratification of the Constitution, the Founders' design for an Electoral College that would be an independent decision-making institution, fully insulated from the influence of voters and composed of highly qualified individuals capable of making a wise choice about who the president would be, had vanished. In its place was the system that survives to this day—a system in which party leaders choose their candidates (more on this below) and produce slates of electors in each state bound to vote for the party's presidential and vice presidential candidates. Voters in each state cast their votes for one of these slates of electors. The slate with the most votes is "elected," and all these electoral votes go to the party's candidates for president and vice president. The candidate with a majority of these electoral votes becomes president, and his running mate becomes vice president.

Many of the Founders participated in this transition, and whether they recognized it or not, this modification of the role of the Electoral College amounted to a fundamental change in their philosophy of the presidency. As Madison had said, the spirit of republican virtue was at odds with the concept of factions, and their hope was that the presidency would stand above the factional fights that would inevitably occur, and in a nonpartisan manner, speak for and pursue the general good of the nation. The

Electoral College was supposed to be a mechanism for maximizing the likelihood of such a nonpartisan presidency, and in his refusal to identify with one of the emerging parties, Washington exemplified such a president. But the election of 1800 made clear that whatever its merits in terms of keeping citizens at arm's length from the process of presidential selection, the Electoral College was now to be an instrument to elevate a partisan to the presidency. Such a person was still likely to be qualified and someone of national repute, but he was most assuredly to be a person who viewed the public interest through the prism of his party's beliefs.

Democratizing the Electorate

The democratization of the Electoral College was accompanied, albeit a bit more slowly, by the expansion of the electorate. The first barrier to fall was the property requirement for voting that was in force in most of the states when the Constitution was ratified. In 1800, only three states (Kentucky, New Hampshire, and Vermont) had universal white male suffrage. By 1830, ten states permitted white male suffrage without qualification, while eight states restricted the vote to taxpayers, and six imposed a property qualification for suffrage. By 1860, just five states limited suffrage to taxpayers, and only two still imposed property qualifications.

It was no accident that the disappearance of property qualifications began in earnest with the arrival of Andrew Jackson on the political scene. Jackson had become a national hero when he led the American military to victory against the British in the decisive Battle of New Orleans in 1815. He became a member of the House of Representatives and later a member of the Senate and, in 1824, was an unsuccessful candidate for the presidency. However, he won the presidency in 1828 and served two terms in office, a period that historians refer to as the Age of Jackson.[4] Before Jackson, the political parties were essentially collections of politicians in the Congress and the various state capitols. In contrast, Jackson and his colleagues in his newly constituted Democratic Party (see below) sought to develop a mass following.

It was in Jackson's political interest and in the interest of the Democratic Party to expand the electorate in order to broaden the party's electoral base. In the South, the Democrats fought against the large plantation owners, advocating, among other things, the elimination of property qualifications for voting, the abolition of imprisonment for debt, and the establishment of free public education. Immigration also contributed to an increase in the size of the electorate, and Jackson was popular with the growing Irish and Scotch-Irish population who, like Jackson, tended to view the British as an enemy. By 1820, Tammany Hall, the Democratic organization in New York City, was dominated by Irish immigrants who had brought with them "an inherent hatred of aristocracy" and were attracted to the Jacksonian commitment to universal male suffrage and easy naturalization policies.[5] With citizenship came the right to vote and larger numbers of people, many with little education and a tenuous grasp of the English language, were admitted to the rolls. Jackson's campaigns catered to the class prejudices of these new and typically poorer Americans, arguing that the rich and more educated leaders looked down on them and did not have their best interests at heart.

In the large states of the Northeast and Midwest, the "Jacksonian politicians organized the now enfranchised masses through conventions, caucuses and committees down into the county, the township, and even the rural school districts."[6] These party organizations provided new arrivals with a connection to their new nation as well as social services in return for their political support. The Democratic machines that ran these cities were instrumental in the expansion of the electorate and their mobilization behind political candidates at every level, but particularly at the local level. There were, however, incidents of reaction against the voting power of immigrants. Connecticut and Massachusetts, for example, enacted literacy tests for voters aimed primarily at Irish immigrants.

The Jacksonian spirit that attacked property requirements for voting and ushered in what Jackson called "the era of the common man" did not extend to African Americans and to women. Through most of the 19th century, both groups were generally denied the franchise; although in a few states, they were allowed to vote if they met property requirements. In the State of New York, for example, African Americans could vote if for a period of one year, they possessed property worth more than $250. The unrestricted right of women to vote began in some of the western states after the Civil War, first in Wyoming in 1869 and in Utah the next year. By 1920, women had the right to vote in fifteen states, and in that year, the Nineteenth Amendment to the Constitution was ratified, enfranchising women throughout the country, regardless of where they lived.

As for African Americans, the road was longer, more difficult, and more violent. Although the Fifteenth Amendment to the Constitution passed after the Civil War declared that the right to vote could not be abridged on account of race, color, or previous condition of servitude, southern states quickly erected various legal barriers to prevent African Americans from voting. Following the precedent set by some northern states to prevent immigrants from voting, the southern states adopted literacy tests for voting, but exempted uneducated whites with clauses allowing them to vote if their grandfathers had been eligible to vote. In 1915, the Supreme Court, in the case of *Guinn v. US*, ruled that such exemptions were unconstitutional for federal elections. In 1889, Florida adopted a poll tax designed to discourage poor people, whites as well as blacks, from voting, and most of the southern states followed suit. Such poll taxes existed in several states until 1966 when the Supreme Court, in the case of *Harper v. Virginia Board of Elections*, ruled them unconstitutional. These legislative acts were backed up by intimidation and terror against African Americans who met the legal qualifications to vote and had the temerity to exercise that right. One of the main goals of the civil rights movement of the 1950s and 1960s was to secure the right to vote, and these efforts reached fruition in 1965, when Congress passed and President Lyndon Johnson signed the Voting Rights Act, legislation that delivered on the promise of the Fifteenth Amendment, albeit one hundred years late. This legislation effectively did away with literacy tests and provided federal supervision of election procedures in the southern states, where discrimination against African Americans remained.[7]

The Nomination Process

In addition to eliminating the independence of the Electoral College and expanding the franchise, the third way in which the presidential selection process was democratized had to do with the method by which the candidates of the major parties were selected. For the first two presidential elections, this was a moot point. Washington ran unopposed for president while several candidates contested for the vice presidency—which would go to the candidate who came in second to Washington. In both 1789 and 1792, that candidate was John Adams. By 1796, political parties had emerged, and although there was no official process for nominating each party's presidential candidate, Federalists coalesced around Adams and Democratic Republicans around Jefferson. In addition to these two men, ten other candidates—six Federalists and four Democratic Republicans—received electoral votes. Because the second votes of Federalist electors were split among their six candidates, Jefferson, who had come in second to Adams in total electoral votes, became vice president. The result demonstrated that the emerging parties had not achieved a level of organization or coherence sufficient to identify a consensus vice presidential candidate. But by 1800, this had changed, with the leaders of both parties agreeing on both their presidential and vice presidential candidates and on a scheme (that as we have seen was unsuccessful) that would produce one less electoral vote for the putative vice presidential nominee. The failure of that scheme produced the Twelfth Amendment.

In the election of 1804, the Democratic Republican ticket of Thomas Jefferson and George Clinton defeated the Federalist ticket of Charles Pinckney and Rufus King by 162 electoral votes to 14. This result spelled the end for the Federalists as a serious opposition party and ushered in a period of de facto one party rule under the Democratic Republican Party. For the purposes of presidential selection, this turn of events created the need for a process for selecting that party's presidential nominee. With no opposition party to contest the general election, gaining the party's nomination was tantamount to election.

The method adopted was the congressional caucus—a process by which the party's congressional members would select its candidate for the presidency. The Democratic Republican caucus of 1808 featured a three-way fight for the nomination, pitting George Clinton, Jefferson's vice president, against two Virginians: James Madison, the secretary of state, and James Monroe, a former governor of Virginia and ambassador to France. Ultimately, the Democratic Republicans endorsed Madison for president and Clinton for vice president. The remnants of the Federalist Party, also using the caucus method, nominated Charles Coatsworth Pinckney and Rufus King. After Madison's victory and his two terms in office, James Monroe, Madison's secretary of state, was selected by the caucus as the next in line for the presidency and also served two terms.

Before proceeding to the 1824 election and the period beyond, it should be noted that for the period from 1809 thru 1824, the president was, in effect, selected by the Congress. Just as the Founders had anticipated when they considered the possibility of congressional selection of the president, the process was characterized by bargaining and favor swapping, as well as a president who was fairly weak and generally in thrall to the members of Congress who had nominated him for the position. And as one would expect, the leaders who selected the president were not very much in touch with the expanding electorate, their policy preferences, and their wishes concerning the presidency. All of this came to a head in the election of 1824 when the Democratic Republican Party splintered, and the congressional caucus was unable to agree on a candidate, setting up a multi-candidate race for the presidency.

In 1824, four Democratic Republicans sought the party's nomination for the presidency—Senators Henry Clay and Andrew Jackson, Secretary of State John Quincy Adams, and Secretary of the Treasury William Crawford. The congressional caucus decided upon Crawford, but the mechanism was already being criticized as undemocratic, and many members of Congress did not participate. In addition, Crawford had serious health problems, which in the view of some, disqualified him. The result was that no candidate could claim to be the party nominee, with all four men seeking support in the Electoral College. In the end, Jackson ended up with a plurality of the electoral votes with Adams close behind. In those states where electors were selected by popular vote, Jackson outpolled Adams by nearly 40,000 votes, demonstrating his popularity with the expanding electorate. However, because no presidential candidate received a majority of the electoral votes (John Calhoun had received a majority of the vice presidential votes because both Jackson and Adams supported him as their vice presidential nominee), the selection fell to the House of Representatives, which was to choose among the top three vote recipients (the number had been reduced from five in the original Constitution to three by the Twelfth Amendment). Henry Clay, the Speaker of the House, had garnered four fewer electoral votes than Crawford, so

Clay was not considered. Clay detested Jackson on a personal level, and his policy priorities seemed closest to Adams. So Clay threw his support in the House to Adams, who was selected despite the fact that Jackson had come out of the election with more electoral votes and substantially more popular votes than Adams. Afterwards, Adams appointed Clay to the position of secretary of state, which, at the time, was still considered to be a stepping stone to the presidency.

Jackson condemned the entire process as an attack on the will of the people and characterized Clay's decision to support Adams followed by Clay's appointment as secretary of state as evidence of a "corrupt bargain." The events of 1824 signaled the end for both the congressional caucus system as a nominating process and the Democratic Republican Party. When the rematch between Jackson and Adams occurred in 1828, they were the only two candidates—Jackson as the candidate of his reconstituted Democratic Party and Adams as the candidate of the newly constituted National Republicans. Unlike 1824, the race was not close; Jackson secured 178 of the 261 electoral votes and outpolled Adams by more than 140,000 popular votes (by that time, only Delaware and South Carolina did not elect their electors).

The 1828 results were a product of a number of factors. First, Adams had been an unpopular president, and, second, Jackson had spent nearly the entire time since the 1824 race was decided campaigning for the presidency. But more importantly, Jackson was the perfect fit for the democratizing electorate. Poorly educated himself, rough in language, lacking in manners, and with a reputation as a war hero and Indian fighter, Jackson connected with the mass public in ways that his predecessors could not, and more importantly, would never consider doing. The French aristocrat Tocqueville, then touring the country, made no effort to conceal his disgust. He called Jackson "a man of violent temper and mediocre talents," someone who "stoops to gain the favor of the majority" and is "supported by a power [i.e., popular approval] with which his predecessors were unacquainted."[8] During his 1828 campaign, as well as his reelection campaign in 1832, the Democratic Party presented Jackson as the champion of the poor against the rich, as the conqueror of the British at New Orleans to the growing Irish and Scotch-Irish population in the country, as the scourge of the Native American tribes, and as the enemy of banks, monopolies, and big business. He attacked the "monied aristocracy of the few" and announced a credo of "equal rights for all, special privileges for none." The historian Wilfred Binkley described the sort of campaigning that characterized the Jacksonian period: "Stump speaking developed into an art and cajolery a profession, while whiskey flowed freely at the hustings." Jackson and his supporters appealed to the class prejudices of the voters, exploiting the "persecution complexes of the masses."[9]

Jackson personifies many of the fears of the Founders in regard to popular election of the presidency. Although he was not a political amateur, having served as a military leader and a member of both houses of Congress, he was not by any means the temperate educated aristocrat that they had hoped would serve. Worse, he exploited his lack of refinement and education to form a bond with the people. His appeals to the emotions and class interests of the voters, his justification of himself as "the people's president," and his commitment to the principle that "the majority should govern" represented exactly the pernicious and intimate relationship between the people and the president that the Founders most wanted to avoid.[10]

Conventions

The Jacksonian period also marked the end of the domination of the nomination process by national elected officials. On the last day of 1831, the anti-Jackson National Republican Party held a convention in Baltimore to nominate Henry Clay as their presidential candidate. The convention was attended by 155 delegates from eighteen of the nation's twenty-four states. Five months later, Andrew Jackson's Democratic Party also held its convention in Baltimore to formalize Jackson's renomination for a second term in office, to select a running mate for him, and to formally adopt its new name. Delegates from all but one of the states attended and selected Martin Van Buren of New York as Jackson's vice presidential candidate.

The national convention initially supplemented, and then replaced, a process that had developed with the fall of the congressional caucus, one in which party members in the various states would put forth a nominee for the presidency. This was the process that had resulted in the multiple candidates and corrupt bargain election of 1824. The purpose of the national convention was to bring the party's various sectional interests and the presidential aspirants who represented these interests together in one place to negotiate their differences and produce a consensus candidate. The delegates to the convention, local and states office holders and other local party activists, were typically chosen by a hierarchy of county, district, and state conventions. County conventions would involve ordinary party voters who would decide on delegates to the district or state convention, which in turn would identify the state's delegates to the national convention. In this respect, the convention was a clear step toward democratizing the presidential selection process, because it involved a much broader group of people than had previously been the case. Although ordinary party voters were involved, the final nomination decision was in the hands of the party leadership assembled at the convention.

The national conventions, in addition to providing a new mechanism for nominating presidential candidates, were instruments for the creation of a national political party structure, which was cobbled together from the various state and local party organizations that supported Democratic and Republican candidates. The convention ultimately became the place where national party rules were formulated and formalized and platforms embodying the party's positions on major policy issues were determined—a role that conventions continue to have today. But most importantly, the convention was the place where the various candidates for the presidency were evaluated, where discussions among party leaders took place, and where those assembled cast ballots to determine who would carry the party's banner in the coming presidential race.

Primaries and Bringing the Voter In

Toward the end of the 19th century, concerns arose about what some considered to be a lack of public influence on the political parties and their nomination processes not just for the presidency, but for state and local offices as well. The Progressive movement, which came to prominence at the beginning of the 20th century, had a rather negative view of political parties and particularly of the party leaders (or, bosses, as they preferred to call them) who controlled the nomination processes at both the state and national levels. One of the reforms that they advocated was a primary system in which rank and file members of the party would decide at the ballot box who they wanted the party to nominate for public office. During the first quarter of the 20th century, such systems were adopted in a number of states.

At the presidential level, the Progressives had come to view conventions as the province of party leaders often more interested in their own status and the political rewards involved with backing a particular presidential contender than with the opinions of the people about who should be president. To gain the nomination, candidates followed a strategy of meetings to solicit the support of local and state party leaders who controlled the delegates to the national convention. Although they undoubtedly needed to convince these leaders that they would be strong and popular candidates, they did not need to make an effort to gain the support of average voters. Rather, they established their electability credentials through their national reputation and by their record of success in gaining previous political offices.

Several remedies were proposed to limit the control of party leaders over the presidential nomination process. The Progressives had proposed a national primary, an idea that did not get very far. But some states adopted presidential preference primaries—elections in which party members would vote for the candidate whom they favored for the party's nomination. In some cases, these preferences were binding on the delegates that the state sent to the national convention, and in other instances, these were simply non-binding "beauty contests" that served the purpose of registering public opinion and informing the delegates about the level of support in the state for the various candidates. Some states moved to have the convention delegates themselves elected in primaries, in some cases with the candidate for the presidency whom the delegate favored listed on the ballot, and in other cases, not. And, finally, some states chose not to have primaries, at least at the presidential level, opting instead for a caucus system in which local party leaders would decide who the delegates would be and often who they would support at the national convention.

These various practices reflect a number of characteristics of the American political party system and its presidential nomination process that persist today. It is always important to remember that the political parties are in many respects extensions of the Constitution's federal system. That is, they are coalitions of state party organizations, each of which retains a certain degree of autonomy over how it conducts its affairs. As the previous paragraph suggests, in this period when the parties' were democratizing their nominating procedures, each state party, rather than the national party, decided whether and how it would proceed. Today, the state parties retain substantial autonomy within the context of national party rules and state election laws. Although national party leaders can exercise some influence, in the end, state legislatures can decide whether or not to have a primary system, when and under what administrative arrangements the primary will take place, and whether or not voting is restricted to registered party members.

The movement toward primaries and a more democratized nominating process opened the door to a new type of presidential politics—the soliciting of public support for the nomination, originally as a way to influence decisions by party leaders as to whom their nominee should be and eventually as a way to determine the nominee. Political scientist James Ceaser refers to the new process as a plebiscitary model, or alternatively, a candidate-centered model, supplanting the party dominance model that had been in force since the Jacksonian period. The conflict between the two models played out in the fight for the 1912 Republican presidential nomination in which Robert LaFollette and Theodore Roosevelt ran as progressive alternatives to the incumbent William Howard Taft. The two progressives did well in the states that held primaries, but Taft did well in the states where the party organizations dominated the delegate selection process. Because there were more delegates from the latter states and because there were two progressive challengers splitting the votes in the primary states, Taft emerged as the nominee. As Ceaser points out, LaFollette's complaints about the outcome in the primary states where Roosevelt did well presaged current complaints about the primary system. LaFollette complained that Roosevelt had done well because he had received money from special interests, had capitalized on his superior name recognition, and had made unprincipled appeals to the voters.[11]

The 1912 race meant that for the next 60 years, aspiring candidates for the presidency would need to run a hybrid sort of race—one that entailed competing in selected primaries while at the same time soliciting the support of the party leaders and regulars who controlled delegate selection in many of the states. The latter were certainly influenced by the primaries, in the sense that they had little interest in selecting a candidate whose performance in the primaries indicated that he would have difficulty winning in November. Sometimes, a candidate's decision to participate in a primary was a sign of weakness, a strategy used by a candidate who had to find a way to convince the party leaders that he could win. Thus, in 1960, John Kennedy entered the West Virginia primary in order to prove that a Catholic could win votes in a state dominated by Protestants

Party leaders were understandably leery of candidates who disdained the party organization and based their claim to the nomination only on the popular support that they registered in the primaries. In 1952, Estes Kefauver, a Democratic senator from Tennessee, won twelve of the fifteen primaries that he entered, but was still denied the nomination, which went to Adlai Stevenson, the governor of Illinois. The power of the state party leaders stemmed from their ability to control the selection of delegates in those states without primaries or with non-binding primaries. In the former, the delegate selection process and the decision about which candidate to back often took place in low visibility private caucuses controlled by the party organization—the proverbial "smoke filled rooms"—and from which outsiders were banned. Local and state party leaders who controlled these caucuses could control their delegates, and in large states with large numbers of delegates, the power of these leaders at the convention was enhanced by their capacity to swing a significant number of convention votes to their preferred candidate.

Under this model, when the conventions took place, there was often some uncertainty about who the nominee would be, particularly when there was no incumbent seeking renomination. Negotiations took place among delegates, state party leaders, and candidates, deals were made, and sometimes the voting process at the convention went on beyond the first ballot. As we will see, under our current system, first ballot nominations are now the rule.

1968–1972

The hybrid system held on through World War II and the immediate postwar period. But then the 1960s happened—the civil rights movement, the Vietnam War and the protests against it, the assassination of two Kennedy brothers as well as Dr. Martin Luther King Jr., and widespread urban unrest. In 1968, at the climax of that extraordinary period of political ferment, Lyndon Johnson, the incumbent Democratic president, was challenged for reelection by a relatively obscure senator from Minnesota, Eugene McCarthy, who ran on a platform centered on ending the war in Vietnam. Although Johnson prevailed in the first-in-the-nation New Hampshire primary, McCarthy did much better than expected, polling 42% of the vote against the incumbent president. That result brought Senator Robert Kennedy into the presidential race and, two weeks later, Johnson suddenly announced that he had decided not to run for reelection.

With Robert Kennedy's assassination the night of the California primary, McCarthy arrived at the Democratic Convention in Chicago having won the most primaries and having garnered the most total primary votes. But McCarthy's candidacy was rejected in favor of Hubert Humphrey, Johnson's loyal vice president, who had not contested any of the primaries but was a strong favorite of the party leadership. The convention took place in the middle of a riot scene, with protestors and police clashing outside the convention center and the delegate hotels. The driving force behind the protests was the war in Vietnam, and the protestors were angry about the nomination of Humphrey, who had supported Johnson's military involvement in that country. Among the political claims made by the protestors as well as by their sympathizers within the party was that the convention and its results did not reflect the views of the people who had voted for McCarthy in the primaries, and the nomination had been conferred on Humphrey by party bosses who controlled their delegations.

For their part, these party leaders were not prepared to turn the nomination over to a senator who was seen as disconnected from the party organization and whose attacks on the war, and therefore on an incumbent Democratic president, they viewed as disloyal and damaging to the party's reputation. It is important to remember that, at this time, most of the Democratic leadership still supported the war in Vietnam, and Johnson and Humphrey continued to be popular among the labor, big city, and party leaders who dominated the convention. The delegates to the convention were mostly older white males, with relatively few seats occupied by women, young people, or people of color, the latter two groups well represented in the anti-war and civil rights movements that had supported McCarthy and Kennedy and disrupted the convention.

The Chicago convention and the subsequent loss of the presidency to Richard Nixon in November generated enormous pressure to make the nomination process more democratic and to take steps to enhance the diversity of the convention. In response, the Democratic Party set up a commission to review its nominating process and make recommendations for reforms. Formally known as the Commission on Party Structure and Delegate Selection, it is more commonly remembered as the McGovern–Fraser Committee, after its co-chairs, then Senator George McGovern of South Dakota and Representative Donald Fraser of Minnesota. The most significant recommendation from the committee was

that all convention delegates had to be chosen in forums tha...
to all party members and conducted within the calendar year o...
tion. States holding primaries had to place the names of qualified...
dential candidates on the ballot, aspiring delegates would need to iden...
their presidential preference, and the distribution of convention delegate...
had to be proportional, in order to reflect the relative strength that the
candidates displayed in the primaries and caucuses. Finally, convention
delegations had to be more demographically representative, giving fair
representation to women, young people, and people of color.

The main impact of these recommendations and the various tweaks
that followed was the movement of many states away from the caucus
and convention systems that were the norm for selecting national convention delegates and toward the primary system. Opening up caucuses
to a broad population, as the new rules required, presented logistical
problems, particularly in large states. The simplest way to conform to
the requirement of openness was to use a primary. In 1968, only fifteen
states held primaries; by 1976, there were twenty-seven such states, a
number that would rise to thirty-seven by 1980, about the same number as today.[12] The requirement of proportionality did away with the
winner-take-all systems that existed in some states, a system in which
the primary candidate with the most votes, even if it was not a majority,
received all the state's delegates. This meant that regional candidates, or
candidates who appealed to a particular ideological wing of the party,
could stay in the race, even if they did not win pluralities in primaries
because they would be able to get a percentage of the delegates commen-
surate with their popular vote total.

Although these were Democratic Party reforms, they also affected the
Republican Party process, particularly on the primary vs. caucus decisions. State governments organize and pay for the primary election, so it
would be inconvenient to provide a primary system for the Democratic
nomination process and a caucus system for the Republican process,
although this in fact has occurred in a few states. State legislatures controlled by Democrats simply legislated a primary system for both parties. State law also determined whether the primaries or caucuses would
be open only to registered members of the party, or to independents,
or in some cases, to any voter no matter the party in which they were
registered. Beginning in 1976, the Republicans also required that their
caucuses be open to all party members who wished to participate. Other
Democratic Party reforms did not apply to the Republicans, particularly
the proportional allocation of delegates and the quota system for ensuring diverse representation in state delegations, although they were certainly free to adopt such procedures if they wished.

In the years following McGovern–Fraser, there have been various
changes in the nominating process in both parties, many having to do
with the sequencing of the primaries and caucuses, and many others at

party designed its own unique process within
by state laws and national party rules. The
angement of the nomination process involves
l fifty states, the District of Columbia, Puerto
an-controlled territories. Candidates need to
s in each state, especially in the case of the
ere is much more state-by-state variation. But
reforms definitely ended the national conven-
party's presidential nominee. Ever since, each
party has nominated as its candidate the person who emerged from the
caucuses and primaries with the most delegate support and has done so
on the first ballot.

Conclusion

Before assessing the current nomination system, it is useful to pause to
review how far we have come from the Founders' vision of the presidential selection process. Initially, the Founders believed that a presidential
aspirant would not need to declare his candidacy for office. They would
not "run" for the office and would not engage in the unseemly activity of
campaigning. Rather, they would accept the nomination and the office if
it was conferred upon them. Conferring the office would be the job of the
Electoral College, a body that would pick a person of national stature and
unimpeachable qualifications. With the emergence of political parties,
the Electoral College ceased to have an independent role, and the nomination process became a party affair, first with the leaders of the party
at the state and national levels deciding upon a candidate to advance,
with the key role being played by the party's members of Congress—the
congressional caucus. With the rise of Jacksonian democracy, the party
still maintained control of its nomination, but with a much broader and
inclusive process that involved local partisans and their leaders, as well
as national office holders who assembled in a national convention to designate a nominee. Early in the 20th century, tentative steps were taken to
involve rank and file voters in the nomination process with the introduction of presidential primaries. Although party leaders continued to dominate the nomination process, popular opinion, as registered in primary
results, became a factor. And after 1968, popular opinion, as reflected in
the results of the primary and caucus systems, came to be the sole factor
determining the party's nominee.

In brief, a system that was at one time controlled entirely by national
and state party leaders evolved into one in which those voters who
choose to participate in primaries and caucuses effectively decide who
the party's presidential standard bearer will be. In 2016, about 60 million voters participated in the primaries and caucuses of the two political
parties. In both races, the candidate with the most votes—a majority

in the case of the Democratic Party and a plurality in the case of the Republican Party—won the nomination. Although the Democratic Party selected Hillary Clinton, the candidate favored by the party's leadership, the Republican Party chose Donald Trump, a candidate who was the first choice of none of the party's leaders and who, even after he received the nomination, failed to gain the support of many of these leaders, including its two living past presidents and the party's most recent nominee for the presidency.

Notes

1 Richard Hofstadter, *The American Political Tradition* (New York: Vintage Books, 1948), 14.
2 This and all subsequent quotes from the *Federalist Papers* carry the number of the paper quoted and the page in the New American Library edition where the quotation can be found. Madison's statement is found of page 78 of *Federalist Paper* No. 10 and is cited as *Federalist* 10:78.
3 I have relied on *The Green Papers* for much of the historical detail in this section. See www.thegreenpapers.com/
4 Arthur M. Schlesinger, Jr., *The Age of Jackson* (Boston: Little, Brown, 1946); See also, Jon Meacham, *American Lion: Andrew Jackson in the White House* (New York: Random House, 2008), 120.
5 Wilfred E. Binkley, *American Political Parties: Their Natural History*. 4th ed. (New York: Alfred A. Knopf, 1962), 126.
6 Ibid., 114–115.
7 Some of these gains were jeopardized by the Supreme Court's 2013 decision in *Shelby County v. Holder* that removed the requirement that states clear changes in their voting procedures with the Justice Department and/or the federal courts, even if they had a record of past voter discrimination.
8 Alexis De Tocqueville, *Democracy in America* (New York: The Modern Library, 1981), 171, 273.
9 Binkley, *American Political Parties*, 132–3.
10 See Meacham, *American Lion*, 120.
11 James W. Ceaser, *Presidential Selection: Theory and Development* (Princeton: Princeton University Press, 1979), 213ff.
12 Elaine C. Kamarck, *Primary Politics: Everything You Need to Know About How America Nominates Its Presidential Candidates*. 2nd ed. (Washington, DC: Brookings Institution, 2016).

5   The Democratized Nomination Process

The changes in the nomination process following the 1968 presidential election meant that national and state party leaders and office holders would no longer decide who the party's nominee would be. Rather, a more diverse group of ordinary voters, local party activists, donors, and interest groups, working through primaries and caucuses, would make that decision, a decision that the party's national convention would simply ratify. The new rules combined with changes in the media environment to transform what, at one time, was a mostly under the radar process to select a nominee into a lengthy, highly visible and very costly public spectacle. And, intended or not, the new rules opened a path to the nomination for people who under the previous arrangements would have not received serious consideration.

Nelson Polsby, a leading scholar of presidential elections, commenting on these rule changes a decade after they came into force, predicted that they would foster party disunity by encouraging a large number of candidates, many with narrow followings, to enter the field. This would reduce the likelihood of a consensus candidate emerging.[1] More recently, Polsby's interpretation has been modified by some who argue that, in addition to the public primaries and caucuses that are covered by the news media, an "invisible primary" takes place within each party. This "primary" consists of candidate endorsement decisions by party leaders, other "policy demanders" affiliated with the party, and big money donors, the latter backing their commitment with the funds necessary to compete in the new process. The "invisible primary," the argument goes, produces a candidate who can unify the various factions of the party, and in this way, the party still decides.[2]

This perspective redefines the concept of the national political party to include not just its office holders and party officials, but also donors, interest groups that traditionally support the party's nominee, and ideologically driven volunteers. In other words, the party that decides includes many more individuals, organizations, and groups than was the case with the pre-1972 arrangements. In that sense, the new system, it is argued, is not quite as wide-open and beyond the control of the party organization as some have suggested.

The 2015–16 Republican Party nomination contest seems to confirm Polsby's viewpoint, while the Democratic Party's experience, for the most part, confirms the "invisible primary" school of thought. In the case of the Democratic Party, endorsements and early money flowed to Hillary Clinton, and the national organization, although officially neutral in the battle between her and Bernie Sanders, in private appeared to have a thumb on Clinton's side of the scale. Nonetheless, the results of the Democratic nomination process were much closer than the invisible primary school would have predicted. Clinton's main opponent, the relatively unknown Senator Bernie Sanders, a candidate with no major endorsements and little in the way of early funding, received 43% of the total votes cast in the primaries and stayed in the race until the very end.

The contest for the Republican presidential nomination was an entirely different matter. Donald Trump, a person who had never held political office, who had become a registered Republican only recently, who was demonstrably ignorant about most public policy issues, and whose campaign for the nomination was characterized by unending personal attacks on anyone in the press or the political world who opposed or criticized him, prevailed over seventeen other candidates, most of whom were more prepared by experience and temperament for the presidency than he was. This result, along with Sanders' near miss on the Democratic side, suggested that the capacity of the party to decide its nominee may have been exaggerated by the invisible primary school of thought. Hans Noel, one of the authors of the book that laid out the party decides thesis, suggested that in 2016, rather than rallying behind a consensus candidate, the party simply tried to stop Trump and failed to do that.[3] As Polsby predicted, the task of identifying an alternative to Trump was made more difficult by the large number of candidates in the field representing different ideological and sectional wings of the party. Many of these candidates had endorsements and contributions from various segments of the party and were to a greater or lesser extent acceptable to the party's leadership, certainly more acceptable than Trump. But with so many candidates contesting the primaries and caucuses, it didn't take many votes to move to a second or third place showing against Trump; so as long as their money held out, those candidates had little incentive to drop out of the campaign and consolidate behind a single alternative to Trump. Instead, these candidates harbored the hope that Trump's candidacy would implode and one of them would be the chosen alternative.

A question to which we will return is whether the 2016 Republican experience was a unique event, the result of a perfect storm of an atypical candidate and deep fissures across the nation and within the Republican Party, or if it is the logical culmination of the post-1968 reforms and a precursor of a new normal for seeking the presidency that will affect both political parties. To answer that question, we will begin with an assessment of the main features of the new nomination process.

The Schedule

Aspiring candidates for their party's nomination now compete in primaries or caucuses in all fifty states, the District of Columbia, and various US possessions. These competitions have at least two purposes. First, they result in the selection of delegates to the national convention who are pledged to vote for a particular candidate, at least on the first ballot. Second, they are tests of the electoral strength of candidates among those who choose to participate, either by voting in the primary or attending a caucus. The schedule for these contests, a product of tradition, state legislation, and party rules, makes little sense from a geographical or political standpoint. Each state process has its own unique character in terms of whether it has a primary or caucus, when the primary or caucus is held, whether participation is restricted to party members or is open to all, how the actual convention delegates are identified, and for how many convention ballots the delegates are pledged to their candidate.

In the case of the Democrats, 15% of the delegates to the convention are not subject to the primary or caucus system. These so-called super-delegates automatically become delegates by virtue of their status as party leaders and office holders, and they are not pledged to a particular candidate. In the case of the Republican Party, each state has different rules about how the outcome of the primary or caucus vote is translated into the percentage of pledged delegates that each candidate receives. Unlike the Democrats, who award delegates in proportion to the results of the primary or caucus, in some states, the Republicans have a winner-take-all system whereby the candidate with the most votes in the primary receives all the delegates from that state. Other states award delegates by congressional district, with the candidate who carries the district getting the delegates. And in both parties, there are examples of complex procedures, especially in caucus states, for selecting delegates that may result in deviations from the results reported on the day the caucuses meet.

New Hampshire always holds the first presidential primary in the nation. This tradition began in 1916 when the state legislature decided to hold a primary to elect its convention delegates; no candidates for the presidency appeared on the ballot or were otherwise involved. But in 1949, a new state law placed the names of prospective presidential candidates on the ballot so that beginning in 1952, the primary became a way for a candidate to demonstrate his potential strength. Since then, New Hampshire has jealously guarded its primary status as the first in the nation, even going as far as passing a state law giving the secretary of state the unilateral power to move the primary date to assure that if another state tried to schedule its primary earlier, New Hampshire would be able to respond so that it would remain first.

In 1972, in response to the McGovern–Fraser reforms, Iowa turned its longstanding caucus system for nominating state and local officials into a presidential event to be held a week before the New Hampshire primary. Because the Iowa event was a caucus rather than a primary, New Hampshire did not see this as a violation of its first-in-the-nation primary entitlement. Since then, the nomination process has started in Iowa, moved to New Hampshire a week later, and then the rest of the states followed in whatever order had been established for that cycle by their state legislatures, the state party organizations, and national party rules. The process begins in early January with the Iowa caucuses and runs through early June when the California primary takes place.

The schedule, particularly as it applies to Iowa and New Hampshire, has been criticized for a number of reasons. Because these states vote first, they have a disproportionate influence on the nomination process. Although candidates who do well in one or both of these two contests are not guaranteed to win their party's nomination, they do gain momentum in the form of media coverage and increased financial contributions, as potential donors come to view them as viable and possibly winning candidates. On the other hand, candidates who do poorly in these contests are probably not going to survive. And for some candidates, just the prospect of not doing well in Iowa forces them out of the race before the caucuses even take place. In 2012, Tim Pawlenty, the governor of neighboring Minnesota and someone consistently mentioned as a viable presidential candidate in the year before the primary, ended his campaign after the Ames Straw Poll—a completely unscientific quadrennial event held in Ames, Iowa at the end of the summer, four months or so before the actual caucuses—showed him in third place. Similarly, in 2016, Scott Walker, the governor of Wisconsin, another neighboring state, who had spent most of his childhood in Iowa and had devoted a great deal of time to campaigning in the state, dropped out of the race before the caucuses in light of polls showing him far behind the other candidates.

Both Iowa and New Hampshire are smaller states that are overwhelmingly white and rural and therefore hardly representative of the more diverse, more urban and suburban populations that characterize the country as a whole. So the schedule gives these two highly unrepresentative states the ability to jump start a candidacy or, in effect, to rule a candidate out of the race before the larger more populous states have a say. It seems less than democratic for the handful of voters in Iowa and New Hampshire to have more influence on who the nominee will be than the millions of voters in states such as New York and California whose primaries take place later and sometimes after the nomination has been decided. In 2016, just over 188,000 people participated in the Iowa caucuses of both parties and just over 528,000 people voted in either the Republican or Democratic primaries in New Hampshire. But in June of that year, 5,252,694 people voted in the Democratic and Republican primaries in California. At that time, the Republican nominee had been identified and the Democratic nominee was all but certain to be Hillary Clinton. There is also evidence that voter turnout in primaries drops once the field has been winnowed and certainly after the nomination has been decided.[4]

In an attempt to balance the influence of Iowa and New Hampshire, the Democrats added the Nevada caucuses and the South Carolina primary to the early schedule, immediately following Iowa and New Hampshire. The goal was to include a more diverse state—Nevada, with a large and growing Latino population and, not coincidentally, the home state of the Democratic leader of the Senate, Harry Reid—as well as a state with a large number of African American voters—South Carolina—to the early voting process. And as early as 1980, many southern states had agreed to hold their primaries on the same day early in March (a day that quickly became known as Super Tuesday) with the hope that this would increase that region's influence on the nomination process.

Primaries and caucuses are two quite different exercises. Caucuses put a premium on what campaign aficionados call the "ground game"— on organization and personal contacts that will get your supporters to the polls. In Iowa, this is a largely retail undertaking, with candidates expected to spend substantial time in all corners of the state meeting likely caucus participants and arranging for those who will support him or her to attend. The "air war"—radio and television advertising—is a part of the caucus process, but it is much more important in a primary where a candidate needs to mobilize a large voter turnout. Caucuses tend to attract a less representative group of participants than primaries. A caucus system requires those who wish to participate to commit a significant amount of time traveling to a caucus site and going through an extended and public process to register the views of the attendees. The people most likely to do this are the more ideological party identifiers, those most actively involved with the party, those with more rather than less education, and those with more rather than less free time.

In 2008, Barack Obama did well in the Iowa caucuses, in part because of his appeal to college students and liberal party activists who flooded the caucuses to support a candidate to whom they had a strong personal and ideological connection. But Hillary Clinton won in New Hampshire and did well in many other primary states, given her stronger support among working class people who were less likely to participate in a caucus. For Republicans, religious conservatives, many of whom see presidential politics through the prism of their cultural concerns, are highly motivated to participate in the Republican caucuses, often to the detriment of more pragmatic and centrist candidates. Religious conservatives are particularly strong in Iowa, and in 2008, Mike Huckabee, the former governor of Arkansas and a pastor with a strong connection to the religious right, won the caucuses, while the two more centrist candidates, John McCain and Mitt Romney, finished third and fourth. In 2016, Ted Cruz and Donald Trump finished first and second in Iowa, while more moderate candidates, such as Jeb Bush and John Kasich, finished sixth and eighth, respectively.

With the exception of Iowa and New Hampshire, the schedule in not etched in stone. Candidates, especially incumbents, have used their influence with the national committees of their parties, as well as with their co-partisans in state legislatures, to manipulate the calendar to their advantage. The southern Super Tuesday primaries, for example, came into being at the urging of President Carter as a way to bolster his chances for renomination in 1980 against Ted Kennedy.[5] Although there is an explanation for each quirk in the primary schedule—historical, political, tradition—the larger point is that as a whole, the schedule makes little or no sense. The argument in defense of the system is that it tests a candidate's ability to draw support in different states with different demographics and that the voters in the early states take their role in vetting the candidates seriously. It also tests his or her stamina as they work their way back and forth across the country seeking support. Although both points are reasonable, they must be weighed against the unfair influence that goes to the voters in the early states, the seemingly arbitrary scheduling of the remaining state contests, the marginalization of citizens of the states that vote later, the huge amount of time and money that such a nomination campaign entails, and, most importantly, the type of candidate whom the process advantages.

The Outsiders

Under the pre-1968 system, candidates without much office-holding or political experience and with little connection to or involvement with national and state party leaders were unlikely to get very far in the nominating process. The new process is much more accommodating to candidates who lack strong ties to party leaders, are relative newcomers to the national political scene, or come from smaller states that at one time were not usually thought of as the source of presidential candidates. Certainly, when the party leadership was in control, they were looking for candidates who could win the general election and who were in concert with the party's main policy positions. But just as important, the party leaders were political and governmental professionals who vetted the credentials and qualifications of perspective candidates in light of the responsibilities of the presidency. They favored candidates with a record of service, candidates who they knew and with whom they had worked, and candidates whose temperament, abilities, and appearance marked them as "presidential." To the extent that the role of party leaders has been attenuated, this vetting is now done in large measure by voters and the financial interests and groups that back each candidate.

When party organizations controlled the nomination process, governors of large states, incumbent vice presidents, and United States senators who had spent some time in that body were the ones usually described as "presidential timber." In general, these men were known quantities with established track records as office holders. Although John Kennedy in 1960 and Barry Goldwater in 1964 were not the first choices of their party leaders, they were visible within the party and experienced at the national level. Kennedy had served three terms in the House and eight years in the Senate when he won his party's presidential nomination, and Goldwater had served two terms in the Senate.

Before the reform era, there were few serious presidential candidates with no previous elective experience. Herbert Hoover had never sought elected office, but he served as head of the United States Food Administration during the First World War and as head of the American Relief Administration after the war, before serving as secretary of commerce in two presidential administrations. Although Dwight Eisenhower had never sought elected office before running for the presidency, his military leadership during and after the Second World War had brought him in contact with much of the political leadership in the nation's capital to whom his qualities and qualifications were well-known and who were therefore confident that he could discharge the responsibilities of the office, particularly in the international arena.

In that era, there was also a bias in favor of candidates from large states. Candidates from Ohio, New York, Illinois, and the like would have received more media coverage and would be more visible than candidates from smaller states. These states also sent large delegations to the national conventions, providing candidates from these states with a leg up for the nomination. And in the general election, the assumption was that the nominee would be favored to win the large number of electoral votes that their homes states were entitled to by virtue of their size.

This bias in favor of known candidates from large states who had established records began to diminish with the post-1968 reforms. George McGovern, the first candidate to benefit from the new nomination procedures, was from South Dakota, a small state seldom in the national spotlight. As a senator, he was from the more liberal wing of the party and was not considered to be among the most influential members of that body. When Jimmy Carter won the Democratic nomination in 1976, his political career consisted of four years in the Georgia State Senate and four years as governor of Georgia. Virtually unknown to the nation at large, the phrase "Jimmy who" appeared regularly in news stories, underlining the candidate's lack of a national reputation. Among the people he bested for the nomination were several veterans on the national political scene, including Morris Udall, an eight-term member of the House of Representatives, and Henry Jackson, who was, at the time, serving his fourth term in the Senate after six terms in the House of Representatives.

With Carter, the nomination process shifted toward governors, some more knowledgeable than others, but all with no experience in national government. Ronald Reagan, Michael Dukakis, Bill Clinton, and George W. Bush were examples of this category of presidential candidate, with Clinton also coming from another small state, Arkansas, not usually connected with presidential politics. But 1988 saw the first signs of still another change. The candidate who came in second to Dukakis, the governor of Massachusetts, was Jesse Jackson, a civil rights leader who had never held any government position, elected or appointed. Drawing heavily on African American voters, as well as members of the more progressive wing of the Democratic Party, Jackson won nine primaries and garnered twice as many votes as Al Gore, a sitting senator and former member of the House. In that same year, Pat Robertson, a conservative evangelical preacher with a large television following, entered the Republican presidential nomination contest. He finished a surprising second in the Iowa caucuses, but he did not do well after that and eventually withdrew. In 1992, when George H. W. Bush sought a second term in the White House, he was challenged for the Republican Party nomination by Pat Buchanan, a conservative newspaper columnist who had worked in the Reagan administration but had never run for office. In 1996, Buchanan also challenged Bob Dole, a United States senator and former majority leader of that body. Although Buchanan lost both times, his anti-trade and anti-immigrant campaign emphasizing cultural issues attracted a significant number of voters and highlighted a growing split within the Republican Party between its mainstream business establishment and its religious and populist wings, a split that presaged the 2015–16 Trump campaign.

The 1992 and 1996 elections also saw the third-party candidacy of Ross Perot, a Texas multi-millionaire who had never run for office but who had acquired some level of public visibility for his involvement with projects devoted to retrieving Vietnam-era missing-in-action soldiers. A frequent guest on television news shows, Perot based his campaign on opposition to the North American Free Trade Agreement and the increasing size of the federal deficit. In 1992, he polled an astonishing 18% of the popular vote and came close to winning the electoral votes of several states. And in 2000, Pat Buchanan was once again on the ballot, this time as the candidate of the Reform Party. Ralph Nader, a consumer advocate and again, a person with no elective or governmental experience, was also on the ballot as the Green Party candidate. Although Nader did not do nearly as well as Perot, he secured enough votes in Florida, which likely would have gone to Al Gore, the Democratic nominee, to cost Gore the electoral votes of that state and the presidency.

Although the candidacies of Jackson, Robertson, Buchanan, Perot, and Nader were quite different in terms of ideology and constituency, they were similar in one crucial respect. All five were people with no governmental experience who had achieved some level of visibility and notoriety through the media. All were political outsiders with ideas and policy proposals that at the time were considered outside the mainstream. None were people who fit the traditional profile of a presidential candidate, and under the old system, none would have been viewed as a serious candidate for the presidency. As we will see, candidates with similar profiles were to follow.

In 2008, Barack Obama, whose previous political experience had consisted of eight fairly nondescript years in the Illinois State Senate and four years as a United States senator (two of which were devoted to campaigning for the presidency), gained the Democratic nomination over a range of veteran Washington leaders, including Senators Joseph Biden and Christopher Dodd, as well as Senator and former First Lady Hillary Clinton. And in 2016, the Republican nomination was captured by Donald Trump, an entrepreneur and television personality, and a person at odds, both personally and ideologically, with the party's national leadership. Trump defeated a huge field of candidates, including five current or former senators, as well as six sitting or former governors. And, for a while, a retired neurosurgeon, Ben Carson, a political neophyte who like Trump had no apparent qualifications for the presidency in terms of policy familiarity, was also viewed as a serious candidate for the office. So was Carly Fiorina, the former CEO of Hewlett Packard who had no government experience and had been quite decisively defeated in her only previous electoral contest for a United States Senate seat. And several of the candidates with office-holding experience did not have much. The candidate who ultimately finished second to Donald Trump was Ted Cruz, who, like Obama, had served four years in the Senate. During his tenure there, he went to great lengths to hone an image as an outsider, attacking both Democratic and Republican leaders as part of the Washington establishment, at one point calling his own party leader, Mitch McConnell, a liar, and encouraging conservative Republicans in the House of Representatives to oppose their Speaker, John Boehner. His strategy paid off, in the sense that he was able to run as an outsider, but he received no support from his Senate colleagues. Their view of him was summarized by Boehner's comment after he left the House, to the effect that he had "never worked with a more miserable son of a bitch in my life."[6]

Given the large number of aspiring candidates, the 2016 Republican nomination contest raised the possibility of a so-called brokered convention that might go beyond the first ballot in order to select a nominee. That had not happened for more than a half a century. Rather than an assembly of party leaders debating the merits and electability of candidates and moving through several ballots in order to select their nominee, under the new rules, a presumptive nominee had been identified before the convention based on the pledged delegates that he or she had assembled through the primary and caucus process. Instead of deciding who the party's nominee will be, the convention has become a four-day infomercial for the party, as it takes advantage of the free television time to showcase its rising young stars and kick off the general election campaign. As a testimony to the obsolescence of the convention as a nominating arena, the brief specter of a brokered Republican Convention plunged party leaders, candidates, and commentators into prolonged discussions about how such a process would work, what the party rules stated, to what extent delegates were free to switch their votes from the candidate who won the primaries or caucuses in their states, and most tellingly, whether it would be "democratic" to select someone other than the candidate who had received the most votes, albeit a plurality, in the primaries and caucuses.

There is no better indicator of the impotence of the Republican party leadership than the fact that Donald Trump, a serial offender of women, Latinos, and Muslims, and the author of the most crude comments about his fellow aspirants for the Republican nomination, and Ted Cruz, by all accounts the most unpopular man in the United States Senate, were the top two finishers in 2016. Rather than doing what he could to avoid what many thought was going to be an electoral and reputational catastrophe for his party, the chairman of the national committee, Reince Priebus, seemed to be at most a referee in the process, apologizing for the excesses of Trump and Cruz, urging people to be nice to each other, and advocating party unity after Trump had secured the nomination.

On the Democratic side, Hillary Clinton ultimately secured the nomination, but only after a long and occasionally nasty contest with Senator Bernie Sanders. As a senator, he called himself an Independent, had proclaimed his belief in democratic socialism, and, like Cruz and Trump on the Republican side, spent a great deal of his time attacking the party whose nomination he was seeking. Again, it is a commentary on the pathetic state of the national party organization that the major challenge to the party's front-runner was someone who, prior to his race, eschewed the label of Democrat. It was also reflected in the inability of the party leadership to get Sanders to drop out of the race early and/or tone down his criticism of Clinton so that the party could unite for the fight against Trump.

In contrast to the Republicans, the Democrats had preserved some level of party control over its nomination process with the creation of super-delegates who could be in a position to head off a disastrous nominee. In 2016, these delegates overwhelmingly supported Hillary Clinton against Sanders, in the process raising criticism—primarily from Sanders backers—that empowering such unelected delegates was undemocratic, despite the fact that Clinton had received many more popular votes in the primaries and caucuses than Sanders had. The Sanders critique of the super-delegates underlines the fact that the movement of the nomination process from a party-centered process to a popular, candidate-centered process did not just take place in terms of rules, but also in the way the voters at large viewed the contest. Simply stated, it is now broadly accepted that the "people"—defined as those who turn up at a caucus or at a primary voting booth—are to decide the party's nominee, rather than those who hold office, or have had extensive experience in government, or have worked for the party over many years. Trump supporters made exactly this democratic claim when, after the primaries concluded, some Republicans were trying to devise a convention scenario that would deprive him of the nomination.

The Sanders people argued as well that because so many super-delegates had announced their support for Hillary Clinton in the midst of the primary season, it created a perception that Sanders could not win the nomination, which in turn became something of a self-fulfilling prophecy. On the other hand, in 2008, most of the super-delegates who had leaned toward Clinton early in the nomination process, many with public endorsements, abandoned her for Obama on the argument that he had emerged from the primaries and caucuses with more support. In fact, when all the primary and caucus votes were counted in 2008, Clinton actually had a few more votes than Obama. As a concession to Sanders and his supporters, the 2016 convention agreed to establish a "unity commission" to revise the rules on super-delegates for the 2020 campaign. Specifically, super-delegates who are not governors, senators, or members of the House (about two-thirds of the super-delegates) would lose their power to vote independently of their state's voters. Instead, they would be required to represent the proportional results of the primary or caucus in their state.[7]

The 2016 nomination process has been seen by some as *sui generis*, the product of a particularly harsh period of voter discontent with the economy and growing income inequality, as well as a sense, fed by eight years of unrelenting attacks by the Republican Party on President Obama, that the government was incompetent and that the nation was on the edge of economic and international catastrophe. Xenophobia, racism, and fear of terrorism also played a role. These factors certainly explain some of what happened, but they miss the larger picture. As the preceding narrative makes clear, party leaders had slowly been losing control over the nomination process ever since the post-1968 reforms. This was not a straight line process, and the organization's candidates certainly prevailed in many cases. But in the fully democratized system that eventually replaced the earlier system, the field was ripe for candidates who, though opposed by party leaders, could connect with the party's most enthusiastic supporters who made up a disproportionate share of the primary and caucus voters.

At one time, candidates needed political experience to appeal to these voters, but changes in the communication industry made it easier for these outsiders to draw attention and support without the help of party regulars. Jesse Jackson, Pat Buchanan, and Pat Robertson were media figures, and as a result, they had their own base of support, independent of their respective party organizations. Barack Obama attracted a great deal of publicity and support as the result of one impressive speech at the 2004 Democratic Convention, as well as his youth, his articulateness, and his status as the first African American with a serious chance to win the nomination. And in 2008, John McCain made his own contribution to the movement toward political amateurism by selecting Sarah Palin, the governor of Alaska, as his vice presidential candidate. Palin's political experience had consisted of two years as governor and a stint as mayor of a very small town in that state. But in the course of the election, she proved to be ignorant on virtually every public policy question on the national agenda and obviously unprepared to become president if the occasion should arise. But Palin also became a media favorite who connected well with less educated voters who liked her homespun style and did not seem to be concerned with her simplistic and uninformed views.

Donald Trump's candidacy built squarely on these trends. The last twenty years had demonstrated that political experience at the national level was no longer an essential qualification for the nomination or for the national visibility that a successful campaign would require. Jackson, Perot, Obama, and Palin had demonstrated that media attention could catapult a person to national prominence and political viability, as it did for Trump, but also for Carson and Fiorina. Bernie Sanders' candidacy is a bit more complicated. Unlike the other candidates mentioned, he had extensive government experience and prior to his race, a rather low media profile. But just as Obama in 2008 was able to generate media coverage and campaign contributions, Sanders was able to do the same thing, in his case exploiting the anti-establishment mood in the country as well as the media interest in having a real, ratings-producing race for the Democratic Party nomination. This allowed him to exploit the democratized nomination process to play to the anger and grievances of the Democratic base in much the same way that Obama did in 2008 and as Trump did on the Republican side in 2016.

The point is that under the pre-reform system, neither Obama's nor Trump's successful nomination nor Sanders' extended but ultimately losing campaign would have been possible. By virtue of the new process, party leaders have precious few options to stop a candidate like Trump whom they do not wish to see at the top of the ticket, but who performed well in the caucuses and primaries. Should such a candidate somehow be denied the nomination, the party would invite a revolt from those voters who supported the candidate and who had been told by the candidates and the media alike that their votes would determine the outcome. Candidates who have been office holders for a brief time, like Obama and Cruz, can no longer be told to wait their turn, that they are not yet ready to be national candidates or to be president, and that there are others who have paid their dues and are more prepared to run and to govern. Rather than waiting, they are able to bypass the party leadership and go directly to the people, whether ordinary voters or local party activists, to seek the nomination.

And the 2016 results, particularly on the Republican side, raise serious questions about the argument that the extended party organization, including donors and affiliated interest groups, have replaced party leaders as the deciders of the nomination process. All through his campaign for the nomination, Trump had virtually no support from major Republican donors and the organized groups such as the Chamber of Commerce, religious conservatives, and pro-life organizations that generally ally themselves with the Republican Party. They viewed him as a loose cannon, a person of uncertain political principles and questionable moral character and, most significantly, as a certain loser in November. Nonetheless, he won, aided of course by his own personal wealth, which handily compensated for his lack of donors. And ultimately, the extended party (or at least most of it) rallied around him. For the Democrats, the party's donors opposed Sanders, viewing him both as a certain loser in the fall, and a person who was hostile to their economic interests. Although some of the party's affiliated labor groups supported Sanders and others remained neutral, most supported Clinton, as did most of the party's African American and Latino leaders. Sanders had very little support among office holders; only one of his Democratic Senate colleagues endorsed him.

Both the Trump and Sanders campaigns were affected by the different rules in each state. In states where voters could participate in any primary that they chose, regardless of their party registration, Trump could draw on disaffected Democrats as well as independents. Sanders had little appeal to registered Republicans but did better among independents and more poorly in those states where voting was restricted to registered Democrats. Another indicator then of the lack of party control is the inability of the party to have, let alone enforce rules about who can and who cannot participate in its nominating process. In sum, rather than awarding the party's presidential nomination to a candidate who has established a record of policy positions and demonstrated competence and personal qualities, the 2016 Republican nomination (and arguably the 2008 Democratic nomination) suggests a process that invites candidates to capture the party's nomination by running a personal, candidate-centered campaign directed not at the party organization, but at those who participate in and finance the primaries and caucuses.

The Marathon

The nomination phase of the selection process has been extended to the point where it now takes much longer to secure the presidential nomination than to contest the general election against the opposition party's nominee. Although actual voting does not take place until January or early February of the election year, aspiring candidates find themselves making trips to Iowa, New Hampshire, and other early primary and caucus states as much as three or four years before the next presidential election. They are there to make friends, do favors, identify allies, and increase their name recognition. They set up "exploratory committees"—devices that allow them to raise money to support these efforts before formally declaring their candidacy. Once they declare, they are then required to register and report their contributions to the Federal Election Commission. The formal announcement of their candidacies can take place anywhere from four months to a year before the Iowa caucuses, which is six to seven months before the convention and almost two years before the national election itself. Barack Obama announced his candidacy in Springfield, Illinois in February of 2007, nearly eleven months before the Iowa caucuses, and twenty months before the election itself.

Jimmy Carter was the first presidential candidate to fully understand the importance that Iowa had assumed under the new rules. When his term as governor of Georgia ended in early 1975, he essentially moved to Iowa, traveling the state, meeting its people, setting up precinct organizations, and recruiting supporters. His opponents, all more experienced politicians, did not recognize the value of doing well in Iowa until it was too late. By the time that they decided to compete there, Carter's organization was firmly entrenched. Although a plurality of Iowa caucus goers voted to send uncommitted delegates to the convention, Carter finished a solid first among those who had a preference among the various candidates. In each subsequent election cycle, there have been candidates who toyed with the notion of skipping Iowa because they didn't view its caucus electorate as politically friendly toward them, but most ultimately decided to compete, because failing to do so would lead the media and other observers to question how serious they were about running.

In more recent years, a new component has been added to the schedule. Candidates who have declared their candidacy or are actively exploring becoming a candidate are now expected to participate in televised debates, many taking place well before Iowa and New Hampshire. Given the fact that this is free publicity, candidates seldom pass on the opportunity to participate. In 2008, the candidates for the Democratic nomination engaged in sixteen debates prior to the Iowa caucus, the first held on April 26, 2007, a little less than nine months before the Iowa caucuses. In 2012, the Republican candidates for their party's nomination engaged in thirteen televised debates before the Iowa caucuses, the first taking place on May 5, 2015, almost eight months before the caucus date. The candidates would engage in seven more debates before the end of the nomination process. Concerned that so many debates had damaged the party's chances of winning in 2012 because they forced the party's eventual nominee too far to the right, in 2016 the party organized "only" seven pre-Iowa debates, the first taking place in the first week of August 2015.

The new nomination process, in other words, has created a permanent campaign for the presidency, a process that begins, for some, not much later than the moment that the current president is sworn into office and sometimes even earlier than that. Certainly, by the time that the presidential election is two years away, serious candidates must be organized, understand where their money is going to come from, and be ready to go. The physical and mental toll on the candidates and their families is enormous. Someone who wishes to be president must, with little exaggeration, commit to being on the road for at least two years, traveling the country, raising money, living in hotels and motels, eating bad food, and giving the same stump speech several times a day—all with the goal of seeking to separate himself or herself from the rest of the announced and potential candidates. In sports terms, it's a marathon rather than a sprint. For office holders such as sitting senators and governors, it means taking what amounts to an unofficial leave from their current position to campaign for a new job. In 2015–16, Governor Christie of New Jersey probably spent more time in New Hampshire than in the state he was elected to govern. The four Republican senators campaigning for their party's presidential nomination missed more than 30% of the roll call votes taken between July, 2015 and July, 2016. Senator Cruz missed 46%, Senator Rubio missed 38%, and on the Democratic side, Senator Sanders missed 58%. The median absence rate for the entire Senate during this period was 2%.[8]

The Money

The nomination phase of the selection process has become a lot more expensive because of the extended time frame and because candidates now need to campaign in caucuses and primaries strewn, seemingly haphazardly, across the nation. As a result, organizational, travel, and advertising costs have increased exponentially, as well as the time that candidates devote to fund-raising. Staff need to be employed and campaign offices opened in the early primary states. Polls need to be commissioned, ads need to be designed, and air time needs to be purchased.

Such expenses are common for any election, but when one is running for the Senate, for example, one needs to do all of this twice: once for a primary and once for the general election. One can use the same staffers and organization for both elections, and although the primary electorate may be different from the general election voters, the local issues that tend to dominate such races will remain the same. But for presidential aspirants, the nomination process requires that this be done in a number of different states, each with its own political culture, its own electorate, and its own series of local issues that voters expect to be addressed. In other words, you do it in Iowa, then again in New Hampshire but with some variation given New Hampshire's political culture and issues, then in Nevada, and on and on until you win or drop out.

The marathon nomination process means that a serious candidate requires significant funds. Having the money, of course, does not guarantee the nomination, but having no money makes it virtually impossible to compete. Under the pre-reform system, a great deal of money wasn't really necessary. A candidate did not have to create a campaign organization and compete in a variety of costly primaries and caucuses. Once the nomination was secured, candidates could rely on the party at all levels to help with the funds necessary to win the election. Not so under the new system. In 1999, George W. Bush raised approximately $37 million to finance his 2000 campaign for the Republican nomination. In 2007, Barack Obama and Hillary Clinton, between them, amassed a total of $221 million for the nomination phase alone, with more money to come as the campaign went on. Again, money doesn't always buy the candidate the love of the voters. In 2007, Rudy Giuliani, the former mayor of New York City, raised more than $61 million to finance his 2008 campaign for the Republican nomination and won no primaries. And in 2016, Jeb Bush raised $100 million for his primary fight, and, like Giuliani, failed to win a single primary or caucus. Ted Cruz, the last candidate standing against Donald Trump in 2016, raised about $182 million dollars directly and through Super PACs supporting him.[9]

The flow of money into campaigns was accelerated by the Supreme Court's 2010 decision in *Citizens United v. Federal Election Commission*. The Court ruled that corporations could spend unlimited money in support of candidates for public office, a right eventually extended to other non-party groups such as unions and trade organizations. Although these groups could not contribute money directly to a candidate and his or her campaign, they could contribute what they wished to so-called Super PACs. These PACs are ostensibly independent of the presidential candidate and are not permitted to coordinate their activities with the candidate or his campaign. In practice, these groups are staffed by people who have been connected with the candidate, and the notion of independent action has been mostly theoretical. Although campaign finance laws restrict the amount of money that a donor can give directly to a candidate, there are virtually no restrictions on how much can be donated to a candidate's "independent" political action committees. And some of these PACs are organized under a separate provision of the Internal Revenue Service code that allows them to keep the names of their donors secret.

The effect of *Citizens United* has further empowered those with a great deal of money. In 2012, Sheldon Adelson, a Nevada casino magnate, almost single-handedly funded Newt Gingrich's campaign for the Republican nomination by giving $20 million to a Super PAC backing the former Speaker.[10] After Gingrich lost, it was estimated that Adelson and his wife spent another $30 million on Romney's losing campaign against President Obama.[11] Unaffected by *Citizens United* was the ability of rich candidates to spend unlimited amounts of their own money on their campaigns. In his losing quest for the Republican nomination in 2008, Mitt Romney spent $42.4 million of his own money.[12] In 2012, he spent less from his own funds but drew upon his friends and contacts in the venture capital business, took in large contributions from the very wealthy, and ultimately raised nearly one billion dollars for his campaign, just a shade under what President Obama raised for his reelection campaign. Often, wealthy candidates loan their campaigns the money they need to start up, with the hope that once contributions start rolling in they can repay themselves. In 2016, Donald Trump boasted that he self-financed his entire primary campaign and did not establish a political action committee, but once he secured the nomination, he sought donations, part of which were used to reimburse him for his own expenditures. He also revisited his opposition to establishing a PAC to receive large contributions.

The full capabilities of the internet for fund-raising became apparent in 2004 when the campaign of Howard Dean, the governor of Vermont and a long-shot candidate, at best, for the Democratic nomination, raised hundreds of thousands of dollars a day via the internet in the weeks right after he announced his candidacy and $20 million overall, with the average contribution amounting to about $100.[13] In December 2007, Ron Paul, a marginal candidate in the Republican field because of his libertarian philosophy and isolationist foreign policy views, raised $6 million though the internet in one day; a month earlier, he raised $4.2 million in one day.[14] These periodic "money bombs" allowed him to stay in the race much longer than one would have imagined given his views.

Internet fund-raising is a further step toward the democratization of the nomination process. It allows candidates who are not necessarily the favorites of those with great wealth, or do not themselves possess great wealth, to compete by amassing the contributions of small donors. Donors who contribute the maximum allowable amount to a candidate usually don't give via the internet, but small donors with more modest resources do. Obama in 2008 and Sanders in 2016 raised more than enough money for their outsider campaigns that way, drawing on a constituency encompassing many citizens who did not regularly make contributions. In January 2008 alone, Obama raised $28 million online, with 90% of the donations coming in amounts of less than $100 and 40% in amounts of $25 or less.[15] Sanders raised $8 million online the day after he won the New Hampshire primary, and during the campaign claimed that $27 was the average donation that he received. Online fundraising has now become an essential component of nomination campaigns. Throughout the primary season, virtually every candidate speaks from behind a podium emblazoned with the campaign's web address, and the speech itself often includes a plea for supporters to visit the web site and contribute.

Empowering the Base

It is clear that the current nomination process is more democratic, in the sense that more people are able to participate, than was the case when the process was dominated by party leaders. In 2008, around 57 million voters participated, just over 30% of the voting age population and 43% of the number of people who would eventually vote in the general election.[16] In 2016, more than 60 million people participated in the primaries and caucuses of the two political parties, a number representing about 29% of the country's voting age population, and about 46% of those who voted in the general election.

The participation numbers in the new nomination process are impressive when compared with the old system that was dominated by party leaders. But these participants also do not reflect the electorate for the general election and sometimes not even the party's supporters. First, of course, in many states, those who are not registered as party members cannot participate. Second, and more importantly, the current system enhances the power of the most committed party identifiers at the state and local levels, the so-called party base, who are the people most likely to turn out to vote, especially in caucuses, but also in primaries. It also enhances the power of narrow interest groups who are particularly important to the party's base. This works in favor of those candidates who can arouse the passion and excitement of these base voters, often candidates with the strongest ideological commitments. While under the old system, ideological purity was somewhat less important than nominating a candidate who could win the general election, under the new system ideology tends to trump pragmatism and centrism. In other words, for many purists, it's more important to be right than to win, or more charitably, they see being right as the way to win.

There were early signs of this at the outset of the nomination reform era. At the 1972 Democratic Convention, the first held under the new system, George McGovern, a person associated with the most progressive wing of the Democratic Party was nominated, despite the concerns of veteran party members that he was the weakest candidate that they could field against Richard Nixon. Nonetheless, McGovern had seized the nomination by winning primaries and besting more moderate veteran politicians such as Scoop Jackson, Hubert Humphrey, and Ed Muskie. Notable as well was the strong showing of George Wallace, the segregationist governor of Alabama, whose race-based ideological appeal to white southerners also played well among some working-class northern whites. The two most ideological candidates in the field—McGovern and Wallace—combined to draw more popular votes than the combination of Humphrey, Jackson, and Muskie.

The importance of ideological purity is apparent in both political parties. Today, it is not possible to win the Democratic nomination for the presidency without being firmly in the pro-choice camp on abortion, just as it is not possible to win the Republican nomination without being firmly anti-abortion. A candidate for the Republican nomination cannot question the wisdom of the National Rifle Association's views on gun control and the Second Amendment, and a candidate for the Democratic nomination cannot question the sanctity of social security and Medicare or the right of unions to organize. The primary system encourages Republican candidates to move as far to the right as possible, and their Democratic candidates to move almost as far to the left. In 2012, Mitt Romney took a much more extreme position on immigration—a hot button issue for the Republican base—than he probably believed in. He also had to explain his reversal from a pro-choice governor of Massachusetts to a pro-life candidate for the Republican nomination, as well as his opposition to the Affordable Care Act—legislation that was quite similar to the health care law that he supported and signed while governor. To address the qualms of the Republican base, he declared himself a "severe conservative" and moved further to the right on these issues than he probably wanted.

In 2016, Bernie Sanders prolonged his race with Hillary Clinton by appealing to the party base with proposals that were further to the left, proposals such as single payer health care, free college tuition, and breaking up the big banks, as well as opposition to free trade agreements. On the latter, he forced Clinton to abandon her support for the Transpacific Trade Partnership, an agreement that she had been on record as supporting. On the Republican side, Ted Cruz, the candidate who came in second to Trump, was the favorite of those primary voters who described themselves as very conservative, and if not for Trump's atypical campaign, Cruz might well have emerged as the party's nominee. More moderate candidates such as Bush, Christie, Kasich, and Rubio made little headway with these voters, despite their conservative credentials.

This bias of the nomination process toward the ideological extremes of each party has adverse consequences for the general election campaign and also creates governing problems for the person who is ultimately elected president. Romney's position on immigration was a problem for him in the general election, as were the less than tolerant positions that he needed to take on gay marriage. And if Sanders had been successful in 2016, his positions would not have been very popular with a general election electorate that was larger, more diverse, and more conservative than the electorate that votes in the Democratic primaries or participates in the caucuses. For a more centrist candidate such as Hillary Clinton, her reversal on trade policy that the Sanders campaign forced was never fully believable to those who viewed this as an important issue, and her switch would certainly have come back to haunt her had she been elected.

Once candidates move to the extremes during the nomination process, they have a very difficult time getting back to the center of the political spectrum where many of those who determine the outcome of the general election are found. The candidate who wins the presidency is then faced with the difficult choice of sticking with the pledges that he or she has made to the primary electorate or engaging in the sort of compromise that presidents need to make in order to govern under our constitutional system. To the extent that our general elections are fought between the more ideological representatives of their political parties, the prospect that the winning candidate can govern in a constitutional system of separate institutions sharing power is reduced. The nomination process, in other words, hardens positions and expands the ideological distances between the two parties, contributing to the gridlock that has characterized the American political system for much of the last two decades.

The Media

The long, open contest for the party's nomination has provided newspapers, television networks, and cable channels, as well as the countless web sites, blogs, and social media platforms that arose as we moved into the 21st century with a continuing story to cover and comment upon. The fracturing of the media landscape and its implications for the presidential selection process will be discussed more fully in the next chapter.

Under the old nominating process, the media coverage of the campaign would come from newspaper stories tracking the movements of particular candidates, or the very occasional segment on a network news program addressing a candidate's statements or his performance in an odd primary. The New Hampshire primary was certainly reported, both in newspapers and on television, mostly because of its novelty as the first-in-the-nation contest and as a debut event for aspiring candidates, but television did not really become a part of the nominating process until the national conventions. With nothing much else on their schedules for the summer, the networks were pleased to provide wall-to-wall coverage of the speeches, silly hats, and raucous demonstrations in the aisles by supporters of the various candidates.

Today, media coverage of the campaigns is dictated by what attracts readers and viewers. Whether played out on the political stage or in sports arenas, people like to see a contest with a winner and a loser, and with some drama and uncertainty about how the contest will turn out. In presidential races under the old rules, there were only two times when there were winners and losers: at the convention, and on Election Day. But the new rules changed that. Now there are more than fifty occasions (actually more than 100, when one considers nomination races in both parties) when there is a winner and often several losers. So the caucus and primary season has turned into a major opportunity to attract readers and viewers, particularly the latter, as newspaper readership declined and television watching increased. Each event provides an opportunity for the networks to declare a winner for a primary and a caucus and assess the consequences of the contest for the nomination process.

Drama and suspense are also staples of television viewing, so coverage of the nomination process often exaggerates the importance of individual contests in order to generate an audience. In 2016, devoted CNN watchers will remember anchorman Wolf Blitzer's breathless announcements of "breaking news," which in many cases were the partial results of a small state primary or a caucus with a handful of delegates at stake. Often lost in the reporting and analysis of primary and caucus results is what has actually been won or lost. A candidate who has been declared the "winner" of the Iowa caucuses may have garnered only 28% of the vote, as Jimmy Carter did in 1976, or 34% of the vote as Mike Huckabee did in 2008. Obviously, the idea of "winning" changes dramatically from the common understanding of the term when two-thirds of the participants vote for someone other than the person who has been declared "the winner." Sometimes people who come in second or third are declared winners because they have done better than expected. This perception is often fed by candidates and their campaign managers who publicly lower expectations so that their candidate can take pride in exceeding them. In the huge 2016 Republican field, finishing among the top five was considered to be a good showing, and finishing second to Donald Trump was considered to be a win. Alternatively, someone who was thought to be a strong candidate could be seen as having failed because he didn't win a primary by a wide enough margin, or because he came in a percentage point or two behind another candidate.

In addition, it is often not clear what exactly has been won. As we have discussed, the role of the primaries and caucuses is to select delegates to the national convention. Under Democratic Party rules, such delegates are apportioned among the candidates in rough approximation to the percentage of the vote that they receive. In 2016, Hillary Clinton's campaign breathed a collective sigh of relief when she was declared the winner of the Iowa caucuses (by four votes) but the close result meant that she received 23 delegates while Bernie Sanders received 21. Had she been declared the loser, her subsequent loss, by a large margin, to Sanders in the New Hampshire primary might have done significant damage to her campaign. The Republican Party has different rules, but only in the case of a few winner-take-all states does winning the primary mean winning all the delegates. When Donald Trump "won" the New Hampshire primary, he received about 35% of the vote, more than double the vote of John Kasich, the 2nd place finisher. But Trump ended up with eleven delegates to the convention, compared with the twelve that were split among the other candidates. Finally, winning in states such as Iowa and New Hampshire, where only a relatively small number of delegates are at stake, is not the same as winning delegates in larger states, but for television, all wins are equal. Wins in the first two states are magnified beyond reason and, in fact, become something of a self-fulfilling prophecy. Because the media tell us how crucial the Iowa and New Hampshire results are, they actually become more important than they should be, given the few delegates at stake.

Even the final results of the nomination process are distorted as commentators forget the relatively narrow electorate that participated and the often split nature of the results in a multi-candidate field. One analysis of the 2016 results notes that, given the fact that about half of those who participated in the nomination process voted for candidates other than Trump or Clinton, the two "winners" of their party's nomination received about 14% in total of the votes of those eligible to participate.[17]

So what exactly is won and lost in these events, in addition to pledged delegates? Most important, what is won is public visibility, the reputation as a winner, status as a serious contender, and likely continued or increased financial donations to keep the candidate in the race. That is why candidates engage in the manipulation of expectations; they do so because they can be perceived as having done well, even if they haven't. Primary and caucus outcomes are seldom reliable measures of actual voter support, given the relatively low turnout in such events. They certainly are not predictive of how well someone will perform in the general election, again, given the low turnout, and secondly, the restriction in many of the states to registered members of the party. Barack Obama won 55% of the vote in the 2008 South Carolina primary, but in the general election he won 45% of the votes in that state, because African Americans constituted a huge share of the Democratic primary vote, but a smaller percentage of the general election voters. Similarly, in 2016, Donald Trump won the Republican primary in New York with 59% of the vote, but lost the state in the general election, receiving only 38% of the vote.

The primary and caucus season has become a sort of television series, if you will, with weekly episodes entitled Iowa, New Hampshire, Super Tuesday, Wisconsin, etc., with a simple plot line and an easy conclusion— one winner and a number of losers. Networks hype each event—in 2016 several cable networks even added a countdown clock to their screen to show the exact number of days, hours, and minutes until the next primary votes would be cast—and suggest that the results will determine if the winner is now firmly on the way to the nomination and the losers on their way to dropping out. Every result, no matter how trivial, is dissected by a panel of "experts" and commentators committed to telling the viewers what it all means. The strength of their analyses is typically undermined, of course, by the results of the next primary or caucus, but that does not dampen their enthusiasm for providing a brand new take on the state of the race.

The primary and caucus television series also runs alongside a second series called the "debates"—televised debates in which candidates square off against each other on the same stage, fielding questions from television news personalities. Debates during the nomination phase of the campaign actually pre-date general election debates. The first one occurred in 1948 when Governor Thomas Dewey of New York and former Governor Harold Stassen of Minnesota, candidates for the Republican nomination, debated a single question: whether the Communist Party should be outlawed in the United States (Dewey said no, Stassen said yes). The debate was carried on the radio. In 1956, Adlai Stevenson and Estes Kefauver held the first televised debate as they battled for the Democratic nomination, and in 1960, John Kennedy had debates with both Hubert Humphrey and Lyndon Johnson on his way to the Democratic nomination. Debates during the primary season have taken place ever since, although incumbent presidents running for reelection typically do not participate.

In recent years, the number of primary debates has increased and the debate season has gone on for a longer period of time. For the 2008 presidential cycle, the first debate was held at the end of April 2007, and with no incumbent in the race, the two parties together held thirty-eight debates (nineteen each) during the nomination season. In 2012, the Republican Party alone held twenty debates.[18] The proliferation of debates and their early start has added to the marathon nature of the presidential nomination process, likely at the expense of both candidate and citizen exhaustion.

Ostensibly, the debates are designed to familiarize viewers with the candidates, their positions, and their style and character. For the candidates, particularly in crowded fields such as the 2008 race for the nomination of both parties and the 2012 and 2016 races for the Republican nomination, the goal is to separate oneself from the field and to be identified as a front-runner, or first-tier candidate, as one moves toward the Iowa and New Hampshire primaries. In 2016, the early debate structure actually contributed to the winnowing of the Republican field. Because the stage could not accommodate all the candidates, the early debates were broken into two segments, with those doing reasonably well in the polls assigned to the prime time slot and those lagging far behind consigned to an earlier and less viewed debate. And in the prime time main event, candidates were arrayed on the stage in the order of the current polling, with the person ahead in most of the polls (typically, Donald Trump) accorded the center spot, those doing less well stationed to his left and right, and those who barely made it to the event on the far edges, underlining their peripheral status in the polls.

Once again, the debates provide an opportunity to declare winners and losers, although in large fields, there may be more than one winner. When viewers and commentators declare someone a debate winner, their stock suddenly begins to rise. When Carly Fiorina did well in one debate by taking on Donald Trump and one of his many sexist remarks, her visibility in the Republican race rose and for a brief time she was considered to be a serious candidate. When Jeb Bush seemed uncomfortable in the debate setting and not very adept at responding to Trump's jibes and insults, commentators were unanimous in the view that he had "lost" the debate, and the assessment of his viability as a candidate began to drop, despite his large campaign war chest and his superior knowledge of the issues. At the same time, Trump's take-no-prisoners approach to the debates seemed to help his position in the race, despite his many outrageous utterances and his obvious lack of knowledge. The larger point is that the rise and fall of candidates as a result of the debates has little to do with matters of substance and policy. These exercises are all about performance and how that performance is assessed by viewers and commentators. At the general election stage, debates, while still about performance, have a substantive dimension to them because, as representatives of different parties, there are typically policy distinctions between the two candidates that are addressed. But during the nomination phase, there are unlikely to be major policy differences, because all candidates come from the same party, and all are appealing to the same group of base voters.

Debates during the nomination season can also have consequences for the general election. To secure his party's nomination in 2012, Mitt Romney had to move far to the right on issues such as abortion and immigration, issues where he had previously established a more moderate position. In a January 2012 debate in Florida, Romney tried to explain his position on immigration by suggesting that undocumented immigrants would leave the country through a process he defined as "self deportation." This infelicitous phrase hounded him throughout the campaign and helped seal his fate with the Hispanic portion of the electorate.

What all of this means for aspiring candidates is that the media is not simply a window into the nomination process for citizens, but more like a fun house mirror, in the sense that it provides a particular picture, often distorted, through which the candidates are perceived and their qualities and positions judged not just by average voters, but by the pundits who make instant declarations of winners and losers. Perception is the name of the game, and candidates who win the perception game by winning primaries and caucuses and doing well, or at least not badly, in debates, will stay in the race and enhance their chances of capturing the nomination.

Although it is risky to generalize from one case, Donald Trump's emergence as the presidential candidate of the Republican Party demonstrates that the two television series that we have identified—the primary and caucus series and the debate series—have very little to do with the qualifications or qualities that one would expect of a presidential candidate. More to the point, his nomination and the close race that Bernie Sanders waged for the Democratic nomination attest to the ebbing of the party organization's control over the nomination process and the movement toward a more chaotic, albeit more open and democratized process, one in which the media, money, public presentation, and the wishes of the party's most ideological members are more important in determining the outcome than the wishes of party leaders, the objective qualifications of candidates for the office, and the selection of a candidate with the best chance of prevailing in the general election.

It is also clear from the 2016 campaign that the various groups associated with the party may be in conflict with each other, as well as with the party's priorities. The commentators on Fox News, as well as other conservative media outlets and personalities, played a more important role in securing the Republican nomination for Donald Trump than the Republican Party leadership, none of whom endorsed Trump until the very end of the process. In recent years, the voices from these precincts had grown increasingly hostile to the party's leaders. They were instrumental in the uprising that cost John Boehner his speakership and also attacked his successor, Paul Ryan, because they thought he too was selling out conservative principles. They were particularly upset when Ryan publicly criticized some of Trump's statements, took his time coming up with an ultimately half-hearted endorsement after he had secured the nomination, and then backed away from the candidate after his recorded comments admitting to a record of sexual assault surfaced.

After its 2012 defeat, the Republican Party commissioned an "autopsy" to discover what went wrong. Among the most prominent conclusions of the final report was that, in view of the changing demographics of the country, the party had to do more to reach people of color, particularly Latinos, who were the fastest growing section of the electorate. The party's reliance on white voters, especially older white voters, was a losing long-term strategy, given both the actuarial charts and the increasing diversity of the country. But in the face of this, the person who emerged as the Party's standard bearer won the nomination by taking the harshest view on the issue of immigration and gratuitously attacking the character of Latinos. Most of his opponents in the nomination process took a similar position, and those who didn't, such as former Florida Governor Jeb Bush, were badly defeated. Although Trump ultimately prevailed in

the general election—although losing the popular vote by
margin—the point is that the objective priorities of the par
be ill served by a nomination process that empowered peopl
who neither knew nor cared about those priorities.

Conclusion

At one time, there was speculation that an amateur candidate with a
great deal of money could run as an independent and win the presidency.
This was the approach that Ross Perot followed, an approach doomed
to failure by the operation of the Electoral College system. What Donald
Trump demonstrated is that under the current rules and in the new media
environment, such a candidate could seize the nomination of a major
political party. This is because when it comes to presidential elections,
the national party of today is primarily, and at best, "in service" to their
candidates.[19] The party "in service" helps ambitious politicians achieve
their goals, but the politicians set the terms of engagement, raise much
of the money that the parties distribute, and always feel free to go else-
where if necessary for what they need. The service party plays the role of
organizing the nominating process and for the most part, staying neutral
as the aspirants, each with his or her own campaign team and financial
backers, slug it out in front of the national media. In 2016, the leaders of
the Republican Party, most of whom were privately appalled at the idea
of Donald Trump as their presidential candidate, did little to stop him.
They were concerned that if they tried to block him, he would run as an
independent, and although he would not win the presidency, he would
hurt the chances of their nominee. So they did everything in their power
to accommodate him in the hope that another, more mainstream candidate would emerge. When that didn't happen, they were stuck with him.

On the Democratic side, Bernie Sanders complained that the national
committee had acted to help Hillary Clinton's candidacy. Certainly,
there were party leaders who did not take Sanders' campaign as a serious challenge to the former secretary of state and wanted to unify the
party behind the presumptive nominee as quickly as possible. Hacked
emails from some party leaders did suggest that they had a preference for
Clinton and the national chairperson, Representative Debbie Wasserman
Schultz, was in open conflict with the Sanders campaign. On the other
hand, it was not at all clear what they did to actually help Clinton. The
voter data bases that the party had created were made available to both
campaigns and there were debates, although in the view of the Sanders
campaign, too few. If anything, Clinton was helped by the rules regarding
super-delegates that were in place long before the 2016 election season
began. Even then, Clinton won more elected delegates than Sanders did,
and had the super-delegates been apportioned on the basis of the primary
and caucus vote, she still would have prevailed. Rather than the rules

hurting Sanders, the real story is that the new rules allowed a person who had never identified himself as a member of the Democratic Party to fight for the nomination right up until the party convention and to exact platform concessions and speaking time as the price for his ultimate support of Clinton.

Once the nomination has been achieved, the candidate, rather than the party, is in charge. The campaign team that helped the candidate to secure the nomination continues on to the general election. That team organizes the field operations, makes the day-to-day decisions about where to campaign and what issues to talk about, and runs the fundraising operation. There is certainly cooperation and communication with the national party, especially in regard to fund-raising, although in Donald Trump's case, there were many reports of a strained relationship between the candidate and the national party. Whatever the case, it is abundantly clear that the candidate and his or her campaign managers are calling the shots. This is symbolized by the location of the campaign headquarters. Barack Obama ran both of his campaigns out of Chicago, Hillary Clinton's 2016 campaign was based in Brooklyn, and Donald Trump's campaign was based across the river in Manhattan. The offices of the national party are, of course, located in Washington, DC.

Clearly, the party in service does not vet the credentials of aspiring candidates or pick the candidate best suited for the job, or even the candidate whose views are most congruent with the party's policy commitments. Rather, the party and its apparatus are, in effect, seized by the candidate who prevails in the nominating process. Although the candidates who have emerged have often been capable people, albeit of varying quality and skills, the process leaves the door open for a candidate who is less capable, as well as a candidate who is less connected with the party and its beliefs. That is the door through which Donald Trump, with the aid of a democratized media environment, walked.

Notes

1 Nelson Polsby, *Consequences of Party Reform* (New York: Oxford University Press, 1983).
2 Marty Cohen, David Karol, Hans Noel and John Zaller, *The Party Decides: Presidential Nominations Before and After Reform* (Chicago: University of Chicago Press, 2008).
3 Emma Roller, "Everything I Learned From Professor Trump." *Washington Post*, July 10, 2016.
4 Lonna Rae Atkeson and Cherie D. Maestes, "Presidential Primary Turnout, 1972–2016." *PS: Political Science and Politics* 49:4 (October, 2016), 755–760. In May, 2017, the California state legislature voted to move its presidential primary to March so that the preferences of their citizens could be registered before the eventual nominee had been determined.
5 Elaine C. Kamarck, *Primary Politics: Everything You Need to Know About How America Nominates Its Presidential Candidates.* 2nd ed. (Washington, DC: Brookings Institution, 2016), 29–31.

6   Danielle Kurtzleben, "Boehner Says He's Never 'Worked With A More Miserable Son Of A Bitch' Than Cruz." www.npr.org/2016/04/28/476016486/boehner-says-hes-never-worked-with-a-more-miserable-son-of-a-bitch-than-cruz

7   David Weigel, "Democrats Vote to Bind Most Superdelegates to State Primary Results." *Washington Post*, July 23, 2016.

8   www.govtrack.us/congress/votes/presidential-candidates

9   www.washingtonpost.com/graphics/politics/2016-election/campaign-finance

10 Theodore Meyer, "How Much Did Sheldon Adelson Really Spend on Campaign 2012?" *Pro Publica*, December 20, 2012.

11 "The 2012 Money Race: Compare the Candidates." http://elections.nytimes.com/2012/campaign-finance

12 Stephen J. Wayne, *Road to the White House 2016*. 10th ed. (Boston: Cengage Learning, 2016), 42.

13 Joe Trippi, *The Revolution Will Not Be Televised* (New York: Harper Collins, 2004), 131.

14 Kenneth P. Vogel, "Money Bomb: Ron Paul Raises $6 million in 24 hour period." *USA Today*, December 17, 2007.

15 Michael Luo, "Small Online Contributions Add Up to Huge Fund Raising Edge for Obama." *New York Times*, February 20, 2008.

16 Drew DeSilver, "Turnout Was High in the Primary Season, But Just Short of the 2008 Record." *Pew Research Center*, June 10, 2016. www.pewresearch.org/fact-tank/2016/06/10/turnout-was-high-in-the-2016-primary-season-but-just-short-of-2008-record/

17 Alicia Parlapiano and Adam Pearce, "Only 9% of America Chose Trump and Clinton as the Nominees." www.nytimes.com/interactive/2016/08/01/us/elections/nine-percent-of-america-selected-trump-and-clinton.html

18 Kyle Kondik and Geoffrey Skelley, "A Brief History of Presidential Primary Clashes." www.centerforpolitics.org/crystalball/articles/eight-decades-of-debate/

19 John Aldrich, *Why Parties: A Second Look* (Chicago: University of Chicago Press, 2011).

6   The Democratized Media

In the middle of the 20th century, there were three major television networks whose entertainment and news programs dominated the airwaves. Most adults read a daily newspaper, and there was a significant readership for weekly news magazines such as *Time* and *Newsweek*. The networks, newspapers, and national magazines served as intermediaries between the population and the political world, reporting on politicians and their doings, government affairs, and the events taking place in the country and around the world. These media outlets and the people who worked for them acted as gatekeepers, determining what was "news" and what wasn't, as well as whose views or candidacy was important and deserved coverage. Although these decisions were made by seasoned editors and journalists, they also were driven, at least in part, by the networks' interest in viewership, the interest of the newspapers and magazines in circulation, and the commercial interests of those who owned these media outlets and those who advertised with them. There was a preference for stories emphasizing personalities rather than issues, conflict rather than consensus, and human interest rather than the public interest, and coverage of people and stories that challenged the nation's economic and political consensus tended to be skimpy. For television, stories with visual content were preferred; news executives quickly discovered that people were less interested in hearing talking heads and more interested in what they could see. Although these biases were not always healthy for the body politic, this information oligopoly nonetheless produced a reasonably standard version of "the facts" that provided citizens and political leaders with a common baseline for discussions of public policy and political candidates.

Democratizing the Media

The first crack in the domination of political news by the established outlets was the emergence of talk radio. Originally aimed primarily at rural audiences, talk radio provided a conservative view of politics and political personalities to those disposed toward these perspectives. Paul

Harvey was the pioneer of this genre of radio journalism with his daily program entitled *The Rest of the Story*, which began in 1976. Harvey "sought to personalize the radio news with right wing opinions, and heart-warming tales of average Americans and folksy observations that evoked the heartland, family values and old-fashioned plain talk. . . . He railed against welfare cheats and defended the death penalty. He worried about the national debt, big government, bureaucrats who lacked common sense, permissive parents, leftist radicals and America succumbing to moral decay. He championed rugged individualism, love of God and country, and the fundamental decency of ordinary people."[1] Contemporary radio personalities such as Rush Limbaugh, Glenn Beck, Sean Hannity, and many others built on Harvey's conservative narrative of the political world with little in the way of serious discussion of the issues, a presumed connection with the values and thoughts of everyday Americans, and a distaste for the forces of cultural and demographic change that they believed were eroding the American way of life.

The second major change in the media environment was the augmentation of the television broadcast networks by cable television, a change that expanded the number of sources of news and information and therefore the choices of viewers. Emerging at the birth of the television age to provide reception to remote areas of the country that could not receive broadcast channels, cable television grew from 14,000 subscribers in 1952 to 53 million subscribers by 1990.[2] By 2013, according to The Nielsen service, the average family received 189 television channels in their homes, although they regularly watched only about 10% of them. Among the cable channels that appeared were narrow gauge news programs designed to appeal to certain audience segments. C-SPAN provided viewers with live coverage of Congress and serious discussions of political issues. CNBC and others concentrated on business news, and CNN, Fox News, and MSNBC devoted themselves entirely to news and politics. These networks provided platforms for prospective candidates, as well as various commentators, that enabled them to reach larger audiences. Viewers, if they wished, were now free to choose a news source, the style and content of which matched their own political and personal interests. And because cable expanded the number of channels that consumers could receive, viewers who were not interested in current events had many alternative and attractive entertainment options from which to select.

Cable broke the monopoly that the networks had over entertainment and news, and the proliferation of options heightened the competition for viewers. In some respects, news became entertainment, and those who appeared on these programs became celebrities. In order to compete, the network news programs were shortened to a half hour, including commercials (so about 22 minutes of actual news). The number of soft news, human interest stories that they carried increased and the amount of time devoted to hard news decreased. They invested heavily in news anchors, male and female, whose appearance seemed to be a more important criterion for their positions than their journalistic ability or understanding of, or concern with, the political world. Cable news shows tried to expand their viewership by creating excitement and conflict, sometimes when neither existed, and sometimes by giving air time to guests with little more than a combative personality to recommend them. In this way, news became a commodity rather than a necessity, and like any commodity, the viewer, as the consumer, was more likely to purchase what he wanted or what made him feel better rather than what he needed.

Fox News came to epitomize this transformation, largely under the leadership of Roger Ailes, its longtime head. As one commentator put it, "Mr. Ailes was a TV guy before he was a politics guy, and then he became a TV guy again. But he recognized, faster than others that on some level TV and politics were the same thing. They fed off the same energy and animal spirits."[3] By catering to and stoking conservative anger and resentments, he and his network prospered, establishing themselves as the go-to place for right wing reporting and commentary, featuring multiple programs offering much the same political slant but fronted by different personalities. Although the network claimed that it was offering "fair and balanced" coverage, its conservative bias was clear. CNN, in contrast, strove (though not always successfully) to stay politically neutral, so when their ratings fell, they moved to a more entertainment oriented strategy by focusing on sensational events and provocative personalities and by labeling virtually every event, no matter how mundane or trivial, as "breaking news."

If democracy and freedom are understood simply as providing multiple choices to citizens, then cable television represents democratization in the sense that it ended the news oligopoly previously enjoyed by the television networks and major newspapers. While at one time Walter Cronkite, the legendary anchor of the *CBS Evening News*, could, with some degree of authority, sign off each broadcast by saying "and that's the way it is," the advent of talk radio and cable television meant that no one was truly in a position to make that statement. Instead, every citizen, drawing on whatever information sources that he or she chose, came to his own conclusions not just on the issues, but also on the facts. The democratization of the media culture eroded the existing information hierarchy and began the movement toward an ethos that said, in effect, that everyone was entitled to their own version of the facts.

The Internet

The next step in media democratization was the rise of the internet and social media platforms—ways for citizens to completely bypass newspapers, cable and network news programs, and their journalists, editors, and commentators. The internet is now home to blogs and web sites too numerous to count. Those trafficking in news and politics run the full range from the sober and fact-based to the lunatic and fantastic. Extremist fringe groups occupy cyberspace alongside standard news sources, reliable reporters, and knowledgeable commentators. Anyone can now call himself a journalist simply by creating a blog and filling it with his own opinions and version of facts and events. Although one can agree that the gatekeepers that existed before the internet restricted the flow of information and often squeezed out positions and ideas that deserved a hearing, the internet is a gatekeeper free zone. Not only is everyone entitled to his or her own version of the facts, but now everyone is able to disseminate this version to the world at absolutely no cost and perhaps at a profit, because if enough people click on your blog, you can actually make money be selling advertising space.

Average citizens regularly recite "facts" and information that they found on the internet. Conspiracy theories and outright falsehoods that, at one time, would have been dismissed out of hand seem to live forever on the internet and, therefore, in the minds of those for whom this is a major source of information. The internet tells us that Barack Obama is a Muslim who was not born in the United States, that Muslim Americans cheered when the twin towers came down on 9/11, that some combination of Jews and the CIA organized various terrorist attacks for their own advantage, and the Sandy Hook Elementary School massacre never occurred, or if it did, it was carried out by advocates of gun control. And in 2016, when Donald Trump's campaign falsely suggested that Hillary Clinton had serious undisclosed health problems, one of Trump's surrogates, Rudy Giuliani, encouraged people to go to the internet to see the proof. These "stories" and countless others that can be found on the internet don't simply stay there; individuals disseminate these stories to their friends through social media platforms, and in their mad rush for viewers and readers, mainstream media pick these stories up, often noting their absurdity, but nonetheless lending them credence by reporting on them.

As people turned to cable and the internet for news and information, advertising dollars followed them there, and the newspaper business declined even further. In 1981, there were 1,730 daily newspapers published in the United States; by 2014, that figure was 1,331, a 23% decline.[4] Those that survived cut their staffs, reduced their coverage of major news stories, and increasingly focused on the local and sensational in order to salvage readers and advertisers. And they also joined the internet, with virtually every newspaper now available online, sometimes requiring internet users to pay to read stories, but often providing their content for free. Websites such as *The Huffington Post* and *Real Clear Politics* do some original reporting and commentary, but for the most part, they simply compile and disseminate stories and articles written for other venues. More encouragingly, foundations, think tanks, and government agencies now have web sites that provide hard data and thoughtful analyses. It would have been much more difficult for interested citizens to find such material in the more controlled and non-digitized media environment of the mid-20th century.

Social media platforms, such as Facebook, provide still another source of news. By enabling peer-to-peer communication, people come to rely on their friends for news and opinion, often on more trivial entertainment or personal subjects, but sometimes on politics and government. Younger people, who seem more addicted to social media than any other demographic, get a disproportionate share of their facts and opinions from what their "friends" tell them or forward to them on Facebook or from the Twitter feeds that they view. Students who would never think of picking up a newspaper are prepared to accept as gospel what someone forwards to them, or what friends might say. Shortcuts to understanding and knowledge are convenient, of course, but not always the most reliable way to gather information. As one analyst concluded, "political information in social media generally lacks strong arguments and coherency and is highly opinionated." In addition, "the tendency to favor interaction with like-minded people is a strong force throughout online social networks."[5] As one observer put it, "we gorge on information that confirms our ideas, and we shun what does not."[6]

The advantage of the internet and social media platforms is that news and information are available whenever people wish to have it, rather than at specific times determined by network programmers or publishing schedules. Younger audiences particularly value this on-demand feature,[7] especially now that their ubiquitous smartphones means not just anytime access, but anywhere access. On the other hand, studies have suggested that while the internet and its associated social media platforms have increased the information available to those who are already politically engaged, it has done little to engage previously uninvolved and uninformed publics. It also makes it easier to avoid information that conflicts with your preconceptions: "if you see something you don't like, you can easily tap away to something more pleasing. Then we all share what we found with our like-minded social networks, creating closed-off, shoulder-patting circles online."[8]

The democratization of the media as reflected in the spread of cable television and the rise of the internet and social media opened the presidential selection process to candidates such as Pat Robertson, Ross Perot, Pat Buchanan, Ben Carson, and Donald Trump—political amateurs able to attract attention and even votes in this new media environment. It also provided access to the nomination process for less experienced office holders who in the past would not have been seriously considered for the presidency because of their meager records of public service—Howard Dean, Barack Obama, Marco Rubio, and Ted Cruz come to mind. Each of these candidates was able to use the fragmented television scene and the wide-open internet to get to voters in a way that would have been possible when the communications industry was controlled by a small number of gatekeepers.

Howard Dean's campaign for the Democratic nomination for president in 2004 is particularly important to an understanding of the role of the new media. Dean, a little known governor of a small state (Vermont) who had taken a vigorous position against the Iraq War, held strongly progressive views on a variety of domestic issues. He was fond of saying that he represented the Democratic wing of the Democratic Party, but he was not given much of a chance to win the nomination. However, his campaign manager, Joe Trippi, was an early adopter of computer technology to political campaigns. He figured out how to generate a large number of small campaign contributions through the internet and how to mobilize supporters through social networking platforms. Trippi concluded his book describing the Dean campaign by asking his readers to "imagine the presidential candidate who is able to continue Dean for America's exponential Internet growth" with millions of citizens all linked up on the internet.[9]

In 2008, Barack Obama was the presidential candidate that Trippi imagined, fund-raising and organizing supporters online, utilizing social media to generate new supporters and keep them in contact with each other, and using technology to organize a sophisticated strategy to identify Obama voters and get them to the polls. And Donald Trump proved to be a master of the media. He seemed to have an instinctive understanding that the more outrageous his comments were, the more likely he was to receive coverage from the ratings-obsessed cable news channels. He also was the first candidate to use Twitter on a regular basis to communicate with and inflame his supporters, to attack and demean anyone who opposed him, and to gain more coverage and notoriety as his more outrageous tweets were reported and discussed on cable news.

The Media and the Conventions

Once upon a time, aspiring presidential candidates might be known and recognizable to only a small segment of the population. Before the age of television, candidates would have to rely on newspaper coverage to gain name recognition, and being visually recognized depended on having one's picture in the newspaper. Those who were able to gain the party's nomination would sometimes be heard on the radio, and as they moved to the general election, they would be seen by the relatively small number of people who attended campaign rallies. This was one reason why presidential candidates typically came from among the ranks of experienced office holders from large states.

The revolution in mass communication that took place in the decades after the Second World War, particularly the emergence of television, changed all that and had a profound effect on the presidential selection process. As television sets found their way into the homes of an increasing number of American families, news programs occupied a significant amount of the air time, and news focusing on the president, and eventually on presidential campaigns, became a regular part of such programming. And because it was television (with an emphasis on the "vision" part of the word), film of presidents and presidential candidates was almost always a part of the story.

Television became directly involved in the presidential selection process in 1948, when the national conventions of the two parties were televised for the first time. The technology was in its infancy, and NBC, the biggest of the networks at that time, decided to cover the conventions, and the other networks went along. The parties, sensing the opportunity to publicize their platforms and their candidates, cooperated by agreeing to hold their conventions in the same city—Philadelphia—in order to reduce the costs of coverage. Although some of the television executives who were involved in the decision to move ahead probably thought of this as a contribution to the civic life of the nation and its voters, it was also less expensive for the network to fill their air time with convention coverage than with more costly original dramas and comedies. In addition, because the networks and their stations were federally licensed, it was politically expedient to go along with the desire of the parties for a few days of free advertising. Finally, NBC's parent company, RCA, was the biggest manufacturer of television sets and saw the conventions as an opportunity to expand its market. Altogether, the 1948 conventions were carried by four networks to eighteen stations in nine cities, mostly on the East Coast.[10]

As it turned out, both conventions had elements of drama that made for good television. On the Republican side, there were five viable candidates for the nomination; it took three ballots for the party to nominate Governor Thomas Dewey of New York, their standard bearer in 1944. He selected one of his opponents for the nomination, Earl Warren, the governor of California, as his vice presidential candidate. All this took place over vehement objections from the more conservative wing of the party, led by Senator Robert Taft of Ohio. At the Democratic Convention, there was initial opposition to President Harry Truman's nomination, particularly from some of the more progressive elements of the party, but in the end, no alternate candidate materialized and Truman was nominated on the first ballot. But the real drama was over the platform, with Hubert Humphrey, the mayor of Minneapolis and Senator Paul Douglas of Illinois, pushing for a strong civil rights plank. When Humphrey and Douglas succeeded—by a very close vote—several southern delegations walked out of the convention and eventually formed the Dixiecrats to run a southern candidate in the general election. All the speeches on the platform issue, as well as the voting and the walkout, were covered by television, interviews were conducted with the major participants, and Humphrey's passionate speech on behalf of civil rights catapulted him to national prominence.

After 1948, television coverage of the national conventions became standard. By 1956, the parties had recognized that the primary role of the conventions was to raise the visibility of the party and its candidates before a national television audience, and to do so, they needed to put on a show that would capture the viewer's attention. The more mundane work of the convention—dealing with national party rules, adopting a party platform, and organizing for the general election campaign—was usually not very exciting, so the parties made a number of adjustments aimed at making the event more "television friendly." A summary of these changes from the Museum of Broadcast Communications tells the story:

> Party officials condensed the length of the convention, created uniform campaign themes for each party, adorned convention halls with banners and patriotic decorations, placed television crews in positions with flattering views of the proceedings, dropped daytime sessions, limited welcoming speeches and parliamentary organization procedures, scheduled sessions to reach a maximum audience in prime time, and eliminated seconding speeches for vice presidential candidates. Additionally, the presence of television cameras encouraged parties to conceal intra-party battling and choose geographic host cities amenable to their party.[11]

The last time that there was any real doubt about the identity of either party's presidential nominee before the convention was 1952. In all thirty-two conventions since then, the candidate has been nominated on the first ballot. And toward the end of the century, the networks, responding to the absence of convention excitement created by the early designation of the nominee and increasing competition from cable entertainment shows, reduced their coverage of the conventions to a few hours a night for each of the four evenings that the convention was in session.

Aside from the nomination itself, there have been many instances of convention drama that would likely have gone unnoticed before the age of television. In 1956, John Kennedy raised his national visibility by briefly challenging Estes Kefauver for the Democratic Party's vice presidential nomination, and by doing so, effectively launched his 1960 campaign for the presidential nomination. In 1968, the riots outside the Democratic Convention in Chicago and the vitriolic debate that they provoked within the convention hall were televised so, in the words of the protestors, "the whole world was watching." It is worth asking whether the "siege of Chicago'" (as Norman Mailer phrased it) would have been such a vivid and memorable event in the pre-television world, when the whole world could not have been watching.

The conventions have also been the scene of memorable speeches by party leaders. In 1964, Barry Goldwater doubled down on his conservative message, asserting that "extremism in the pursuit of liberty was no vice." In 1984, Mario Cuomo delivered a moving keynote address in which he challenged President Reagan's idea of America as a shining city on the hill by noting that there were two cities, one of which was not doing very well in Reagan's America. In 1988, Bill Clinton's long and windy address was interpreted, incorrectly as it turned out, as career ending, and Pat Buchanan's fiery speech at the 1992 Republican Convention touched off the culture wars and in the view of some, contributed to George H. W. Bush's reelection defeat by painting an extreme view of the Republican Party. And, of course, Barack Obama's stirring keynote address in 2004 launched his improbable rise to the presidency. Certainly, there were important convention speeches before television—William Jennings Bryan's "cross of gold" speech at the 1896 Democratic Convention comes to mind—but they are known only to historians and are seldom remembered or quoted. The examples above, and many others could have been included, are memorable because they were seen and heard and commented upon in front of a national television audience.

Once the locus of the nomination process moved from the convention to the caucuses and primaries, the conventions became solely about showcasing the party, its nominee, and its leaders. The goal was to project an image of a unified party, so disruptions such as the southern walkout of 1948 or the Chicago riot twenty years later needed to be avoided. Another goal was to energize the party's base, which was represented by the assembled delegates, as well as those watching on television. To accomplish this, the work of organizing and planning the convention required the same skills that would be necessary to produce a television show. The convention needed to be carefully staged—from the visuals that would provide the background for the speakers, to what speakers would wear and say, and in what order they would say it. Things needed to run smoothly and on time in order to make certain that the most important speeches of the evening were delivered before the largest television audience.

Those in charge of the convention—typically some combination of national party officers, representatives of the candidate designate, and professional show producers—plan every moment of every evening. Once the television networks abandoned gavel-to-gavel coverage of the conventions beginning in the 1980s, each evening of the convention could best be viewed as an episode in a four night prime time miniseries, with a theme for each episode, specified speakers assigned to address the theme, and slickly produced videos set to uplifting music to highlight the theme, to extol the candidate, and to criticize the other party and its candidate. And, as is the case with every television show, each episode had to feature a star or two to attract the attention of the viewers and the television commentators. The final night (or episode) centered on the candidate's acceptance speech as the culminating event, drawing together the various themes and arguments featured on the first three nights and ending with music and, more recently, the dropping of multi-colored balloons from the ceiling.

And speaking of stars, it is not just the party's political stars—their most popular and attractive office holders on the national and local scene. Conventions now routinely feature addresses and performances by actual celebrity entertainers, thereby further blurring the lines between politics and entertainment. Sometimes these things go well; other times, not so much. In 2012, the actor and director Clint Eastwood gave a bizarre prime time address at the Republican Convention in which he rambled at length to an empty chair that he said represented President Obama. No one knew exactly what his point was, but his speech ran so long that Mitt Romney's acceptance speech—the ostensible highlight of the evening—was delayed and, in some respects, overshadowed by speculation and commentary about Eastwood's performance. In 2016, the Republican Convention featured addresses by somewhat less than famous television personalities—an obscure soap opera star, a 1980s child star whose career had hit the skids, and a reality television star from Duck Dynasty, a show with a narrow appeal to southern good ole boys. The Democratic Convention in contrast, had an all-star lineup that included Meryl Streep, a bevy of Broadway actors, and musical performances by Paul Simon and Katy Perry, among others. The point is that the conventions are now strictly media events, with presentations and entertainment designed to attract the attention, arouse the excitement, and play to the emotions of the audience. And as is the case with all television shows, the important thing is less what is said, but how it plays, and, most crucially, how it is reviewed by the eager and easily excitable panel of commentators assembled by the television stations.

Finally, the conventions provide a visual portrait of each party's constituency. As the cameras panned the Republican Convention in both 2012 and 2016, the visual was a sea of white faces with a pronounced bias toward an older demographic. The image from the Democratic Convention, particularly in 2016, was much more diverse, with Latinos and African Americans making up more than half of the convention delegates. Speakers at the Democratic Convention came from virtually every ethnic, racial, age, and gender group, underlining the party's diversity, in contrast to the Republican Convention's distinctly monochromatic image.

From this perspective, if Emmys were awarded for best convention of the year, the 2016 Democratic Convention would win hands down. Speakers stayed on time and gave the speeches that they were expected to give, videos highlighting the candidate and disparaging her opponent were professionally done, and the themes of optimism, hope, and patriotism were emphasized, in comparison to the dark assessment of the state of the nation and the world that Donald Trump and his supporters presented at the Republican Convention. On the first night of the convention, Michelle Obama was the featured speaker; on night two, it was former President Clinton; on night three, Vice President Biden and President Obama; and on the fourth night, the candidate herself, introduced by her daughter. The first night also included a prime time speech by Bernie Sanders, a concession that the Clinton team made to the Sanders campaign in return for Sanders urging his supporters to support (or at least not verbally oppose) Clinton. The various speeches highlighted the themes of the Clinton campaign: that the country was stronger together and that Donald Trump was unworthy of the office of president. Most memorably, on the last night of the convention, a Muslim American husband and wife whose soldier son had died a hero in the Iraq War delivered a powerful rebuke to Trump's attacks on Muslims and their patriotism. Clinton followed with an acceptance speech (timed to start precisely at 10:30 p.m. eastern standard time to ensure the maximum prime time audience) that attempted to project a sense of optimism about the future of the country while acknowledging the problems that the nation faced. Naturally, she included a number of critiques of Trump, as well as allusions to the history-making nature of her candidacy as the first female nominee of a major political party.

Donald Trump's convention, in contrast, was notable for the absence of most national Republican leaders. Neither of the two living former Republican presidents, nor the party's last two presidential standard bearers showed up. In their place were testimonials to Mr. Trump's character by his family and incessant attacks on Hillary Clinton's character and honesty, attacks that bordered on the crude and violent, with "lock her up" being the preferred chant from the convention delegates. The animosity toward Clinton, obviously a pre-existing condition among the delegates, was stoked by the two most prominent Republicans who spoke, Chris Christie, the governor of New Jersey, and Rudy Giuliani, the former mayor of New York, both of whom used their time primarily to attack Clinton rather than extol the virtues of their nominee. Politically, a great deal of attention was paid to the speech by Ted Cruz, one of the candidates who Trump had insulted and vanquished in the primaries, in which Cruz passed on the opportunity to endorse Trump, urging the delegates and the viewing public to vote their conscience, a position accompanied by a chorus of jeers from the convention floor. While the Clinton campaign had agreed to give Sanders a prime time spot only after his full-throated endorsement of her candidacy and his promise to try to calm down his supporters among the delegates, Cruz, inexplicably, was accorded a prime time spot without such assurances and apparently without anyone vetting his speech. The most well received speech was by Trump's wife, Melania Trump, although the glow of that speech vanished quickly when it was discovered that a small portion had been copied from a convention speech that Michelle Obama had delivered. That, of course, became the story, rather than the nice things that Mrs. Trump said about her husband. Trump's acceptance speech dwelled on what he believed to be the terrible state of the nation, its vulnerability to terrorism and crime, and the weakness of its incumbent leaders. He included a memorable line announcing that "I and only I can fix this." The line was taken out of context (he was talking about fixing what he called a "rigged system" rather than the nation's problems), but that assertion of unilateral power and responsibility provided talking points for the Clinton campaign, as well as the media.

Whether or not the conventions make much difference to the election outcome is hard to say. It may be that the convention constitutes the first opportunity for many voters to see and hear the candidate, and so they have the effect of crystallizing the views of those who have been only occasional followers of the campaign. Specialists in polling argue that the fluctuations that take place right after the conventions should not be taken too seriously and that what counts is what the polling looks like weeks afterwards. The 2016 Republican Convention was followed by a small bump in the polls for Donald Trump, a bump that quickly receded, in part because the Democratic Convention started only a few days after the Republican Convention ended. The Democratic Convention was followed by a substantial climb in Hillary Clinton's polling numbers, a climb that persisted well after the convention, but eventually receded. And, of course, the outcome of the 2016 election suggests that good conventions and good poll numbers do not necessarily translate into Electoral College majorities.

Televising the Campaign

In the previous chapter, we discussed the role that the media plays in the nomination process. The network and cable television outlets hype the debates, exaggerate the importance of each caucus and primary, and fixate on the horse race. They focus on unique candidates, like Barack Obama in 2008 and Donald Trump in 2016, and emphasize conflict and drama, rather than policy and substance. It seems clear that how the nomination fight is reported has some impact on the results, as the networks loudly proclaim the "winner" and the "losers" of each contest, no matter how few votes constituted the plurality, and how few or how many convention delegates were won.

Once the conventions are over and the candidates have been formally nominated, the television networks and cable channels cover the campaign, typically with a news team assigned to each candidate reporting on campaign stops, the issues addressed in the stump speech, and the multiple "horse race" stories that inevitably emerge in every national campaign. Campaign stops in one city have now become national events, in the sense that a clip or sound bite from that appearance usually makes it on to the networks' national news programs. And the emergence of cable news networks has magnified the impact of the campaigns. Outlets such as CNN, MSNBC, and Fox devote huge portions of air time to both the race for the party's nomination as well as to the general election race.

From the point of view of the cable and the broadcast networks, the most important consideration about their coverage of the presidential race is the size of their viewing audience, a figure which translates into the money that pays their bills and rewards their stock holders. This concentration on ratings affects television coverage of the campaign in a number of ways. Viewers are drawn to reports on the horse race (i.e., who is out in front and by how much and how a particular event affects the race) and by reports on campaign strategy, the latter being of special interest to the more politically engaged.[12] That means, first, that every new poll that comes out is hyped as breaking news, despite warnings from those who do polls for a living that a single poll reveals very little about the state of the race. In fact, there is evidence from a study of the 2008 election that television news was more likely to report on polls that showed a tight race between Obama and McCain than on polls in which one candidate had a large lead. In addition, television news spent more time reporting on odd surveys that showed a closer race than seemed warranted by the bulk of the polling data; also more time was devoted to surveys that showed a big change from previous polls. Naturally, one seldom hears in such reports disclaimers about margins of error in polling, or the quality and track record of the organization doing the polling which, if fully considered, may mean that the reported big change was perhaps not so big or, in the case of a survey outlier, not really representative of an actual change in public opinion. But a big change is, of course, more dramatic than the steady or relatively small fluctuations that one usually sees when election polls are viewed in the aggregate. And, not surprisingly, it is the dramatic rather than the mundane that generates ratings.[13]

In addition to hyping the polls, every policy issue addressed by the candidate and, indeed everything that the candidate says, is viewed in terms of whether or not it will help or hurt his electoral chances. Television commentators create viewer interest by focusing on small or ultimately extraneous matters in the candidate's background, as they look for scandals or the hints of scandals. Embarrassing or sensational incidents from a candidate's recent past become continuing news stories. Hillary Clinton's role in Benghazi and her use of a private email server or Donald Trump's mocking of a disabled reporter were constantly referred to during the coverage of the 2016 campaign, even though there was nothing new to report on either of these issues. Later in the campaign, Trump's recorded comments from eleven years before bragging about his sexual assaults on various women and the confirming testimony of several of his victims became, for many weeks, the sole issue discussed. In contrast, precious little attention was afforded to Trump's lack of knowledge about the policy issues facing the nation, his failure to offer any plans to deal with the national maladies that he talked about at each campaign stop, or the outsized influence of extreme right wing advisors on his campaign. Although the reports of personal indiscretions speak to the character of the candidates and should not be minimized, they are accorded far more coverage than the qualifications and experience that each candidate would bring to the presidency or the policy issues that citizens continue to claim are most important to them.

Finally, the candidates who get the most coverage tend to be those who say the most provocative things. Candidates whose speeches are heavy on the details but short on one-liners receive less attention than the candidate who says outrageous things or has come up with a snappy sound bite. Donald Trump's presidential campaign is the prototype of this phenomenon. Throughout the Republican nomination process, Trump, compared with his competitors, received far more attention and far more free air time from all the network and cable news programs, in no small part because of his incessant stream of nasty remarks and personal attacks. As one former television news anchor observed during the 2016 campaign when she saw Trump's first speech after his loss in the Wisconsin primary covered live by three cable news networks as breaking news:

> In all these scenes, the TV reporter just stands there, off camera, essentially useless. The order doesn't need to be stated. It's understood in the newsroom: Air the Trump rallies live and uninterrupted. He may say something crazy; he often does, and it's always great television.[14]

This same commentator reports that television executives were thrilled with the high ratings that Trump pulled in. During the campaign for the nomination, in a field of seventeen candidates, he received 50% of the free exposure on network and cable news. The CEO of CBS, Les Moonves, was widely quoted as saying that the 2016 campaign in general and Trump's candidacy "may not be good for America, but it's damn good for CBS."[15] In other elections, the comments that got Trump all this coverage might have been disqualifying for a presidential candidate—mocking a war hero of his own party, racist remarks about Mexicans and Muslims—but Trump, aided and abetted by the news media, leveraged these comments to make himself omnipresent on television and to mobilize a sufficient number of supporters so that he could prevail in a multi-candidate race for the nomination. And because of the free media, he was able to accomplish this by spending almost nothing on television ads.

The internet is another source of free media, and, as noted earlier, it epitomizes the fully democratized media environment. As a gatekeeper free zone, fake news stories have as much access as actual news stories, and outright lies have as much access as accurate reporting. Everyone with a cell phone or a computer can now call herself a journalist. Anyone can write a news story—real or fake—and post it on her blog or Facebook page, or pay a fee and have it appear on multiple web sites. Anyone with a smartphone can film an incident or event, post it on YouTube, and have it disseminated. When Hillary Clinton fell ill at a campaign event in September, she was helped to her car by Secret Service members. The video of that event spread instantaneously across the internet, feeding the fake news story that she had serious undisclosed illnesses, rather than a more mundane case of the flu. In the final weeks of the 2012 campaign, a cell phone video surfaced of Mitt Romney speaking to a group of donors. In the video, he said that forty-seven percent of the American people were "takers" who paid no taxes and were dependent on the government for handouts. The video, replayed countless times on network and cable news shows and with thousands of views on YouTube, fed the image that the Obama campaign had been creating of Romney as a rich man out of touch with the concerns of average working Americans.

Beginning in 1992 and every four years thereafter, The Pew Research Center for The People and the Press has asked survey respondents where they get most of their news about presidential campaigns, allowing each respondent to name up to two sources. In 1996, 72% said television and only 3% said the internet. But in the 2012 survey, 47% said the internet, compared with 67% saying television, with the latter more likely to mention cable rather than broadcast television. The rise of the internet seems to have come primarily at the expense of the print media; in 1996, 60% mentioned newspapers, but in 2012, that figure was only 20%. Presumably, many of those who had been reading newspapers in hard copy in 1996 were now reading those same papers on the web, so the demise of newspapers as a source of information may be a bit exaggerated by these numbers.[16]

The Debates

If there were questions about the impact that television would have on the presidential selection process, the 1960 campaign resolved them. The Republican Party nominated Richard Nixon, Eisenhower's vice president, and the Democratic Party turned to John Kennedy, a young senator from Massachusetts who had kept a fairly low profile during his time in Congress. Kennedy, as mentioned in the previous chapter, had won his party's nomination largely through the old-fashioned process of gaining the support of major party leaders in big industrial states.

By 1960, 90% of American households owned a television set, and television entertainment and news had become a major component of American culture. The party conventions and the presidential campaigns were now fully covered, but the key innovation for that election year was televised debates between the two candidates. Much has been made of the first debate between Kennedy and Nixon, with the prevailing narrative being that Kennedy did well because he looked younger and more dynamic that Nixon. Some of this was explained by Nixon's health; he had a serious knee injury prior to the debate and probably an infection. He also refused makeup, and was visibly perspiring during the debate. In addition to the optics, because Nixon was the much more experienced leader, the debates presumably helped Kennedy by placing him on the same stage and therefore on an equal footing with the vice president. Most people concluded that Kennedy "won" the first debate, although Nixon was thought to have won the next two, with the fourth ending in a draw. Of course, these are all impressions; unlike an election, there are no votes to count to determine who really won or lost, so winning and losing is rather arbitrarily decided by reporters and commentators, as well as campaign aids assigned to spin the results. In any event, before the first debate, Nixon was slightly ahead of Kennedy in the polls, but after the debate, Kennedy moved ahead. The impact of Nixon's ostensibly better performance in the remaining debates was diminished by the fact that the audience was much smaller for those debates than it was for the much anticipated first debate. For those who hadn't figured it out before, the 1960 election made clear that how a candidate looked and how he came across on television would now be a consideration as one assessed the chances for a winning candidacy.

As for the debates themselves, the jury is still out on exactly what effect they have on voter decisions, but it was clear from the first presidential debate that they added an unpredictable element to the campaign. Convinced that Nixon had lost the advantage of his political experience by agreeing to debate his younger and less well-known opponent, Lyndon Johnson in 1964 and Nixon in 1968 and 1972 refused to participate in debates. The debates returned in 1976 when President Gerald Ford, who, in the wake of Watergate was looking at a very close election, agreed to debate Jimmy Carter. It was in one of those debates that Ford committed a major gaffe when he suggested that the Eastern European countries were not really under the control of the Soviet Union. Again, there is little empirical support for the conclusion that this cost Ford the election, but the publicity around his statement certainly did not help his campaign.

From 1976 on, televised debates became a regular part of the general election campaign and the nomination process as well, as discussed in the last chapter. These events have been watched by large audiences—an average of 60.5 million people for the 2008 debates and 64 million for the 2012 debates.[17] In 2016, the Clinton–Trump debates drew an average audience of 69.8 million viewers. The debates are promoted by the television stations in much the same way that sports stations hype the World Series or Monday Night Football. Sports metaphors are a staple of the hype; candidates "face off" or "square off," "instant replays" of key interchanges are shown repeatedly, and instant (and highly unscientific) polls, along with comments by panels of experts and panels of ostensibly undecided voters, tell us within a few minutes who "won" or "lost" the debate. Their impact on the outcome of the election is uncertain; even when a candidate does poorly, as both George W. Bush and Barack Obama were thought to have done in the first debates of their respective reelection campaigns, their performance does not "change the voting preferences of their most partisan supporters or shift the sentiment of most independent voters."[18] But what debates can do is support the pre-existing dispositions of voters who see their views of their preferred candidate confirmed, even when he or she may not have done particularly well.

As is the case with conventions, debates are less about substance and more about performance. For voters, the most memorable portions of presidential debates are how a candidate looks on television, his confidence and body language as he responds to questions, the one-liners that he is able to deploy to attack his opponent, and, of course, the gaffe— the truly absurd statement, or the statement open to misinterpretation, such as Ford's Eastern Europe remark. In 1980, Ronald Reagan's affable "there you go again" response to Jimmy Carter's assertions about his conservative positions was more memorable than Carter's critique. In 1988, Michael Dukakis, the Democratic candidate, was visibly shaken by a harsh question about his position on capital punishment, framed by the inquisitor in terms of what his reaction would be if his wife were a murder victim. And in the vice presidential debate that year, after the Republican candidate, Dan Quayle, compared himself to John Kennedy, the Democratic candidate, Lloyd Bentsen, put Quayle in his place with the rejoinder that he, Bentsen, had known and worked with John Kennedy, and Quayle was no John Kennedy. In 1992, George H. W. Bush seemed uncomfortable during his debate with Bill Clinton, sneaking looks at his watch a number of times, seemingly hoping that it would be over soon. In 2000, Al Gore's audible sighs of frustration with what he viewed as George W. Bush's uninformed statements projected an image of intellectual elitism that played badly against Bush's less polished, but everyman presentation style. And in 2012, Barack Obama seemed uncomfortable and disengaged in his first debate with Mitt Romney, but in the second debate, Romney tried to defend his record on women's issues with an artless statement that he had "binders full of women" to consider for government appointments.

The point of all this is that these examples of memorable debate moments had nothing to do with public policy questions, with what the candidate intended to do if elected, or most importantly, with the candidates' preparedness for the job of president. When candidates prepare for these debates, they train themselves to avoid or deflect difficult questions and to "pivot" to their stump-speech talking points. The rules for the debate are agreed to beforehand by both campaigns; they deal with time limits for each response and more mundane issues such as the height of the lectern for each candidate and whether or not the networks can show split screen shots so that the viewing audience can see candidate's reacting to their opponents comments. These rules are designed to reduce the possibility of errors, an impolitic or inappropriate comment, or a poor visual that will be the major take away from the event.

The campaigns try to influence the analyses of the debates by lowering the expectations for their candidates prior to the debate and meeting with the press moments after the debate to "spin" what has just happened into a narrative that explains how well their candidate performed and how he or she exceeded the pre-lowered expectations. The rise of social media, the instantaneous analyses that hit the internet, and the ease with which various parts of the debate can be played back on smartphones and tablets may magnify the impact of a particular debate compared with the times when one had to wait until the next day's newspapers to read the commentary.

Research by political scientists and other analysts suggests that debates have a relatively minor impact on presidential races. By the time that the debates got underway, most voters have made their decisions, so there are relatively few persuadable voters out there. The first debate (usually there are three) is the most watched, and in the short term, it moves polls by less than two percentage points, usually in the direction of the candidate of the party that does not hold the White House.[19] But often, the impact of a debate on the race is short term. In 2012, President Obama was perceived to have done poorly in the first debate with Mitt Romney, and his four-point lead in the polls prior to the debate disappeared. But in the weeks following the debate, he regained the lead that he had held before that debate.

Prior to the first debate of the 2016 race, the polling numbers for the two candidates seemed to be converging, and some were characterizing the race as tied. But during the debate, Trump frequently interrupted Clinton, was goaded by her into a number of controversial statements, seemed to lose interest in the proceedings as the debate went on, appeared completely unprepared to deal with any specific policy issues, and, at the end, was caught flat-footed by Clinton's citing of sexist comments that he had made to a Latina beauty contest winner. Trump sputtered in response, and in the aftermath of the debate, he tweeted numerous attacks on the woman rather than letting the issue blow over. After the first Clinton–Trump debate, the commentators were unanimous in their view that Trump had lost and devoted most of their time to his comments about the beauty contest winner.

The outcome and influence of a debate is determined by how it is reported. As John Sides noted in the *Washington Post* the day before that debate, "news coverage helps 'frame' or interpret politics for average voters. For better or worse, we 'outsource' some of that interpretive labor to reporters and political commentators."[20] The impact of the debate typically has less to do with what one actually sees happening on the stage and more to do with an amalgam of the spin and the commentaries that come to dominate the newspapers, the 24/7 cable news outlets, the political web sites, and the legions of social media feeds. In the aftermath of the first debate, Clinton opened up a substantial lead in the polls. Trump did only slightly better in the second and third debates, and Clinton's poll numbers stayed relatively high. But after the last debate, several external events, especially an intervention by the director of the FBI, lowered her poll numbers to about her pre-debate lead. As we know, these polls fairly accurately predicted her popular vote victory, but they failed to anticipate Trump's Electoral College win.

Advertising

Television is also a vehicle for campaign advertising. In 1968, as Joe McGinniss reported in his book on *The Selling of the President*, the ad people who persuade the public to buy certain cars, smoke certain cigarettes, and use certain cosmetics were fully incorporated into Richard Nixon's presidential campaign.[21] Their role in that and all future campaigns was to create, cultivate, and market an image of the candidate who employed them. Richard Nixon, who had been rejected by the American electorate in 1960 and by the California electorate in 1962 when he ran for governor in that state, was in drastic need of an image makeover. McGinniss describes in detail how the image makers went about that process, how they worked to shake the "loser" image, as well as the sense that Nixon was a mean and ruthless person who put politics above principle. Efforts were made to create a "new Nixon," a warmer candidate with the experience to govern, which was an effort that paid off with his 1968 victory.

Today, television advertising constitutes a huge portion of a candidate's budget at both the primary and caucus stage and the general election. In 2012, the total cost of advertising by candidates, the parties, and non-party groups was $950 million.[22] Professionals are hired to design commercials, to test them with focus groups, and to select the stations, media markets, and times at which they will be aired. Air time can be expensive as well, depending heavily on the size of the market and the length of the commercial. Given the cost of air time and the notoriously short attention span of voters, thirty-second ads shown multiple times are preferred to less common longer ads that provide more detail. Obviously, when ad people are in charge, the created image often falls far short of reality. It is only slightly hyperbolic to say that the candidate is presented in ways that qualify him for sainthood and his opponent is drawn in terms more fitting for a criminal. These "contrast" ads are sometimes defended as a way to highlight the policy differences between the candidates, but their real intent is to define both the candidate and his opponent to the advantage of whoever is paying for the ad.

The internet and social media have added a new dimension to advertising. In every campaign, there are ads that are designed only for the internet and never get on television. When a campaign posts an ad on its own or its party's web site, there is no cost beyond the production costs. When ads are placed on web sites owned by other entities (newspapers, blogs, Facebook, etc.), there is a charge, but it is substantially lower than for a television ad. While spending on television ads accounts for about half of advertising expenditures, internet ads and radio ads each account for about 10%.[23] These ads can help a candidate to reach a specific audience—for example, if you want to reach men, advertise on sports web sites. They are also a particularly effective way to reach young people who are more inclined to get their information from the internet rather than from television news or newspapers. And when those who see internet ads place links to them on their Facebook page and disseminate them to their "friends," the ads can metastasize to an even larger audience. Internet ads are also picked up by partisan or ideological web sites that favor one candidate or the other, thereby further extending their reach, and they are sometimes reported as "news" in the mainstream press or on cable channels. In the wake of the 2016 election, Facebook came under criticism for providing a platform for the broad dissemination of "fake news stories," including assertions that Donald Trump was endorsed by the pope (he wasn't), that Hillary Clinton had purchased a $200 million house in the Maldives (she didn't), or that Clinton and her close advisor, Huma Abedin, were lovers (they aren't).[24]

Although casual historians and journalists like to focus on the memorable ads from presidential campaigns, it is difficult to determine how effective these are in changing minds or votes. The 1964 Democratic ad suggesting that Barry Goldwater would start a nuclear war, the Willie Horton ad deployed against Michael Dukakis in 1988 to prove that he was soft on crime, and the Swift Boat ad used against John Kerry in 2004 to suggest that he wasn't really a war hero are all part of the lore of presidential campaign history. If there is a consensus among those who have actually studied the issue, it is that ads have the effect of mobilizing those people who are already disposed toward supporting a particular candidate and that through selective perception, these voters filter out negative information about their candidate that comes from the ads of his opponent. On the other hand, even if most voters are not affected by ads, the few who are could make a difference in a close race, so no candidate can take the risk of eschewing the ad war completely. In fact, some argue that the nasty attack ads that each campaign launches against its opponent are designed to discourage the participation of the undecided voter who might go in any direction in the voting booth, and energize the committed voters so that the most dependable partisans end up comprising a disproportionate share of the final electorate.

The uncertainty about the effect of debates and advertising on voting behavior is in some respect beside the point. The real lesson is that the entire television show—by which I mean the news coverage, the debates, and the advertising campaigns—along with the internet and the post-1968 rules changes signify the movement from a party-dominated process of presidential selection to a more democratized candidate-centered system. The main focus now is always on the candidate—what he says, what he looks like, his curated image—and less so on the party or the party's positions. People who aspire to the presidency are told to lose weight and to adopt their speaking style so that they can connect with a mass audience. Extensive polling is part of each campaign, with the goal of finding phrasing for the candidates' positions that are most likely to resonate with the voters, as well as the most fruitful lines of attack against one's opponent. Their speeches are written with fully prepared, focus group-tested sound bites designed to catch the attention of television news producers. As we have said, the debates, rather than an exchange of views, provide an opportunity for candidates to demonstrate how smooth and confident they are in responding to questions, and how facile they are with the zinger designed to savage one's opponent.

In fairness, in-depth discussions of policy are very difficult to have in the context of an election campaign, given the complexity of the policy challenges facing a modern nation and the general lack of policy sophistication that characterizes most voters. Asking a candidate to outline, or better yet explain, his position on entitlements, health care, or the Middle East in the course of a brief speech, debate response, or interview is unlikely to be successful. The most one would get is a set of platitudes and generalities (we need to work toward a balanced budget, we need to assure quality health care, we need to support a peace process in the Middle East, etc.) and few specifics. If a candidate went much deeper, most voters would be lost, and many votes would likely be lost, because complete answers would reveal that there are no easy solutions to many policy challenges and that each solution will have winners and losers. As Mario Cuomo, the former governor of New York once said, "we campaign in poetry, but we govern in prose." And most voters listen only to the poetry because either they cannot grasp the prose, or because if they understood the prose, it would make them less inclined to support a candidate.

Although partisan loyalties continue to explain a great deal of the variance in voting behavior, candidate characteristics are now a more significant factor. Harry Truman would have been an unlikely candidate in the age of television and debates; he was diminutive in size, his voice was unpleasant to listen to, and he was, at best, an uncertain public speaker. Whether or not Franklin Roosevelt could have been elected given his physical disability is an open question; at least, it would have been discussed today, but it was not really addressed when he was a candidate. On the other hand, Donald Trump would have been a very unlikely candidate in an earlier day, but he was the perfect candidate for the modern media environment.

The Media and the Public

There is a reason why it's called the mass media. Unlike science, philosophy, or modern dance, television, radio, Facebook, and Twitter are intended for everyone, no matter what they know, their status in society, or the interest that they pay to the world of politics and government. No special training or educational attainment, or even effort, is required to watch, participate, or enjoy. Television watching is an essentially passive process that makes no demands on the citizen's intellect or critical thinking facilities. Social media requires little more than looking at your telephone or laptop, clicking on an icon, or composing a 140-character, syntax-free message that can contain emojis and abbreviations, the meaning of which are known primarily to those who participate in these practices.

Much has been made of the opportunities that the new media can offer for enhanced citizen activism, especially among younger people, but there is a strong tendency among that demographic to indulge in what some scholars refer to as "slacktivism"—online actions performed in support of a political or social cause but requiring little time or involvement, such as signing an online petition.[25] As one study of how young people use the internet concluded, "what they do online does not reflect a strong interest in politics." Instead, "on line entertainment is the biggest draw for youth."[26] Of course, the internet and social media are not just for the young. Although there is ample reason to believe that a good deal of the time that adults spend on their laptops and smartphones is devoted to the same pursuits as young people—amusement and entertainment, shopping, and personal gossip—it is also clear that an increasing percentage of the population depends on the internet for news and information. There have certainly been times when the new media has abetted citizen activism by connecting like-minded people with one another, thus facilitating a political movement, as occurred in several countries during the Arab Spring, and this seems to have occurred in both the Trump and Sanders campaigns. The rise of outsider or amateur presidential candidates also has been facilitated by the new media's capacity to link geographically dispersed supporters. The uniformity of views displayed by Trump supporters in Idaho and Alabama may have as much to do with their mutual commitment to certain websites than to their own conclusions about the candidate and his policies.

Most citizens, young and old, are in no position to check what they see on their various screens against the facts of the real world. Many rarely even wonder whether what they see and think corresponds to reality or not; to a large extent they simply take what they see as reality. This absence of critical thinking is further exacerbated by the trend among many media users to select outlets whose biases confirm their existing view of the world. Social media privileges information that "friends" "like" or forward. When conservatives listen to talk radio or watch Fox News, they hear what they want to hear, the same as progressives do when they watch *Rachel Maddow* or *The Daily Show*. As one media analyst put it, "each of us constructs a custom informational universe, wittingly (we choose to go to the sources that uphold our existing beliefs and thus flatter us) or unwittingly (our app algorithms do the driving for us). The data that we get this way, pre-imprinted with spin and mythos are intensely one-dimensional."[27]

On the other hand, there is some evidence that these custom informational universes more accurately characterize the habits of the relatively small number of citizens who are the most politically committed, especially those who are most committed to the Republican Party. A sizable fraction of total political news consumption by Republicans is devoted to conservatively aligned outlets like Fox News and Breitbart, sources that are very rarely visited by Democrats. Alternatively, many people make only modest efforts to seek out coverage that is consistent with their preferences or to avoid uncongenial information in the real world, where other factors like convenience, habit, and recommendations from friends on social media often matter more. For the most part, these less intensely partisan citizens learn about political news from mainstream, relatively centrist media sources, not ideological websites or cable channels.[28]

Politics and Entertainment

In many cases the line between politics and entertainment has become so blurred that it is impossible to tell where one ends and the other begins. The emergence of *The Daily Show* erased the line entirely. Jon Stewart and his colleagues tackled real political issues in what they frankly referred to as a "fake" news program, in the sense that they had no reporters (except fake ones) and did no investigative work beyond the imaginative culling of the efforts of other media organizations. They went for both the serious and the profane, for the facts as well as the laughs, and they succeeded to an extraordinary degree. On several occasions, the points made on Stewart's show were reported as serious political commentary in mainstream newspapers. College faculty members who had long since given up on getting their students to read the newspapers found that they could spark a political discussion in their classes simply be referring to the previous night's *Daily Show*. In one study, 14% of 18–24 year-olds said that they regularly watched *The Daily Show*, compared with 4% of those 25 years or older. The percentage of the younger cohort who regularly watched network news programs was in the middle single digits.[29]

Stewart's success produced more political/entertainment shows, several starring people who got their start with Stewart, such as Steven Colbert, John Oliver, and Samantha Bee, along with others like Bill Maher. Although Fox was never explicitly about entertainment, its penchant for provocative personalities such as Bill O'Reilly and Sean Hannity—people like Stewart and his colleagues who did no reporting and had no journalistic training but attracted viewers because of what they said and the earthy way in which they said it—suggests that they were in the same game of putting on an entertaining, personality-driven show. Like Stewart, they discovered that the more outrageous or controversial they were, the higher their ratings would go.

Fox went a step further in the process of merging entertainment with politics by becoming, for all intents and purposes, an appendage of the Republican Party and more particularly, the right wing of the party. During the 2016 campaign, Hannity was a strong supporter of Trump who was a regular guest on his show, and he also appeared at his campaign rallies. More generally, if one wants to be the Republican nominee for president, you cannot have Fox as an enemy. In the early days of the republic, newspapers were frequently house organs for a particular political party or faction, often trafficking in what we would call today fake news and ad hominem attacks on political opponents. But Fox's blatant, no apologies alliance with the Republican Party is the first time that an entire network has become part of a major party's coalition.

Fox is also emblematic of a revolving door between the political and the media worlds. Failed Republican candidates, such as Mike Huckabee and Sarah Palin, have been rewarded with shows on Fox after their losing campaigns. And when Donald Trump parted ways with his first campaign manager, Corey Lewandowski, CNN hired him to comment on the presidential race. Although officially separated from the campaign, Lewandowski continued to consult with Trump privately and was receiving severance money from the campaign. And in Trump's last campaign shuffle, he turned to Steve Bannon, the executive chairman of Breitbart News, a media outlet even further to the right than Fox, to be the executive director of his campaign. After Roger Ailes was forced to step down from his post at Fox because of sexual harassment charges, he became an unofficial consultant to the Trump campaign. During the 2016 election cycle, David Axelrod, who managed both of President Obama's campaigns, was a commentator on CNN, as was Donna Brazile, who took a leave from that gig in July when she was appointed chair of the Democratic National Committee. Later, CNN severed its tie with Brazile after hacked emails suggested that she had shared debate questions from CNN moderators with Hillary Clinton. And on MSNBC, Joe Scarborough, a former member of the House, publicly toyed with the idea of a presidential run and then spent a good deal of the campaign in a war of words with Donald Trump—or more exactly, a war of tweets on Trump's part.

The political/entertainment shows also introduced a coarser dimension to political discourse, in part because words and images can be used on cable stations that would not be permissible on broadcast stations. Stewart, Oliver, Bee, and Maher regularly employ offensive language in their monologues. Conservatives like Hannity, Glenn Beck, Rush Limbaugh and Laura Ingraham regularly engage in over-the-top nastiness, conspiracy theories, rumors, and character assassination. The goal is to entertain through offense and provocation in the manner of radio shock jocks, and thus lower discourse to the level of ordinary people, as opposed to the elite.

Coarseness is not restricted to political commentators. Televised entertainment shows, particularly those on cable, but increasingly on the networks, regularly use vulgarity, and they are much more permissive than they once were about sexual topics and references. The internet has no restraints at all when it comes to these topics and terms. It is not too much of a stretch to say that because of this media environment, Donald Trump's multiple marriages, his blatant, documented misogyny, his racist attacks on various groups, and his vulgarity, although much criticized, did not prove to be disqualifying because Americans had come to accept such discourse as normal rather than deviant. As Jonathan Martin of *The New York Times* put it, "with American culture increasingly coarse and ever more obsessed with celebrity, the country's politics were bound to eventually catch up. Less than 25 years after Bill Clinton shocked some by unabashedly answering a question on television about his underwear preferences, Mr. Trump purposefully brought up the size of his penis in a television debate." And in Clinton's case, it wasn't just the boxers or briefs episode; despite the graphic and highly publicized details of his relationship with White House intern Monica Lewinsky, Bill Clinton left the presidency with a job approval rating of 65%. As one observer whom Martin interviewed put it, "Trump is reflecting a culture that is more crass, more accepting of vulgarity, and more attuned to pop culture."[30]

Trump's popularity is also related to the entertainment media's ability to turn objectively bad people into sympathetic characters. In the 1990s, *The Sopranos* turned a brutal killer into a sympathetic everyman who struggled with his family and his personal anxieties, while at the same time running a mob engaged in every imaginable form of mayhem. A decade later, the American public fell for Walter White, the hero of *Breaking Bad*, a chemistry teacher turned drug king, who made a fortune manufacturing crystal meth and participated in several brutal killings along the way. As one scholar has noted, these examples suggest "a clear appetite for bad behavior" among American television viewers. "In an era when

so many institutions have become broken, from the economy to our politics, we find some kind of comfort in the person, no matter how ruthless,
who shows the drive to get things done—no matter what—without letting that brokenness stand in his way."[31]

The willingness to accept and encourage such discourse is understandable for a mass media that is driven by ratings, and the evidence is that
a brew of comedy and crudeness works, just as for the cable and network news stations, scandals, the horse race, conspiracy theories, and
provocative and often unsourced reports work, especially if the notion of
"works" means viewers. Serious and sober discussions of public events of
the sort that Bill Moyers used to do and Charlie Rose still does on PBS—
politics without the entertainment component—are viewed by far fewer
people than the current raft of shows that specialize in politics as entertainment. Similarly, as network news programs fought to keep their viewers, they shrunk the portion of the air time that they devoted to complex
policy issues and substituted human interest issues, the scandal de jour,
and wall-to-wall coverage of various disasters, natural and manmade.

The effect of this media environment is to reduce all politics to a virtually fact-free zone in which the loudest, funniest, and/or vilest voices
prevail. In the words of one observer of the social media scene, "users
have a propensity for humor and goofiness that make gaffes and zingers
central points of political discussion."[32] This is an environment tailor-
made for a candidate like Donald Trump who came to national attention
in so-called reality television. Trump, who openly disdains civil discourse
and uses demeaning terminology to put down his opponents, dominated
the mass media during his primary campaign for the Republican nomination. The more times he referred to his opponents as liars, low energy,
losers, or made misogynist and racist comments, the more free air time
and attention he received. His daily (sometimes hourly) 140-character
Twitter attacks on his opponents and on those who had accused him
of dishonesty or sexually predatory behavior and his penchant for "re-
tweeting" supporting tweets from his followers or endorsers were faithfully reported by respected media outlets. Many networks allowed him to
regularly call in to their stations for interviews or comments rather than
actually appearing, a courtesy that no one remembers being afforded
to other candidates. By one commonly quoted estimate, the value of
Trump's air time, if he had had to pay for it, was $2 billion. One analysis
of media coverage for January and February 2016 concluded that for
every dollar Trump spent on advertising, he received $189.90 of free
media time; for Hillary Clinton, the figures was $26.60 for every dollar
she spent, and for John Kasich, one of Trump's vanquished Republican
opponents during the primaries, the figure was $2.70 of free air time for
every dollar that he spent.[33]

Trump knew exactly what he was doing. More than other candidates,
he understood the populist power of Twitter. While the literate and

intellectual among the citizenry mocked the idea of dealing with complex public policy or electoral issues in 140 characters, the larger population, few of whom would wish to work their way through a lengthy newspaper analysis or a policy paper, enjoyed the truncated summary or the nasty attack. He also understood that the mass public was more interested in entertainment than in policy, more interested in the profane than the sacred, and more interested in the fake world of reality television than in the real world itself. The glut of these shows on the broadcast and cable networks constitutes the electronic version of pulp fiction, an escapist fantasy world for those who do not care to engage with current events, who live their lives vicariously through the participants on such shows, or who, at some unconscious level, merge the fantasy with the real world. Trump's fantasy world in which he is brilliant, informed, rich, handsome, and successful becomes the truth for a segment of this population, any data to the contrary notwithstanding.

Trump boasted, probably accurately in this case, that if it were not for his candidacy, the record viewership of the Republican debates and the news programming around them would not have occurred. His opponents for the Republican nomination, who for the most part refused to engage in this type of rhetoric, were either slighted or ignored, and certainly serious discussions of real issues virtually disappeared. In a media version of Gresham's law, "bad" political discourse drove out the "good."

Citizens fully acclimated to this media environment see little wrong with Trump's approach; although they may not vote for him because they do not like him or what he says, his behavior is congruent with the media culture in which we live, a culture that too frequently devalues civility and rewards someone who, to use some of the favorite phrases of his supporters, "tells it like it is," and doesn't care about "political correctness." People lined up for hours to attend his events, just as people line up for a *Jerry Springer Show* episode featuring sexual and physical confrontations—because they want to see the show. They sat and waited for the outrageous statement for which the candidate is known, and seemed bored to tears when his advisors forced him to read a more carefully stated policy speech from a teleprompter. Like a good entertainer, Trump displayed a keen sense of when he was losing his audience, and when he saw this happening, he would deviate from his set speech and toss out some surefire lines to excite the crowd. They got caught up in the call and response aspect of his rallies—Build the wall! Lock her up!—and for many it was a cathartic event, allowing them to vent their anger and frustration, not dissimilar in this respect to a revival meeting. Sometimes Trump's ad lib approach led to him stepping on the theme that his speech was supposed to hit. In early September, Trump was giving a speech in which he was trying to project a more moderate tone on the issue of immigration, but the people to whom he was speaking were not interested in nuance. Sensing that, Trump returned to his more inflammatory

tone on immigration, leaving his audience happy but his su
opponents confused about where he actually was on the issu

Conclusion

Just as the presidential selection process has become fully democratized,
the mass media has undergone a similar and parallel process. At one
time, the dissemination of political news and information was tightly
controlled by a small group of media journalists who decided what the
public needed to know. Although this gatekeeping function undoubtedly
narrowed the range of information available to citizens, the information
that was transmitted was of relatively high quality. With the arrival of
multiple broadcast and cable channels, and especially the internet, the
old information oligopoly was destroyed and replaced by an anarchic
multitude of television and internet sources of news and information. But
the price for this has been a decrease in quality control, because without
any information hierarchy, all opinions have an equal claim to validity.

The other dimension of media democratization has been a race to the
bottom as television and newspapers compete for the largest number of
viewers and readers, and as websites compete for the largest number of
visits and clicks. There are certainly outlets that strive for higher standards, including newspapers such as *The New York Times* and *The Wall
Street Journal*, and television stations such as PBS and C-SPAN. But it
will come as no surprise that the circulation of these newspapers is stag-
nant, their revenues are declining, and many of their stories are read on
the web rather than in hard copy. Similarly, the ratings for news shows
on PBS and C-SPAN would not allow these programs to survive on commercial as opposed to public television.

Media participants understand that in order to attract people, the sensational, the scandalous, and the personal need to be emphasized over the
mundane, the analytical, and the institutional. Short-term stories with
simple messages, as well as drama and human interest, trump stories that
require complex explanations and policy details and those that end up
with no clear winners and losers. People are attracted by entertainment
and entertainers, not by dry analysis, no matter how detailed or well-
reasoned it might be. The democratized presidential selection process fits
well with this new media environment. The lengthy and public nomination process in which each party engages provides countless opportunities for drama, as winners and losers are announced on a regular basis.
The conventions that conclude the nomination process merge politics
and entertainment, with the primary goal of putting on a good show for
the viewers.

Presidential candidates must adapt to an environment that requires
them to connect with the voters. In 1992, Bill Clinton turned his campaign
around by going on late night television shows, playing his saxophone,

and answering the boxers or briefs question. Barack Obama, before and after his elections, was a regular guest on *The Daily Show*, *The Colbert Report*, and various late night talk shows. And Donald Trump, whose second career after real estate was reality television, was a made-for-television candidate. He provided cable news with whatever it needed. If they wanted sensational, he gave them personal attacks on his opponents, outrageous statements about entire ethnic and religious groups, and a promise to build a wall. If they wanted earthy, he gave them sex scandals and vulgarity. And, most importantly, he delivered viewers.

Admittedly, there is more than a little intellectual elitism to this critique of popular culture and its infiltration of the political world. There are echoes of the platonic notion that argued that democracy would fail because most citizens would be unable or unwilling to deal intelligently with the great issues of the day and that democracy's commitment to equality would come at the expense of expertise and merit. There are also the echoes of the concerns voiced by the Founders who rejected the notion that the "mob" could play a productive governing role. Committed democrats should reject this critique out of hand in favor of the notion that the cultural and political preferences of the people, no matter how inarticulate or vulgar they might be, are all that should matter. But doing so does not obviate the need for a sober assessment of the implications of the fully democratized presidential selection process for the quality of our presidents and the stability and survival of our political system.

Notes

1 Robert D. McFadden, "Paul Harvey, Homespun Radio Voice of Middle America, Is Dead at 90." *New York Times*, March 2, 2009.
2 California Cable and Telecommunications Association, "History of Cable." www.calcable.org/learn/history-of-cable/
3 James Poniewozik, "Roger Ailes Fused TV With Politics, Changing Both." *New York Times*, July 21, 2016.
4 www.statista.com/statistics/183408/number-of-us-daily-newspapers-since-1975/
5 Daniel Gayo-Avello, "Social Media, Democracy, and Democratization." *IEEE Multimedia* 22:2 (April–June, 2015), pp. 10–16.
6 Farhad Manjoo, "How the Internet Is Loosening Our Grip on the Truth." *New York Times*, November 2, 2016.
7 Doris Graber, "Adapting Political News Top the Needs of Twenty-First Century Americans." In W. Lance Bennett and Robert M. Entman, ed. *Mediated Politics: Communication in the Future of Democracy* (Cambridge: Cambridge University Press, 2001), 439–441.
8 Manjoo, "How the Internet Is Loosening Our Grip on the Truth."
9 Joe Trippi, *The Revolution Will Not Be Televised* (New York: Harper Collins,2004), 223.
10 See Reuven Frank, "1948: Live . . . From Philadelphia . . . It's the National Conventions." *New York Times*, April 17, 1988.
11 Sharon Jarvis, "Presidential Nominating Conventions and Television." www.museum.tv/eotv/presidential.htm.

12 Shanto Iyengar, Helmut Norpoth, and Kyu S. Hahn, "Consumer Demand for Election News: The Horserace Sells." *Journal of Politics* 66:1 (February, 2004), 157–75.

13 Kathleen Searles, Martha Humphries Ginn, and Jonathan Nickens, "Here's Another Reason Not to Trust TV News Reports About Election Polls." *Washington Post*, August 23, 2016.

14 Campbell Brown, "Why I Blame TV for Trump." *Politico Magazine*, May/June, 2016.

15 Ezra Collins, "Les Moonves: Trump's Run is 'damn good for CBS.' " http://www.politico.com/blogs/on-media/2016/02/les-moonves-trump-cbs-220001

16 Stephen J. Wayne, *Road to the White House 2016*. 10th ed. (Boston: Cengage Learning, 2016), 212. Also see www.people-press.org/2012/11/15/low-marks-for-the-2012-election/.

17 Wayne, *Road to the White House 2016*, 221.

18 Ibid., 224.

19 Harry Enten, "Trump May Have More to Gain From the First Debate Than Clinton." http://fivethirtyeight.com/features/trump-may-have-more-to-gain-from-the-first-debate-than-clinton/ September 26, 2016.

20 John Sides, "Here Are 5 Keys to Watching Monday Night's Debate Between Clinton and Trump." John Sides, *Washington Post*, September 26, 2016 www.washingtonpost.com/news/monkey-cage/wp/2016/09/26/here-are-the-5-keys-to-watching-monday-nights-debate-between-clinton-and-trump/.

21 Joe McGinniss, *The Selling of the President, 1968* (New York: Trident, 1969).

22 Wayne, *Road to the White House 2016*, 226.

23 Philip Rosenstein, "Borrell Predicts $350 Million More in Political Ad Spend." www.mediapost.com/publications/article/272593/borrell-predicts-350-million-more-in-political-ad.html.

24 See Max Isaac, "Facebook in the Cross Hairs After Election, Is Said to Question Its Influence." *New York Times*, June 12, 2016; Max Read, "Donald Trump Won Because of Facebook."http://nymag.com/selectall/2016/11/donald-trump-won-because-of-facebook.html.

25 Gayo-Avello, "Social Media, Democracy, and Democratization."

26 Janelle Ward, "Exploring How Young People Use the Internet for Political Participation." In Richard Scullion, Ronan Gerodimas, Daniel Jackson, and Darren Lilleki, eds. *The Media, Political Participation, and Empowerment* (New York: Routledge, 2013), 200–1.

27 George Saunders, "Trump Days," *The New Yorker*, July 11 and 18, 2016, 54. See also Cass R. Sunstein, *Republic.com 2.0* (Princeton: Princeton University Press, 2009).

28 Brendan Nyhan, "Relatively Few People Are Partisan News Consumers, But They're Influential." *New York Times*, September 7, 2016.

29 Jody C. Baumgartner and Jonathan Morris, "Stoned Slackers or Super-Citizens: *The Daily Show* Viewing and Political Engagement of Young Adults." In Amarnath Amarasingam, ed. *The Stewart/Colbert Effect: Essays on the Real Impact of Fake News* (Jefferson, NC: McFarland and Co., Inc., 2011), 67.

30 Jonathan Martin, "Anything-Goes Campaign an Alarming Precedent." *New York Times* September 18, 2016.

31 Julian Zelizer, "Why Donald Trump Is the Next Walter White." www.cnn.com/2016/05/30/opinions/trump-as-tv-anti-hero-julian-zelizer/.

32 Gayo-Avello, "Social Media, Democracy, and Democratization."

33 Michael O'Connell, "Political Ad Spending to Hit $11.7 Billion in 2016; Trump's Free Coverage Unprecedented." *The Hollywood Reporter*, March 31, 2016 www.hollywoodreporter.com/news/political-ad-spending-hit-117-879699.

7   Charisma, Demagoguery, Populism, and Celebrity

The democratized presidential selection process requires presidential candidates to establish a relationship with the electorate rather than simply a relationship with party leaders and office holders. At the risk of stating the obvious, those who prevail in the process are those who are able to get the most votes. The democratic hope is that citizens will use this power to nominate and elect candidates who are qualified for the office and whose policy positions appeal to their sense of the nation's interests. The Founders' fear was that the attitudes and, therefore, the votes of citizens would be manipulated by candidates who appealed to their passions rather than to their reason and to their narrow, often selfish interests, rather than to the public interest. The performance of the now fully democratized process for winning nomination and election to the presidency, abetted by a fully democratized media environment, suggests that the fears of the Founders were more prescient than the hopes of the democrats.

James Madison, who often articulated the fears of the Founders, rued the vicious arts by which elections are contested. Contemporary and critical discussions often use terms such as charisma, populism, and demagoguery to describe these arguably less virtuous ways that candidates use to connect with the voters and solicit their support. More recently, the cultural concept of "celebrity" has entered the political lexicon as a way to describe candidates who rely on their public image rather than their record of accomplishments or their positions on the issues. Each of these different, yet related, terms helps us to understand the perils of our current presidential selection system.

Charisma

The term "charisma" traces its origins to the New Testament, where it refers to a person with divine powers manifested in a capacity to prophesize, to heal, or to speak in tongues.[1] The German sociologist Max Weber expanded, and to some extent, secularized the concept, discussing a leader who "possesses charisma by virtue of magical powers, revelations, heroism, or other extraordinary gifts."[2] Exploiting these characteristics, such a leader seeks to convince his putative followers that these "gifts" make him uniquely qualified to lead and that following him is not just in their interests, but it is their duty.

Today, the term charisma has acquired an even broader meaning than Weber's formulation. Modern commentators have discussed charisma in terms of a leader's "ability to articulate a compelling vision of a bright future," and others have suggested that the term implies a capacity to inspire followers "to perform above and beyond the call of duty by appealing to their emotions and enduring motives."[3] From this perspective, a charismatic leader is one whose connection with his followers is based on his personality, his rhetorical skills, and his ability to arouse their passions, and not on his objective qualifications to lead, his ideology, or his ability to address specific policy questions. Weber argues that such leaders are more likely to emerge during a time of crisis because the "extraordinary gifts" that they convince their followers that they possess are essential to deal with these out of the ordinary situations. Such leaders typically employ language and rhetoric rife with symbols calculated to persuade citizens to follow them. They attach themselves to important events in their nation's history, they refer to past glories, condemn past humiliations, and promise future greatness.[4] If they are successful, the masses virtually "surrender themselves" to such heroic leaders.[5]

Charismatic leaders need not actually possess extraordinary talents or skills or have viable plans for the future of their countries. Because they traffic in rhetoric and symbols rather than in actions and concrete solutions, the feasibility of any actions that they propose to take is not considered by their followers; rather their success or failure is calculated in terms of their ability to serve the psychic needs of the individual citizen—to convincingly and consistently articulate and deploy words and symbols that provide comfort and reassurance, and the appearance, if not necessarily the reality, of action.[6]

Today, the concept of charisma has been watered down by popular commentators to the point where it is often used simply as an antonym to "dull." Candidates are referred to as charismatic if they can strike a responsive chord among those who listen to them and if they seem to generate a high level of excitement among those to whom they speak. Various American presidents, including Franklin Roosevelt, John Kennedy, Ronald Reagan, and Barack Obama, have been described as charismatic. The term has also been applied outside the political or leadership arena. As one scholar has put it (only a bit hyperbolically), charisma has become a label attached to "pop musicians, movie stars, sports heroes, TV personalities, glamorous models, and, on occasion, notorious rogues."[7] In this sense, charismatic leadership becomes akin, at one extreme, to a cult of personality and, at the other, to the more modern concept of celebrity, a term that we will consider later in this chapter.

But for our purposes, the heart of charisma, whether in Weber's telling or in its more expansive modern version, is the direct and intimate relationship that it assumes between leaders and followers, a relationship unmediated by political institutions such as political parties or governmental bodies, a relationship based entirely on a personal and emotional connection. Weber distinguished charismatic leadership from what he called "legal domination," or depersonalized leadership characterized by accepted procedures for leadership selection and by permanent, collective governing institutions, such as bureaucracies and legislative bodies. Charismatic leadership, in contrast, emphasizes the singular and personal qualities of the leader. Although modern nation-states are almost by definition characterized by legal domination, the concept is always in tension with the personalized and potentially charismatic leadership associated with the singular presidency.

Empowering the people to select their leaders is an invitation to charismatic leadership, especially in a time of perceived crisis when many citizens may come to see existing state institutions and incumbent leaders as insufficient for the task of governing. In such an environment, voters become especially vulnerable to the appeal of a candidate who markets himself as a special leader with unique abilities to solve the problems of the nation and who asks voters to accept this claim as a matter of blind faith. Some theorists argue that citizens of modern societies are increasingly vulnerable to these leaders. The security that they offer compensates for the byproducts of modernity, particularly the breakdown of primary and secondary groups such as the family, community organizations, and religious institutions.[8]

Demagoguery

Charismatic leadership and demagoguery are close cousins. Typically, the demagogue identifies himself with popular and patriotic symbols and names and vilifies those whom he identifies as the enemies of the nation and its people. As a candidate for office, the demagogue fans the fears of the public by exaggerating both the problems that the nation confronts—because he knows that it is the fear itself that evokes support from the followers he seeks—as well as his capacity to solve those problems. He promises order and safety to replace chaos and danger, pride in place of humiliation, superiority in place of inferiority, leadership in place of inertia, strength in place of weakness, hope in place of despair, and a return to the mores of an idealized past in place of what he depicts as the political and cultural chaos of modern society.

As was the case with charismatic leaders, people are more likely to turn to a demagogue in times of crisis or rapid change. Under these circumstances, citizens will feel threatened—by a sudden loss of economic status, by civil disorder or criminal activity, by a menace from a foreign power, or by societal changes that threaten their values. As an individual comes to believe that he lives in a world that he can neither understand nor influence, a desire to attach oneself "to reassuring abstract symbols rather than to one's own efforts becomes chronic. And what symbol can be more reassuring than the incumbent of a high position who knows what to do and is willing to act, especially when others are bewildered and alone?"[9] Individuals thus choose to "escape from freedom"[10] by turning to a more authoritarian "man on horseback" who promises to provide purpose, stability, protection, and, most importantly, reassurance. Such leaders need not necessarily deliver solutions for the problems that the nation faces. Rather, individuals are prepared to accept and support a leader who is able to "dramatize his competence," and to "appear to be in command."[11]

Demagogues often adopt what the historian Richard Hofstadter called a paranoid style. "The central image is that of a vast and sinister conspiracy . . . set in motion to undermine and destroy a way of life." The demagogue is "always manning the barricades of civilization. He constantly lives at a turning point: it is now or never in organizing resistance to conspiracy. Time is forever running out. . . . He does not see social conflict as something to be mediated and compromised, in the manner of a working politician. Since what is at stake is always a conflict between absolute good and absolute evil, the quality needed is not a willingness to compromise but the will to fight things out to a finish. Nothing but complete victory will do."[12]

While charismatic leaders can be salutary or harmful for a nation, the demagogic leader is always dangerous for the body politic. Certainly, history has many examples of charismatic leaders who did not resort to demagogic tactics. Mahatma Gandhi, the Dalai Lama, Nelson Mandela, Franklin Roosevelt, and Charles De Gaulle are leaders who in different ways and under different circumstances could be classified as charismatic leaders who were not demagogues. On the other hand, Adolph Hitler, Juan Peron, and Hugo Chavez can be viewed as both charismatic and demagogic. And in American history, George Wallace in the 1960s, Pat Buchanan in the 1990s, and Donald Trump in the 2010s were aspiring leaders who attempted to establish a link with the voters by fanning and exploiting their fears and prejudices.

Elements of the demagogue's paranoid style can be found in Donald Trump's repeated assertions that we are "losing our country," unless we act it will be "too late," and this is our "last chance to take back our country." During the 2016 Republican primaries, Ted Cruz articulated a similar perspective, arguing that there were absolute rights and absolute wrongs and that his consistent refusal during his brief Senate career to compromise with the Democrats or even with his own co-partisans was an act of principle. Trump and Cruz depicted themselves, to use Hofstadter's term, as manning the barricades against forces that they believed were determined to destroy the nation.

Because democratic societies, especially those with elected presidents, legitimize leadership through popular support, these systems can prove a fertile ground for both charismatic and demagogic leaders. Both forms of leadership, after all, rely on establishing a direct connection to the people, and electoral success comes from an excited and committed set of followers. But are there ways to establish that connection that do not rely upon the singular powers claimed by the charismatic leader or the prejudices fanned by the demagogue? One of these techniques is often labeled populism, another concept with a long history and an evolving meaning.

Populism

The populist movement that emerged in the United States in the late 19th century was critical of the concentration of wealth and political power in the hands of banks and moneyed interests. In that sense, it was the direct heir of Jacksonian democracy in its edification of the common man and its vilification of economic elites. A more modern definition of populism views it as an ideology "that considers society to be ultimately separated into two homogeneous and antagonistic groups: 'the pure people' versus 'the corrupt elite' and which argues that politics should be an expression of the general will of the people."[13] Another scholar suggests that populism exalts "the purity of the people as a condition for a politics of sincerity against the quotidian practice of compromise and bargaining that politicians pursue."[14] In its concentration on class interests, populism intersects with aspects of democratic socialism, as evidenced in Bernie Sanders' campaign attacks on banks, international trade agreements, and the power of money in American politics and its presidential elections.

But populism also has taken on demagogic tones. In some areas of the United States, particularly the South, the late 19th century populists coupled their economic message with racism, xenophobia, and conspiracy theories involving Catholics and Jews, along with allegations of nefarious conspiracies by overseas economic powers to subjugate the United States. In contemporary Europe, parties and political leaders who have opposed their countries' membership in the European Union and have used racist language to attack the EU's immigration policies, while identifying with the grievances of their countries' native working class have been referred to in the press as populist.

Populism, like charisma, has come to have a broader meaning. The term is now used to describe any politician who tailors his appeal to less educated voters at the lower end of the socioeconomic scale. In some instances, the candidate exhibits his populism by making common cause with the resentment toward elites that people of this status sometimes exhibit, whether those elites are economic powers on Wall Street, government bureaucrats, or the more intellectual or cosmopolitan classes and the media outlets with which they are associated. Populist candidates play on the notion that the political system and the culture at large is dominated by these elites whose interests, views, and values are at odds with those of the average citizen. These candidates, like their 19th century forebears, depict themselves as tribunes of the people and exponents of the class and cultural grievances of average citizens.

One reason why populist appeals succeed is because they tap into the American ethos of equality that Tocqueville and others observed. They also succeed among voters who feel that they have been left behind economically. Modern communication technology has played a role in stoking such a sense of relative deprivation. At one time, citizens had relatively little contact with those who were not of their social class. They heard about the lives of rich people, of course, but they seldom saw it up close. Although economic segregation remains a fact of American life, television has brought the different lifestyles of the rich and sometimes famous into everyone's living room. Reality shows that center on the lives of the wealthy feed the sense among those with less that there are others who are living much better and easier lives than they are. When viewers see people in New York City and Los Angeles buying multi-million dollar homes on the cable show *Million Dollar Listing* and vacation homes priced in the high six figures on *House Hunters*, some of more modest circumstances who are struggling to make ends meet are bound to feel a degree of envy. The ubiquity of products advertised on television creates an inexhaustible desire in citizens for the newest automobile, the latest smartphone, or upgraded kitchen appliances and counters, a desire that many people are not financially able to satisfy.

Although there is much in American culture that works against such class resentments—the notion that those who have wealth deserve it because they have worked hard to earn it, that money does not buy happiness, various religious incantations that suggest the evils of wealth and the nobility of the poor—nonetheless, some degree of class envy is inevitable, especially in a context in which, objectively speaking, economic inequality has visibly accelerated and the "creative destruction" that is central to capitalism often leaves the destruction more immediate and more visible than the creativity. Populists convince people who are unhappy with their lives that they are not to blame for their situation; rather, they are told that they are victims of actions and events beyond their control, an argument that is sometimes difficult to refute. Populists often foist the blame on foreign interests who have taken advantage of the country through unfair trading practices or domestic economic elites who they say are benefitting from the economic pain of those lower on the socioeconomic ladder, or on government leaders who, they argue, are doing the bidding of the well-off and/or are looking out for themselves rather than the people.

Modern American populism also has a cultural dimension to it. Populists rail against intellectuals and media elites whose values and actions the say are out of touch with those of "average Americans." For those who believe the world is changing too quickly and that traditional values are being eroded or even swept away, contemporary populist rhetoric offers a reaffirmation of those values as they harken back to a different and presumably better time. They play on the nostalgia that people have for an idealized past, the problems of which they have airbrushed away. In their rhetoric, they paint a picture of a crumbling society in which the old and presumably better ways have been shunted aside. This rhetoric sometimes takes a demagogic turn when their cultural argument highlights a past when the country was whiter, when women knew their place, and gays were invisible.

Populism in America also has taken on an anti-government dimension. Americans have always been suspicious of government, beginning with Jefferson's aphorism that the government that governs best governs least. This has combined with a resistance to taxation that has been part of the culture since the birth of the Republic. Many candidates for Congress, as well as the presidency, have designed their campaigns around a theme that argues that the federal government is corrupt, inefficient, spends too much money, and doesn't respond to the needs of the people. As the political scientist Richard Fenno observed of House candidates, they run for Congress by running against Congress, promising that if they are elected they will clean up the mess in Washington or, to use the contemporary meme, "drain the swamp."[15] Not surprisingly, when citizens hear their leaders articulate the consistent theme that the national government is broken, they come to believe that. In 2015, only 19% of Americans said they can trust the government in Washington to do what is right; only 3% responded "just about always" to that question while 16% said "most of the time."[16] Populists exploit these attitudes by conveying the idea that the problems that people are experiencing are partially attributable to the government, thus setting up an oppositional relationship not just between the people and powerful private interests, but between the people and those whom they have elected to govern.

Other forms of populism are less connected with public policy or specific political or cultural grievances. As one scholar has put it, populists "reject linguistic styles and postures that are distant from those that the people share and practice in their everyday lives," and opt instead for a popular or direct style of expression.[17] This more benign aspect of populism is commonplace in all presidential campaigns. It manifests itself in gestures and speaking styles that candidates employ to suggest to voters that they are indeed one of them. Candidates kiss babies, shuck their ties and dress in casual clothes when campaigning in rural areas, and stuff themselves with local dishes that are put before them. They try to signal their connection to the common people by the way they speak. Barack Obama, a highly educated man who has frequently been accused of intellectual snobbery by his opponents, regularly drops his "g's" when in campaign mode ("We're goin' to provide health care for all Americans"), switches to black vernacular when speaking to African American audiences, and in one colossal failed attempt to demonstrate his affinity for white working-class men during his 2008 campaign, went bowling, an exercise that clearly demonstrated that his sport was basketball. During the 2016 contest for the Republican nomination, candidates such as Ted Cruz and Mike Huckabee sought to reinforce their everyman credentials by talking about their affection for and their facility with guns, Governor Scott Walker of Wisconsin spent a lot of time riding his Harley-Davidson motorcycle, and Governor Chris Christie of New Jersey pumped up the volume on his regular Jersey guy persona.

It isn't clear that this approach wins many voters, but it's also clear that candidates whose rhetoric and style is too abstruse or abstract for average people may have difficulty with many of these voters. The American people certainly want to have a president who is more intelligent and informed than they are, but they do not want to have that intellectual superiority made explicit. Thus, candidates engage in this form of benign populism because they worry that if they don't, they will be perceived as talking down to the voters. In 1952 and 1956, Adlai Stevenson's campaign for the presidency was hampered by the perception some voters had that he was too intellectual and unable to understand them and their concerns. Similarly, one scholar reports a 2014 exchange with a British cab driver concerning Nigel Farage, at that time the leader of the right wing United Kingdom Independence Party. The cab driver had regularly voted for Labor candidates but was impressed by Farage who, despite his wealthy background and elite school education, frequented pubs and seemed to talk *to* him, not *down* to him and not *about* him. Although he claimed not to endorse the man's racist views, he felt that Farage understood his worries, and "speaks my language."[18] Similarly, in the 2000 presidential campaign, some commentators said that George W. Bush was a person whom people would rather have a beer with than the more cerebral Al Gore. And in 2016, many poor white voters seem to have supported Donald Trump because his language about trade, immigration, and people of color suggested that despite his own wealth and lifestyle, he understood their economic pain and their sense of cultural loss.

But candidates who practice benign populism need to be skillful in doing this, lest they risk appearing condescending or looking less than genuine. In 1988, the Democratic nominee, Michael Dukakis, looked ridiculous when he put on a helmet and got into a tank to demonstrate his affinity for the military. Such was also the case with Obama's ill-considered bowling expedition in 2008. And in 2012, Mitt Romney was pictured in Iowa in a plaid shirt and jeans standing with his leg perched on a bale of hay. It took only a quick glance at the picture to see how uncomfortable this venture capitalist multi-millionaire was in that setting, how determined he was not to move his leg until the event was over, and how unlikely it was that he had ever been that close to a hay bale in his life.

As was the case with charisma, populism has become a fairly elastic concept, incorporating campaign rhetoric that appeals to cultural and racial resentments (George Wallace, Pat Buchanan, Donald Trump), class resentments (Bernie Sanders and Donald Trump), and a campaign style that seeks to reassure the average voter that the candidate can relate to them and their lives. Bill Clinton, an acknowledged policy wonk, was also a master at projecting empathy, convincing voters that he "felt their pain." In 1992, when his campaign for the Democratic nomination was in trouble, Clinton became the first candidate to appear on late night television, and rather than discussing politics, he played his saxophone. Musically, it was far from a virtuoso performance, but it was a political success, allowing him to reach and connect with an audience that does not read policy papers and does not watch C-SPAN. Today, candidates, as well as incumbent presidents, regularly appear on such shows, placing themselves on the same level as the celebrities who are the usual guests.[19] This practice is an indicator of the growing nexus between celebrity culture and politics and further underlines the connection between entertainment and politics. As the social commentator Neil Postman put it thirty years ago, "political figures may show up anywhere at any time, doing anything without being thought odd, presumptuous, or in any way out of place. Which is to say, they have become assimilated into general television culture as celebrities."[20]

Celebrity Politics

The easiest way to understand the meaning of celebrity is to begin with the idea of fame. By fame, we mean being widely and positively known. Our history is told in terms of famous people, people whose names are known and fondly thought of by large numbers of Americans. Presidents such as Washington, Jefferson, and Lincoln are famous; monuments to them are found in the nation's capital, and schoolchildren know who they are and why they are important. Charles Lindbergh and Babe Ruth are famous for what they accomplished in the fields of aviation and baseball. But these historically famous people are, of course, no longer with us. The essence of their fame lies in what they did (or were said to have done) years ago, and their case for fame rests on the fact that the memory of who they were and what they accomplished has endured over the years.

But being a celebrity differs from being famous in two ways. Although celebrities, like famous people, are widely known, they are not always thought of in a positive way. Al Capone is known and remembered, but he is certainly not remembered fondly; for people like Capone, the antonym of famous (infamous) applies, but in his time, he was a celebrity.

In addition, while fame implies a record of past accomplishments, the people whom we typically think of as celebrities are contemporary, rather than historical figures. Although celebrities may be widely and favorably known, this status has been conferred upon them only recently, it is far from permanent, and it is not necessarily connected with anything enduring that they have done. To use Andy Warhol's phraseology, most celebrities enjoy fifteen minutes of fame. In most cases, their claim to fame has a limited shelf life, but while it lasts, they have a large audience interested in the things that they say and do. The list of current celebrities comes, for the most part, from the entertainment worlds of music, television, the cinema, and sports—Justin Bieber, Jennifer Aniston, Meryl Streep, and LeBron James are examples. As celebrities, they regularly get their picture in the newspaper, they adorn the pages of magazines such as *People* and *US*, they amass Twitter followers in the hundreds of thousands, and because stories about their professional and personal lives seem to be of inordinate interest to large segments of the population, they sell publications and generate ratings for cable television stations and internet clicks for web sites. Certainly, some celebrities may eventually become famous, but we won't know that for many years, perhaps not even during their lifetime.

We have also witnessed an explosion in the number of people who are considered to be celebrities, a phenomenon connected in part with the fractionalization of the media that we discussed in the previous chapter and in part with our cultural commitment to equality, a commitment that serves to widen the circle of people whose lives we are supposed to care about. The profusion of media outlets makes it much easier for people to rise to prominence than it was in an earlier time when there were fewer outlets and greater control. The ceaseless, often vicious war that cable and network television channels, web sites, and social media platforms wage for viewers, visits, and clicks exploits the public interest in celebrities. The world of reality TV has constructed a business model centered on celebrities as commodities to be created, managed, marketed and, eventually, discarded to make way for new products.[21] The *Real Housewives* franchise has metastasized to different cities with changing casts of characters, each seeking to monetize their celebrity status by creating and endorsing product lines and striking deals with various print and online outlets that specialize in this material.[22] Although reality television shows appear on the major networks, the real impetus for their expansion has been cable television and the need of an increasing number of channels to fill their air time. Reality shows are low budget ways to do this, because they use amateur talent and bare bones scripts.

The celebrity culture is congruent with democracy in the sense that people attain celebrity status by a form of popular approbation and because virtually anyone can claim to be a celebrity. It is difficult to think of someone as a celebrity if only a few people know or care to know about them. To gain that visibility, they are carefully packaged and marketed by those who have a stake in the celebrity production industry. Alternatively, they do or say outrageous things. The public registers its interest not by voting, but by buying magazines and tabloids that feature the celebrity, tuning in to the television shows that feature them, following them on Twitter, and clicking on internet stories about them. In some cases, the public actually does vote, as was the case with *American Idol*, where winners were identified through votes from viewers. In May 2012, 132 million people voted for the next American idol, 10 million more than voted in the 2008 presidential election.

A claim to celebrity status rests on attaining a level of popular visibility. One need not do anything important or accomplish anything of substance to earn celebrity status. Here, at last, we have the connection to the political world. The first step toward a successful campaign for any office, but especially the presidency, is for a candidate to raise his name recognition. Briefly stated, people have to know who you are before they will consider voting for you. Celebrity status is a short cut to name recognition; building on the fact that they are already known, some celebrities become candidates themselves. Donald Trump's candidacy is the most striking example of a celebrity capitalizing on his visibility to his political advantage. Others who have done so include John Glenn, the astronaut who became a senator from Ohio and, for a time, a presidential candidate; the actor Arnold Schwarzenegger, who became governor of California; the comedian Al Franken, who became a senator from Minnesota; Elizabeth Warren, who rose to celebrity status from appearances on *The Daily Show* and then ran successfully for the Senate; and Fred Thompson, who had a movie career before being elected to the Senate from Tennessee.

In the time immediately following his 2004 keynote address to the Democratic Convention, Barack Obama became an instant celebrity. By that I mean that he did not have to seek out media coverage; the media sought him out, chronicling his every step as he began his career in the Senate and plotted his run for the presidency. The half-life of celebrity reputations is relatively short, and the celebrity business is always on the lookout for the next new thing. Obama's combination of youth, rhetorical skills, a compelling and unique personal history, and his status as the first non-Caucasian who could be taken as a serious candidate for the presidency attracted enormous interest from the media and then from large segments of the population. His opponents seeking the nomination, virtually all better known than he, could not generate that same level of interest. Ironically, Hillary Clinton, who had parlayed her own celebrity status as First Lady into a successful run for the Senate in 2000, was no longer a celebrity by the time she ran for president in 2008. She was just a hard working politician who had been around for some time, while the celebrity business had moved on to the next new personality.

In 2008, after Obama secured the Democratic nomination, he traveled to Europe, where he was greeted with the sort of crowds that one usually associated with rock stars, or at least incumbent US presidents, not candidates. His general election opponent, Senator John McCain, sought to deploy the celebrity label against Obama, running ads associating him with frivolous celebrities such as Britney Spears and Paris Hilton, and suggesting that he was no more prepared than these "famous" women for the responsibilities of the presidency. This approach fell flat. As one observer put it, "the Republicans did not understand that Obama's rising celebrity status was helping him become more popular, getting him more attention, support and, eventually, votes from a population that is generally attracted by celebrity status and culture."[23]

Interestingly enough, the 2008 campaign saw another instant celebrity emerge in the person McCain selected as a vice president, Sarah Palin, a previously obscure governor of Alaska. McCain's advisors thought that she had the potential to be a "star" (a term now in more common use in politics, perhaps unconsciously denoting the increasing connection between entertainment and politics), and because she would be a rather surprising pick (and only the second woman to be on a presidential ticket); they hoped that she would attract the sort of attention to the McCain campaign that Obama was attracting to his campaign. Like Obama, Palin was young—forty-four—she looked good on television, and she seemed to possess a populist ability to speak to the average person. As the campaign had hoped, these characteristics, along with a strong acceptance speech at the Republican Convention, turned her into an instant celebrity, much more interesting to the media and the American public than the party's presidential nominee who had been around seemingly forever.

Unfortunately, as often happens with celebrities, in Palin's case there turned out to be nothing beneath the surface. She proved to be virtually ignorant about basic political and policy facts, she was inarticulate when not reading from a prepared text, and various unflattering stories about her family and her brief time as governor surfaced as well. Given the financial crisis that was to hit the country in September 2008, President Bush's low public approval ratings, and national exhaustion with the wars in Iraq and Afghanistan, the Obama–Biden ticket likely would have prevailed in 2008, even without Palin's presence on the ticket. But Palin certainly proved a significant distraction for the Republican campaign, and for many voters, her selection as McCain's running mate suggested extraordinarily poor judgment on the part of a presidential candidate whose strong suit presumably was how much more experienced he was than his opponent. As for Palin, after the defeat of the Republican ticket, she resigned her position as governor of Alaska to cash in on her celebrity status with a reality television show of her own, a commentator spot on Fox News, and generously remunerated speaking engagements around the country.

Trump's lack of knowledge about public affairs was as apparent, perhaps more so, as Palin's, and his personal history made the foibles of the Palin family seem rather tame by comparison. It may be that Palin might have done better at the top of the ticket, or it may be that female celebrity/politicians are held to a different standard than males. But in terms of the things she said during the campaign and the sort of crowds that she attracted, Palin's candidacy seems in retrospect to be a precursor to Trump's. Traveling to a small southern town and speaking to a largely white audience, she reveled in being among "real Americans." She condemned what she liked to call "the lamestream media" and supported the idea that Obama was a secret Muslim. Just as was the case with Trump eight years later, the crowds she attracted were large and enthusiastic, and they responded well to her populist themes and her no-frills way of speaking to them.

At one point, being widely known was a necessary condition for becoming a viable presidential candidate, but the rise of celebrity culture means that it can be a sufficient condition for a successful run for the presidency. Barack Obama's celebrity diminished the importance of his lack of governmental experience and made room for him to display the intelligence, knowledge, and articulateness that served him so well in his campaign and in office. Donald Trump's celebrity status seems to have eliminated the concern that not only did he have no political or governmental experience, but he also had no knowledge of government, seemingly no interest in becoming more knowledgeable, and his demeanor was light years removed from what any fair-minded person would declare presidential. As the celebrity culture of the entertainment industry came to intersect with the political world of presidential selection, we have seen the displacement of traditional political skills (bargaining, compromise) and their replacement by those of media management.[24] As Postman argued, politics becomes all about appearance and image, so that we reach a point where cosmetics replaces ideology "as the field of expertise over which a politician must have competent control."[25]

Donald Trump

Donald Trump's candidacy has elements of charisma, demagoguery, populism, and celebrity. Trump's celebrity status, assembled through a nearly constant media presence in the years before his candidacy, is what propelled him into the presidential race, accounted in large measure for the incessant media fascination with his candidacy, and explains the attachment of some of his followers who seem drawn by the persona that he displays. Trump succeeded because he understood and exploited the nexus between successful entertainment and successful politics. One Democrat described the attachment of many to Donald Trump in this way: "it's just that we've always enjoyed the show. It's entertaining to hate him, to like him and to imagine being him."[26]

As is the case with charismatic leaders, he tells his followers that he has extraordinary abilities—superior intelligence, verbal toughness, vigor and strength, and an unparalleled ability to make good deals—that uniquely qualify him to solve the nation's problems. According to Trump, he knows more about the Islamic State than the generals do. He knows more about the tax code as well, so he is best suited to fix its inequities. But he offers little in the way of concrete policy proposals; instead, he simply demands that voters support him as an act of faith in him personally. His candidacy focused entirely on himself—not on the party of which he is the ostensible leader and not on an identifiable set of principles and policies. He asks people to believe him and in him, despite the fact that he regularly changes his positions on major issues, denies that he took certain positions in the past, even in the face of irrefutable evidence to the contrary, and presents no feasible policy proposals to address the problems that he identifies. He promises economic growth rates that have never been achieved, indicates against all reason that Mexico will pay for a wall across the southern border, and defies basic mathematical principles by promising huge tax cuts, the protection of social security and Medicare, and the quick paying off of the national debt. He displays none of the historical, political, or policy knowledge, or even the intellectual curiosity, that would seem to be a prerequisite to at least understanding the issues that he is talking about, let alone dealing with them.

As is the case with other demagogues, he rouses his followers with apocalyptic claims about the state of the nation and with crude attacks on minority ethnic groups, established politicians, and even the political system itself. He referred to immigrants from Mexico as criminals and rapists; he suggested that Americans who are Muslims be put under surveillance and that no more Muslims should be admitted into the country; and he sought, for years, to delegitimize the first African American president with the false claim that he was not born in the United States and therefore ineligible to be president. In addition to his racist and sexist language, he implicitly and sometimes explicitly encourages his followers to violence. Employing the demagogic idiom of the paranoid style, he argues that governing elites have pushed the nation toward a political, economic, and cultural abyss, and that he and he alone has the ability to prevent the country from falling over the edge. He accused Hillary Clinton of meeting "in secret with international banks to plot the destruction of US sovereignty in order to enrich these global financial powers." In an interview with CNN shortly after he announced his candidacy, he said "I'll be honest with you. I want to save the country. Our country's going to hell. We have a problem. I want to make America great again. And to do that, you have to be bold, you have to be strong."[27]

As is the case with populists, he packages himself as the voice of those who have fallen behind economically or are nostalgic for the past, and attributes their problems and anxieties to a vast conspiracy among elites in Washington, academia, and the media, as well as malevolent international forces. To his followers, his vulgarity and insults project a persona of a guy who talks like real Americans talked before the onset of "political correctness." They say that they appreciate the fact that "he tells it like it is." His campaign specifically targeted the less educated segments of the electorate, particularly white people. His populist appeals to this class attribute the loss of blue collar jobs to poorly negotiated trade deals and to an influx of undocumented immigrants, especially from Mexico. In a throwback to the southern populists of the late 19th century, he combines this racism with appeals to the class resentment of blue collar workers, especially white men, by attributing their problems to cultural changes engineered by intellectual elites and foreign countries and to an atmosphere that has elevated women and people of color to a preferred position.

In this sense, Donald Trump's candidacy for the presidency is a realization of the worst fears of those who created the office and, in many ways, the logical culmination of the democratization of the presidential selection process. Those who believe in democracy stipulate as a matter of principle that presidents, as well as other office holders, are to be chosen by the people. But years of research by scholars into the political attitudes, behavior, and knowledge of the American people demonstrates that more than a third do not vote, and of those who do, most have only a casual understanding of the political world and virtually none have a firm grasp or a deep knowledge of the domestic and international issues facing the nation. The most reliable predictor of how people will vote is their party affiliation, and as the most recent analysis of this topic argues, "partisan preferences and voting patterns were powerfully shaped by group loyalties and social identities.... it appears that most people make their party choice based on who they are rather than on what they think."[28] And, of course, when it comes to winning a party's nomination, party identification is not a factor, so the choice of the voter comes down to the candidate himself.

We know that people have a stronger, more constant relationship to the entertainment world, broadly construed, than they have to the political world. Combined with the lack of political and policy information that characterizes so many citizens, it should not be surprising that the populism of the lowest common denominator and the emphasis on celebrity that characterizes the entertainment industry should become the tools for political advancement by aspiring politicians. Those who are steeped in this industry know what will play to the larger public. It may be a homespun way of speaking or a winning personality and style. It may also be an attack on an already marginalized portion of the population or an appeal to the naked self-interest of the voters. Or it can be an appeal to the social identities of portions of the population who feel aggrieved by cultural and economic changes. It can be an appeal to national anxieties, or it can be simply saying and doing things that have never been said and done before by a presidential candidate, which by itself makes news. Not to put too fine a point on it, but it is worth saying that none of these approaches to gathering votes has obvious policy content, has a clear relationship to the public interest, or speaks in any but a negative way to the qualifications for office of the candidate making these appeals. The name of the game, after all, is to gain the approval of as many voters as possible, and the goal of the game is to win. If voters respond to what they perceive to be the personal qualities and styles of candidates or to the candidates' appeals to their prejudices or passions, then that is perhaps the necessary, albeit bitter, fruit of democracy.

Trump's rhetoric drew a picture of a country that was failing, both internally and internationally, and he promised to "make America great again" by "putting America first" in all of his decisions and policies. In doing so, he invoked the time-honored themes of nationalism as a way to motivate voters, and he sold himself as a strong leader, an approach with a long history of success among voters who believe, correctly or not, that their country and their way of life is at risk.

These themes suggested historical parallels between the rise of fascism in Germany and the rise of Trump. And although Trump is not a fascist in the sense that he subscribes to a coherent ideology that characterized such movements, there is something to be said for the similarities between his words and his movement and the movement that propelled European fascists to power in the 1930s. Hitler came to power by promising to restore Germany's greatness after the humiliation of the Treaty of Versailles. He singled out Jewish citizens as enemies of the state and the source of the country's internal weakness and economic travails. He attacked the incumbent political leadership for its failures to deal with the nation's challenges, for their corruption, and for overseeing Germany's loss of status as a great power. He offered himself as the strong leader who would sweep away the incumbent politicians, rid the country of its internal enemies and therefore its problems, and restore its prominence as a great nation. As one commentator put it, "successful fascism was not about policies but about the strongman, the leader in whom could be entrusted the fate of the nation. Whatever the problem, he could fix it. Whatever the threat, internal or external, he could vanquish it, and it was unnecessary for him to explain how."[29]

Hitler invented the concept of the big lie, advising in *Mein Kampf* that it is wise to fabricate "colossal untruths," because the listeners would not believe that one "could have the impudence to distort the truth so infamously."[30] Trump seemed to follow this advice, making wildly inaccurate statements about the condition of the nation and the positions of his opponents and regularly denying that he had taken positions that ample evidence indicated that he had. *Politifact* classified 70% of Trump's most controversial statements of 2015 as either mostly false, false, or "pants on fire" lies.[31] He said that he opposed the Iraq War from the start, even in the face of recordings to the contrary. Based on no evidence, he characterized Hillary Clinton as a person who wanted undocumented immigrants to be treated better than veterans. He maintained that Clinton was the first person to raise the question of whether or not President Obama was born in the United States when, in fact, she never did, while Trump's rise to prominence among the right wing was a direct result of his championing this cause for several years. And the lies continued after his election victory when, for example, he claimed that the only reason that he did not win a plurality of the popular vote was because millions of people had voted illegally, all presumably for Clinton. Of course, there was no evidence for this claim and, quite the contrary, election officials from both parties from all over the country said that there were virtually no incidents of voter fraud. A week or so later, he claimed that the murder rate in the United States was "the highest it's been in 47 years," while FBI figures indicated that the murder rate was among the lowest in the last 50 years. And in March 2017, he asserted that President Obama had wiretapped him and his campaign, a claim that was refuted by the director of the FBI, the director of the National Security Agency, and both the Democratic and Republican leaders of the House and Senate Intelligence Committees.

Trump's obsession with the birther issue exemplifies the conspiracy aspect of the paranoid style that demagogues adopt. Beginning in 2011, Trump was the primary advocate for the idea that President Obama was not born in the United States. He demanded to know why the president would not produce his birth certificate. When he did produce a birth certificate, he suggested that it was forged and claimed to have dispatched private investigators to Hawaii, the president's place of birth, who he said "could not believe what they are finding." Of course, he never indicated what they had found and it is not even clear that there ever were investigators. When the director of the Hawaii state health department died in a plane crash, Trump tweeted that it was "amazing" that he died while others on the plane survived. He encouraged hackers to go after the president's college applications where, he suggested, the president's real, non-United States birthplace would be found. According to a count by ABC news, Trump tweeted his view about the president's birthplace sixty-seven times, spinning a tale of a giant conspiracy to keep the truth from the American people.[32]

As one writer put it, Donald Trump, "does not so much struggle with the truth as strangle it altogether. He lies to avoid. He lies to inflame. He lies to promote and to preen. Sometimes he seems to lie just for the hell of it. He traffics in conspiracy theories that he cannot possibly believe

and in grotesque promises that he cannot \
out, he changes the subject—or lies larger."
lie hypothesis (or in Trump's case, perhaps tl.
is that more American voters viewed Trump a
than they viewed Clinton—this despite the fac
checkers found many fewer factual errors or lie
than in Trump's. As Hitler suggested, who would b
could be so "impudent" as to lie so obviously and r

Although Trump did not have the political infrastr ...
fascism, he did employ some of the more unsavory tac. ...ose movements. He did not have an army of brown shirts, but the red hats that he and his followers wore served the same purpose. At his rallies, he singled out protestors in the audience, encouraged his followers to engage in violence against them, urging them at one time to rough up those who demonstrated against him and promised to pay their legal bills. He verbally attacked members of the media covering his campaign, with many of these journalists reporting that Trump supporters had harassed them physically and verbally. He suggested to the National Rifle Association that their only option for protecting their gun rights in the event that Hillary Clinton was elected was to engage in violence against judges and perhaps against Clinton herself, and several of his surrogates repeated that theme.

Finally, Trump's rise has paralleled a resurgence of nationalism in Europe, as reflected in the rising support, especially among less educated voters, for anti-immigrant parties in France, Germany, and Eastern Europe, and public discontent with the EU. Some of the same anti-immigrant attitudes that propelled Brexit in England, Marine Le Pen's National Front in France, and Victor Orban's Fidesz Party in Hungary are reflected in Trump's attitudes toward immigration in the United States. Trump endorsed the Brexit movement and one of its leaders, Nigel Farage, returned the favor by coming to the United States to endorse Trump. Both men cited their anti-immigration platform and their desire to "take back" their countries and their sovereignty. After he was elected, Trump made the gratuitous suggestion that the British appoint Farage as ambassador to the United States. Her Majesty's government was not amused.

Conclusion

Although analytically distinct, the concepts of charisma and demagoguery have this in common: both focus on the singular leader as the answer to individual and national problems. Both emphasize a personal bond between leaders and followers. Such a bond can be forged by a claim of extraordinary powers and a promise of strong leadership to deal with moments of crisis or with deep-seated citizen dissatisfaction with their own status or the state of the nation. It can also be forged by identifying s of complex problems, causes that focus on the nefarious of despised groups or on domestic or international conspiracies. e have been charismatic leaders who have forged a bond with their followers in more gentle ways—by projecting empathy with citizen concerns, identifying with the lives and problems of those with less, or simply by speaking eloquently and intelligently to the fears and hopes of the discontented. Populists can also address serious issues, such as income inequality, and they can connect and identify with the concerns of the disadvantaged. But there also are populists who seek support by playing the demagogue, appealing to the prejudices and emotions of the voter.

The calculus in regard to celebrities is a bit more complicated. Celebrities have a public persona, one often carefully curated by public relations representatives or established through the roles that they play in the entertainment industry. It is never clear, however, if the public persona is an accurate portrayal of who these people really are. Was John Wayne really the tough guy that he played in most of his movies and Tom Hanks the nice guy he plays in most of his? When Curt Schilling became a hero in New England for pitching the Boston Red Sox to a World Series victory, did anyone know or care about his far right views on political issues? It seems that many take celebrities at face value; what they see of these people on television is, they believe, what they will get. This allows voters to project their hopes onto the celebrity's public persona. Donald Trump is rich and famous, so he must know how to make us rich as well. Sarah Palin is a hockey mom, so she must know and empathize with the concerns of all suburban mothers. Mike Huckabee is a minister, so his politics should reflect the morality of his station.

The larger point is that the rise of celebrity candidates who have the ability to exploit the media and connect directly with the people has lowered the bar in regard to stature and experience as a qualification for the presidency. It may be that the presidency, the highest office in the land, has become something of an entry-level position. Barack Obama was an unlikely presidential candidate, given his nearly total lack of experience at the national level. As it turned out, the intelligence and demeanor that he displayed in office allowed him to perform reasonably well, although he would likely admit that having a bit more experience in national affairs before assuming office would have been helpful. In the case of Donald Trump, we have a candidate with no experience in politics at either the state or national level who has demonstrated neither the intelligence nor the demeanor that the office demands. Yet he won the Republican Party's nomination as well as the election against several candidates, many of whom had far more experience and policy intelligence. The question is whether Obama and Trump are simply blips or if something has fundamentally changed about the qualifications that we expect presidential candidates to have.

It may be that the saturation coverage of the presidency and presidential campaigns and the decisions by incumbents and candidates alike to traffic in celebrity-like interviews on late night television have demystified the office. This process began during the Kennedy administration. Here was a young president with a young wife and very young children. They made for great television. Mrs. Kennedy invited television cameras into the White House for a tour, and cute pictures of the president with his children appeared in the press. After the Kennedy administration, presidents and their families became much more accessible to the media, and the president came to be presented as an everyman, rather than an extraordinary person doing a very difficult job.

As one writer put it, "the modern chief executive must now be able to present a version of himself that is as audience-friendly as the persona of an entertainment star . . . In addition to his more solemn duties, the president of the United States is expected to perform the functions of a professional showman. . . . No longer does a president stand apart on a remote civic pedestal, isolated from the hurly-burly."[34] President Obama fully embraced this approach. "He has used to his advantage every possible venue and media outlet,"—networks, cable, daytime programs such as *The View*, talk shows hosted by Jon Stewart, Jimmy Fallon, and David Letterman, as well as Facebook and Twitter. "Through it all, he has projected an image of an unflappable leader, a nice guy and family man."[35]

There has always been a certain mystique about the presidency. The men who have occupied the office have been expected to exhibit a certain degree of gravitas, of dignity and seriousness about the office and its responsibilities. Attempts to present presidents and presidential candidates as regular guys undermine that quality and convey the implicit message that anyone can do the job. When Bill Clinton and Barack Obama decided to sit down on the couches of television hosts, they placed themselves on a par with the celebrities, like Donald Trump, who usually inhabited those precincts. It should not be surprising then that some voters drew an implicit equivalency of sorts between presidents and celebrities, contemplating perhaps for the first time, that the latter could do the job of the former.

Notes

1 This discussion of charisma closely follows Michael L. Mezey, *Presidentialism: Power in Comparative Perspective* (Boulder, CO: Lynne Rienner, 2013), chapter 6.

2 Reinhard Bendix, *Max Weber: An Intellectual Portrait* (Garden City, NY: Doubleday, 1962), 294.

3 Cynthia Emrich, Holly H. Brower, Jack M. Feldman, and Howard Garland, "Images in Words: Presidential Rhetoric, Charisma and Greatness." *Administrative Science Quarterly* 46:3 (2001), 527.

4 Murray Edelman, *The Symbolic Uses of Politics* (Urbana: University of Illinois Press, 1985), 6.

5 Bendix, *Max Weber: An Intellectual Portrait*, 300.

6 See Edelman, *The Symbolic Uses of Politics*, 77.

7 Gary Dickson, "Charisma, Medieval and Modern." *Religions* 3:3 (2012), 763.

8 William Kornhauser, *The Politics of Mass Society* (New York: The Free Press, 1959), 212.

9 Edelman, *The Symbolic Uses of Politics*, 76.

10 Erich Fromm, *Escape From Freedom* (New York: Holt, Reinhart, and Winston, 1941).

11 Edelman, *The Symbolic Uses of Politics*, 77–78.

12 Richard Hofstadter, *The Paranoid Style in American Politics and Other Essays* (New York: Alfred A. Knopf, 1965), 29–31.

13 Cas Mudde, "Conclusion: Some Further Thoughts on Populism." In Carlos de la Torre, ed. *The Promise and Perils of Populism: Global Perspectives.* (Lexington: University Press of Kentucky, 2015), 437.

14 Nadia Urbinati, *Democracy Disfigured* (Cambridge: Harvard University Press, 2014), 151.

15 Richard Fenno, *Home Style: House Members in Their Districts* (Boston: Little, Brown, 1976).

16 Pew Research Center, November 23, 2015. www.people-press.org/2015/11/23/1-trust-in-government-1958-2015/

17 Urbinati, *Democracy Disfigured*, 145.

18 Ruth Wodak, *The Politics of Fear: What Right Wing Populist Discourse Means* (London: Sage Publications, 2015), 125.

19 Kenneth T. Walsh, *Celebrity in Chief: A History of the Presidents and the Culture of Stardom* (Boulder, CO: Paradigm Publishers, 2015), 9.

20 Neil Postman, *Amusing Ourselves to Death* (New York: Viking, 1985), 135.

21 Graeme Turner, "Reality Television and the Demotic Turn." In Laurie Ouellette, ed., *A Companion to Reality Television* (New York: John Wiley, 2014), 313ff.

22 June Deery, "Mapping Commercialization in Reality Television." In Laurie Ouellette, ed. *A Companion to Reality Television* (New York: John Wiley, 2014), 18–20.

23 Douglas Kellner, "Barack Obama and Celebrity Spectacle." *International Journal of Communication* 3 (2009): 722. See also Mark Wheeler, *Celebrity Politics* (Cambridge, UK: Polity Press, 2013), 104–6.

24 John Street, "Celebrity Politicians: Popular Culture and Political Representation." *British Journal of Political and International Relations* 6 (2003): 440.

25 Postman, *Amusing Ourselves to Death*, 10.

26 Jonathan Martin, "Donald Trump's Anything-Goes Campaign Sets an Alarming Political Precedent." *New York Times*, September 17, 2016.

27 Eric Bradner, "Donald Trump: 'Our Country is Going to Hell.'" www.cnn.com/2015/07/14/politics/donald-trump-iran-republicans/

28 Christopher H. Achen and Larry M. Bartels, *Democracy for Realists: Why Elections Do Not Produce Responsive Government* (Princeton: Princeton University Press, 2016), 264.

29 Robert Kagan, "This Is How Fascism Comes to America." *Washington Post*, May 18, 2016. Also see Peter Baker, "Rise of Donald Trump Tracks Growing Debate Over Global Fascism." *New York Times*, May 28, 2016.

30 See Ronald Bailey, "Donald Trump and the Big Lie Strategy." http://reason.com/blog/2015/11/24/donald-trump-and-the-big-lie-stratagem; see also, http://www.jewishvirtuallibrary.org/excerpts-from-mein-kampf

31 www.politifact.com/personalities/donald-trump/

32 Ryan Struyk, "67 Times Donald Trump Tweeted About the 'Birther' Movement.'" http://abcnews.go.com/Politics/67-times-donald-trump-tweeted-birther-movement/story?id=42145590.

33 David Remnick, "Introducing a New Series: Trump and the Truth." *The New Yorker*, September 2, 2016.

34 Alan Schroeder, *Celebrity-in-Chief: How Show Business Took Over the White House*, (Boulder, CO: Westview Press, 2004), 3–4.

35 Walsh, *Celebrity in Chief*, 9.

8   Democratization and Presidentialism

There are several characteristics of our current political landscape that would have astonished the men who wrote the Constitution. Three are particularly relevant to our discussion. The first, of course, is the democratized presidential selection process, something that most of the Founders would have contemplated with undisguised horror. The second is the power and prominence of the federal government. Even men like Alexander Hamilton, who in his time favored a strong central role on financial matters, would have been surprised by a national government as deeply involved in issues such as health, education, housing, and social welfare and with the power to fund its operations by levying taxes on income. The third, a product of the first two changes, is the transformation of the American presidency from a relatively restricted office with limited powers to the dominant office in the land. On this issue, the Founders probably would have been divided. Hamilton made no secret of his desire for a strong executive who would provide energy for the government and ensure national security against foreign powers. His *Federalist Paper* co-author, James Madison, voiced his concern that the legislature was the more dangerous branch of the government, that it was an institution whose power needed to be checked, presumably by the president. But many others at the convention found it difficult to conceive of a strong executive that would not display monarchic tendencies, and a dominant presidency would have worried them.

The Transformation of the Presidency

The vague description of presidential power contained in Article II of the Constitution has been filled out by the precedent-setting actions of a succession of presidents, as well as by acts of Congress, that have expanded the authority of the office. These enhanced presidential powers are usually defended as an unavoidable necessity given the complexities of public policy and the realities of leading, governing, and protecting the modern nation-state. Whatever the justification might be, it is clear that American presidents have come to enjoy a capacity to influence and determine public policy that is well beyond the expectations of the men who designed the office. This transformation of the presidency has been driven by three factors: the expanding role of the national government, the increasing importance of international issues, and the democratization of the office.[1]

At the beginning of the 20th century, progressives argued that the federal government should play a role in dealing with social problems such as child labor, as well as establishing fairness in economic matters. These ideas accelerated during the New Deal with the passage of legislation providing, among many other things, for social security for widows, surviving children, and the elderly; regulation for the agricultural and banking sectors of the economy; and public works jobs to reduce unemployment. The movement toward an activist federal government reached a crescendo with Lyndon Johnson's Great Society initiatives. And with each new policy area that the federal government claimed some jurisdiction over, the federal bureaucracy expanded; new agencies were created or the mandates of existing agencies were broadened so that each of these new policy areas could be administered. A decision that the federal government should take some responsibility for the health of its people and the education of its children led to the creation of the Department of Health, Education, and Welfare, which later became the Department of Health and Human Services when education assumed its own departmental status. Legislation that made the goal of cleaner air and water a federal responsibility led to the creation of the Environmental Protection Agency.

As a result, the president, by virtue of his constitutionally specified role as chief executive, now presides over a federal bureaucracy comprised of more than 400 departments, agencies, and sub-agencies that employ nearly 2.7 million civilians and about 1.5 million uniformed military members. By comparison, the federal government employed about 53,000 civilians at the end of the Civil War, and 950,000 people at the outbreak of World War II. Because public policy has become more detailed and technical, many of the laws that Congress enacts are phrased in broad terms, typically specifying goals and providing the agencies with a great deal of discretion in developing the rules and regulations that give effect to the law. Presidents, through executive orders, can require an agency to take actions that they believe to be consonant with the law, or that are in pursuit of what they believe to be their unilateral power.

As the size and authority of the federal government increased, Congress gave the president the responsibility to construct an annual budget for its consideration. The White House staff was increased to provide the president with expertise on the multiple policy areas coming under the purview of the national government and with assistance in overseeing the activities of the expanded executive. To an increasing extent, Congress and the public looked to the president as the initiator of major policy proposals, and members of his staff became involved in drafting complex pieces of legislation for submission to Congress.

Although the Constitution was vague about the scope of presidential power, the Founders anticipated a more dominant role for the president in the international than in the domestic policy arena. The president is designated as commander in chief of the armed forces; he is charged with negotiating treaties with foreign countries and is empowered to appoint foreign ambassadors and to receive the credentials of the ambassadors appointed by other nations. In a series of decisions that he made during his presidency, George Washington effectively seized the power to determine the foreign policy of the United States, a power his successors expanded. And President James Polk, in the Mexican War, and President Lincoln, during the Civil War, established the principle that the role of commander in chief meant not just that they were in charge of the military during war time, but that they also had the unilateral right to deploy American troops, even without a declaration of war by Congress.

During the country's first century, the United States was not an international power. Secured by large oceans to its east and west, the country was, for the most part, isolated from the European and colonial wars that marked that period. But during the 20th century, the United States became involved in two wars in Europe and several conflicts in Asia. By mid-century, the United States was part of a complex series of alliances with countries around the world and a prominent participant in a number of international bodies. A standing military was established with soldiers and bases around the world, an enterprise that now accounts for an expenditure in salaries, supplies, and equipment that typically comprises about 20% of the country's annual budget outlays.

Today, the president's role as commander in chief allows him to commit American military might around the world for the protection of American lives or interests, to preserve the national security of the United States, or because the president wishes to support a friendly nation or intervene against a perceived enemy. In the post-9/11 world, Presidents Bush and Obama have assumed the right to use military force whenever they wish against a suspected terrorist, and in at least one case, a person who was an American citizen. The president's foreign policy role enables him to enter military and economic agreements with foreign countries, and diplomatic interactions with foreign leaders on economic and strategic concerns consume a large portion of his time and responsibilities.

Globalization, as reflected in multiple international trade agreements and in organizations such as the United Nations, the World Bank, and the International Monetary Fund, has elevated the importance of foreign economic policy. As the United States involved itself more deeply in the world, both militarily and commercially, and as the fiscal and banking systems of the world became more fully interdependent, the number of purely domestic issues began to decline and the number of policy areas with international dimensions to them increased. Today, immigration, trade, banking, environmental policy, cybersecurity, and terrorism are only a few examples of policy areas with both domestic and international components to them. Were these issues purely domestic, the president's claim for authority might be weaker, but to the extent that they are seen as international issues, the president's claim to power is strengthened.

Democratization and Presidential Power

There is a connection between this transformation in the power of the presidency and the democratization of the presidential selection process. In the three decades after the political parties eliminated the independent role of the Electoral College, presidents were nominated by their co-partisans in Congress through the congressional caucus system. Not surprisingly, these three presidents—Madison, Monroe, John Quincy Adams—proved to be largely subservient to the congressional majorities to whom they owed their office. Popular election, on the other hand, provided the president with a constituency independent of the Congress. Andrew Jackson was the first president to take advantage of this change, frequently citing his popular support as a democratic defense for the many controversial actions that he took. Three decades later, Lincoln justified the extraordinary powers that he assumed during the Civil War by citing his "rightful masters, the American people," rather than the Constitution or congressional authorization as the source of his authority. This was a reversal for Lincoln who, as a young Whig member of the House, had rejected such a theory of presidential power, arguing for congressional supremacy over the executive.

By the 20th century, presidents, as a matter of course, defended their exercise of power in democratic terms, as a reflection of the voice of the people. Theodore Roosevelt asserted an expansive and controversial view of presidential power, arguing that the president could do anything that was not specifically prohibited by the Constitution rather than only what was specifically authorized by the document. In justifying this position, he cited his responsibility as "steward of the people" to do all he could for the people, a responsibility that trumped a narrow reading of the Constitution's description of presidential power. Using his "bully pulpit," Roosevelt sought popular support for his view of the presidency and for his policies by going directly to the people, a practice that nearly all his 20th century successors followed.

The democratized selection process did not only provide a justification for an increase in presidential power; it also contributed to a central role for the president in American political culture. Today, the United States, as well as other countries with presidential systems, exhibits a broadly shared public perception that makes the president the focal point of the nation's politics and views him as the person primarily responsible for dealing with the challenges before the country. One leading scholar, speaking of Latin American presidencies but in terms that apply with equal force to the United States, summarized this phenomenon in the following terms: "The president is taken to be the embodiment of the nation and the main custodian and definer of its interests." The president is thought to be "the individual who is most fit to take responsibility for the destiny of the nation."[2]

This perspective is apparent in the manner in which American history is remembered by its citizens. The story is told in terms of great presidents and their accomplishments, almost as if no other institutions or leaders, or no contextual factors were involved. The names and events are familiar—Andrew Jackson and the creation of popular democracy; Lincoln, the Civil War and Emancipation; Franklin Roosevelt and the Great Depression, the New Deal, and World War II; Lyndon Johnson and the Great Society; and Ronald Reagan and the end of the Cold War. The area on and around the National Mall in Washington, DC, has memorials to Washington, Lincoln, Jefferson, and Franklin Roosevelt, and one to honor Dwight Eisenhower is in the planning stage. An island in the Potomac is named after Theodore Roosevelt, and the main airport for the nation's capital is named after Ronald Reagan. Around the nation, highways, airports, and schools bear the names of past presidents.

Children at an early age can name the current president (and probably no other office holder), and they are taught to memorize the names of his predecessors. When they move beyond reciting the names to learning something about past presidents, they generally receive a sugarcoated version of the man, a version that is often more myth than reality. They are unlikely to learn that George Washington did not cut down any cherry trees and probably told more than a few lies in his time in office. Jefferson will be discussed as an icon of republican liberty, and not as a slave holder, a double-dealing politician, and as we learned definitively in recent years, the father of several children conceived with one of his slaves. It's not at all clear that Lincoln was born in a log cabin—although Jackson probably was—and his unilateral actions during the Civil War, though arguably necessary to preserve the Union, set a precedent for some of his successors to act in violation of the Constitution if they thought that national security demanded it. Franklin Roosevelt, thought to be the 20th century's greatest president, ordered the confinement of Japanese Americans in detention camps for the duration of World War II, a part of his legacy usually elided in popular accounts of his presidency.

The mass media accords more attention to the presidency than to any other political institution, and as we have seen, for nearly a two-year period, presidential campaigns receive wall-to-wall coverage by cable and network television outlets, as well as the various internet and social media sites. Coverage of presidential campaigns far exceeds that accorded to congressional elections and certainly state and local election contests.

As a result, presidential elections are characterized by greater interest and higher voting turnout than any other American election.

Popular expectations for the welfare of the nation and for the satisfactory performance of its political system focus on the presidency, often to the exclusion or at least the marginalization of other public officials and political leaders. When the American people were polled one week before Barack Obama's inauguration in 2009, more than 80% believed that their new president would work effectively with the Congress and that he would manage the executive branch wisely, 79% pronounced themselves optimistic about the next four years under President Obama, and overwhelming majorities said that Obama would be a good president, that he would bring real change to Washington, and that he would make the right decisions on the economy, Iraq, the Middle East, and protecting the country from terrorist attacks. At the same time, 78% of the population reported that they had a favorable opinion of Obama, with only 18% reporting an unfavorable opinion.[3]

All this was remarkable given the fact that Obama had prevailed in a tough, often bitter, election campaign, winning just under 55% of the popular vote. Equally remarkable was that the popular belief in Obama's abilities to deal with all these challenges seemed to be largely a matter of faith rather than a reasoned assessment based on past performance. After all, Obama had served only two years in the United States Senate prior to announcing his candidacy for the presidency, and before that, his only government experience had been as a rank-and-file member of the Illinois state legislature.

This nearly blind faith in the capacity of our presidents has something to do with the fact that they are the political descendants of the great presidents of the past, men whose presidencies have been accorded a near mythic quality. In other words, we believe in presidents because we have been taught to do so. But our faith in a new president also has much to do with how they campaigned for office. In our era of populist, often demagogic, appeals to voters and the charismatic disposition of candidates during their campaigns to emphasize their extraordinary qualities and abilities, presidential candidates promise the stars and the moon to citizens. They campaign almost entirely in the first person singular, their oratory promising major changes that will follow directly from their election. Candidates talk about what they will personally do, ignoring the fact that there are policy areas that are generally controlled by states and localities and that there are a limited number of things that they actually can do without the agreement of Congress, or the Supreme Court, or even the bureaucracy that is under their ostensible control. And they minimize or even ignore the fact that there are various foreign actors and economic forces over which they can exert little or no influence. Their campaigns are notable for the simple solutions that they offer for complex problems, for the soaring rhetoric of the best orators, and for the dearth of achievable policy specifics. Rather, campaigns seem designed to evoke personal trust from the voters, trust that is built on the ability of the candidate to identify and connect with the voters and their concerns.

The result is that voters are encouraged to believe that by electing a president, they can change their world. Their need to believe this becomes even more palpable when they are convinced that the nation is facing a crisis. Then, they are especially vulnerable to the appeals of a charismatic candidate who offers himself and his special powers as the savior who can rescue the country from disaster. The demagogic candidate is more polarizing, more disposed toward conspiracy theories, and often more apocalyptic, identifying particular groups or countries or cultural forces that are responsible for the crisis, arguing the necessity for immediate action against these enemies, and offering his strong leadership as the only way to eliminate these threats. Populist candidates often do the same thing; although some will traffic in the prejudices of the demagogue, for the most part they concentrate their fire on the larger economic and cultural elites that they assert are responsible for the looming disaster. And when crises or government failures cause a turn against politics and a wholesale rejection of the current governing class, as they sometimes do, an opening is provided for celebrity candidates with little or no experience in government. It also provides an opening for more established politicians, such as governors, who have had no experience in national politics or on the international scene, but nonetheless claim that they have the ability to "clean up the mess in Washington." All these candidate types raise public expectations for their presidency to unreasonably high levels. And all, inevitably, will disappoint those who have supported them.

Constraints

In some countries, power is allocated in a way that allows presidents to meet the expectations of the voters and fulfill most of the promises that they made, but that is not the case in the United States, where power is dispersed among a number of different institutions and actors with the express intent of frustrating unilateral actions on the part of office holders. The transformation in the scope of presidential power may have weakened some of these constraints, but they certainly have not disappeared. Congress can modify or even reject the president's budget, ignore his policy proposals, and refuse to approve his nominees for judicial and executive positions. This is especially the case when presidents must contend with one or both chambers of Congress controlled by the opposition party. The federal courts can nullify a presidential decision that they view as contrary to the law or the Constitution, as they did with President Trump's early executive order restricting travel to the United States from several Muslim nations. And despite the greater presidential powers in foreign and defense policy, he cannot control the actions of other countries nor the response of the public, the press, or Congress to what he does in the international arena.

Even the bureaucracy can frustrate the president's attempts to bring it under his control, despite his constitutional role as chief executive. Because of its size, both in terms of employees and agencies, it can be difficult for the president and his aides to even know, let alone control, what is happening in each corner of the bureaucracy. Because the bureaucracy houses long-serving experts in their policy area, they usually know more than the president and his people do. Rather than the president controlling the bureaucracy, presidents become dependent on the bureaucracy for this expertise. Finally, the president's control of the bureaucracy is limited by the fact that most employees are civil servants whose jobs are protected by law so that they cannot be removed if their political views are different from those of the administration. While the president's term in office is limited, bureaucrats are part of the permanent government; most were there before the president arrived in office, and most will be there after he leaves.

As a result of these constraints, all presidents experience policy disappointments during their time in office. For Obama, these included his inability to close the detention facility at Guantanamo and a failure to get Congress to act on gun control, the minimum wage, climate change, or immigration reform, or any of a number of initiatives designed to address the needs of the urban poor. His predecessor, George W. Bush, failed to get reforms of social security and other entitlements and also failed to advance his own proposals on immigration reform.

How Presidents Respond to Constraints

Once the constitutional and other real world checks on their powers become apparent, presidents can react in two ways. One approach is to accept the constraints, abandon or modify their more controversial promises, and try to work within the system to seek compromises where one can with other actors and branches of government. An alternative approach is to act unilaterally in order to achieve what cannot be achieved through the constitutional system. Successful presidents usually combine these approaches, negotiating when they must and acting unilaterally when they can.

The first approach is the one envisioned by the Founders. They hoped that their system of interlocking checks would produce moderate policies borne of the compromise that a system of separate institutions sharing power necessitated. They assumed that if compromises could not be reached through negotiations, it had to mean that the policy proposal was a bad or dangerous idea. However, the negotiating approach may well be alien to the new type of candidate that the democratized selection process produces. For the charismatic and the demagogue, compromise is not a viable option. After all, he has trumpeted his unique set of special powers that supposedly equip him, and only him, with the knowledge of what the right answers are. So, by definition, others who disagree with him are wrong and therefore should not be accommodated. The demagogue has constructed a world of enemies and dark conspiracies, so to compromise with these forces is unacceptable to him and to those who follow him.

It may be comforting to think of the demagogue as someone who stirs up hatred simply as a way to get elected but who is at heart a more moderate person who really doesn't believe most of what he said during the campaign. Having accomplished his electoral goal, the hope is that a more moderate president will emerge. It may be just as comforting to think that the charismatic leader is simply pulling a con job on his followers. He knows that he has no special powers and no easy solutions; rather, he simply has to convince the voters to believe in him. Once in office, the hope is that he will revert to a normal sort of politics. In Obama's case, once in office a more "normal" politician did emerge, one who recognized that public policymaking was more complex than a campaign based on hope and change suggested and who worked hard, though not always successfully, to achieve consensus. It is too early to tell whether this also will be the case with Donald Trump, although the early signs from his first weeks in office were not encouraging.

But even if normal governance once these people are elected does come to pass, there are still significant risks for the body politic. The demagogue, who it turns out did not really mean it, has opened wounds and divisions in the society which no amount of post-electoral moderation will cure. The charismatic who turns out not to be that special or gifted, or the populist who cannot deliver on his promise to tear down the walls of economic privilege, will have raised and then disappointed the hopes of those who voted for them. Having been promised that their enemies will be vanquished and that their problems will disappear, voters will expect this to happen, and when it doesn't, the result is a population even more alienated from their political system than they were before they turned to such a leader.

Barack Obama's administration exemplifies the dangers of the charismatic candidate. Having run a campaign on the theme of hope and change and inspiring so many to believe that a new politics would emerge from his election, his moderation once in office and his willingness during his administration's first two years to negotiate with his opponents proved disheartening to many of his more ardent followers. His failure to achieve all that he had promised—in fairness, due in large measure to the unwillingness of Republicans in Congress to compromise with him—contributed to the alienation that helped produce Donald Trump in 2016.

In the days after Trump's victory, the newspapers were full of stories of people who voted for him in the belief that he would bring the factories and jobs that had gone overseas back to the industrial heartland and that he would restore the coal industry and coal miners to their former status in society. Others believed that the Affordable Care Act would be repealed but that they would still be able to get affordable coverage, even if they had pre-existing conditions. And still others believed that more than ten million undocumented individuals living in the country illegally would be rounded up and deported. And some believed that he would simply be a strong leader and that strength, as ill-defined as that concept might be, would be sufficient to solve our national problems without doing damage to their own interests or to the constitutional system.

The same newspapers, however, were full of stories indicating the improbability of Trump delivering on these promises. Factories were not coming back and some that had announced that they were leaving claimed that Trump's election would not alter their plans.[4] Coal was not coming back, no matter how many EPA regulations were gutted, as the country turned to cheaper, cleaner, and abundant natural gas as well as various non-fossil fuel alternatives. Trump appointed a cabinet top heavy with billionaires whose records in the private sector did not display a particular empathy for workers and others at the lower end of the economic scale. And in regard to Obamacare, after six years in operation, 20 million people who had been previously uninsured were now covered, and health care providers, employers, and insurance companies made major adjustments to adopt to the requirements of the law. Repealing it, though legislatively easy, would be incredibly disruptive to an economic sector that accounted for 20% of the gross national product. Replacing Obamacare with a new law that would ensure that those newly covered would continue to be covered at prices that they could afford would prove to be challenging. And in the days immediately following Trump's victory, talk of a deportation force that would round up people illegally in the country disappeared to be replaced by a policy to deport undocumented people who were members of violent gangs—a policy already in force under the Obama administration.

In sum, presidents who succumb to the constraints of the real world imposed by the constitutional system and multiple independent actors, domestically and internationally, run the risk of increasing the alienation of a citizenry. They feed the narrative that politicians say one thing when they are campaigning and do something different after they are elected, and in doing so, they encourage a turn against democratic politics and its politicians. Ironically, such an attitude leads voters to a search for a new savior, someone who can break up the established patterns of political and governmental behavior. Many voters who chose Barack Obama in 2008 because he promised change did not vote in 2016, voted for Bernie Sanders in the Democratic primaries, and even for Donald Trump in the general election because, they said, Obama did not bring the change that they had hoped he would.

Unilateralism

A second option for a president whose promises and priorities have been frustrated by constitutional and political realities is to attempt to expand their powers and to act unilaterally. Presidents do so first because it is in the nature of an office holder to seek to aggrandize his power so that he can have a greater influence on events, and, second, because they wish to provide themselves with the capacity to meet the inflated public expectations that our presidential history, as well as their presidential campaigns, have fostered. As presidents seek to expand their power, they employ their rhetorical skills, amplified by electronic technology, to encourage popular support both for their policies and for enhanced presidential power. They engage in what scholars have called a permanent campaign, in the sense that once in office they continue to devote a great deal of their own and their staff's time to communicating with the public and soliciting their support. The campaign never stops; it simply changes its focus from generating votes to generating policy support and high levels of presidential approval. Jeffrey Tulis notes that the permanent campaign in effect replaces the framers' intent to establish a healthy distance between the president and the public by a de facto "second constitution" that "puts a premium on active and continuous presidential leadership of popular opinion."[5]

In the weeks after his inauguration, Trump continued his use of Twitter, every day sending out attacks on his critics along with self-congratulatory messages to the more than 23 million people who follow him on this platform. In one of his tweets four years before he ran for president, when he had about two million followers, he said that "It's like having your own newspaper," an accurate reflection of the decline of newspapers and the rise of the media. His tweets regularly provide his version of political events, often varying sharply from undisputed facts as reported by mainstream journalists. Whether by tweet or oratory, presidents proffer a decidedly democratic argument for this activity. It is important, they say, to generate popular support for them and for their policies, even if to do so they need to use half-truths, or even lies; after all, that is what got them elected. If these efforts succeed, they can assert that they and what they wish to do represents the will of the people. Therefore, deference to the president and to his agenda is required if his, and by extension the people's, policy goals are to be achieved.

Because presidential powers are so vaguely defined in the Constitution, presidents have been able to interpret the document to provide a justification for taking unilateral action when they have been stymied by other institutions. President Obama took a number of such steps in regard to undocumented residents when Congress proved unwilling to act. Young people who had come to the country as children (so-called "dreamers") were given legal status via executive order. Obama also ordered an expansion of this program to family members, although that step was put on hold by the federal courts. When Congress refused to pass legislation protecting gay citizens from employment discrimination, an executive order from the president prohibited the federal government from doing business with any company that did not offer such protections. Similarly, when Congress refused to pass an increase in the minimum wage, he issued an executive order requiring federal contractors to pay their workers at least $10.10 an hour. When Obama wanted to secure an agreement with Iran and with other world powers to halt Iran's nuclear program, he did this through an executive agreement rather than a treaty so that the Senate would not have to act on it.

The temptation for a president to take unilateral actions may be irresistible. It would not be surprising if they come to believe in their own monopoly on truth and wisdom, having repeated it so many times to the voters to whom they have made so many promises. Presidents tend to discount congressional resistance as partisan, and they become impatient because they know that their time in office is limited. One study of executive orders suggests, not surprisingly, that presidents are more likely to act unilaterally when Congress is gridlocked or when Congress is poised to act in a manner opposed by the president.[6] Often, a president's supporters will urge him to take unilateral action, ignoring the fact that once a president of whom they approve takes such action, the precedent is there for a subsequent president whose views they may disagree with to take similar action. Democrats who did not perceive presidential overreach when Barack Obama issued executive orders have been appalled when Donald Trump has done the same thing.

Unilateral actions on the part of the executive, no matter what the policy reason for it, carry substantial risks to the political system. At the extreme, a tyrannical executive can make arbitrary decisions about what the law is, can decide to implement it in an unfair or even brutal manner, and can avoid being held to account for his actions. Such a person could assume not just the role of executor of the law, but also the roles of determining what the law is and judging the guilt or innocence of those charged with violations, tasks that modern political systems typically assign to non-executive agencies, such as legislatures and judiciaries. Like Machiavelli's prince, such a despot would not be simply above the law; he would embody the law. The great task of constitutional government, as it arose during the period of the Enlightenment, was to constrain the discretionary power of such a prince by requiring his actions to conform with the law and by identifying institutions, such as parliaments and courts, that would be beyond his control and would be in charge of deciding what the law is and whether or not it was being applied fairly.

This concept of a constitutionally constrained executive is threatened by the direct ties between the president and the population that came about through the democratization of the electoral process and the fragmentation and democratization of the electronic mass media. The omnipresence of presidential candidates, as well as presidents, has resulted in the personalization of government and politics, an increased emphasis on charisma rather than demonstrated competence, on rhetoric rather than deeds, on image rather than substance, and on the passions evoked by demagogues and populists rather than moderation and reason. This concentration on the presidency encourages many citizens to think of the president and the government as one and the same thing. Presidential candidates emphasize their own commitment and ability to bring about needed change, implicitly marginalizing constitutional niceties and the roles of the other political institutions and actors with whom they will need to work, and minimizing the intractability and durability of many of the problems before the country.

In challenging or difficult times and in times of danger or crisis, people are especially inclined to turn to the president for leadership, protection, reassurance, and answers, and in return they are often willing to accept broad discretionary presidential power. Not surprisingly, during war time and other international threats, the disposition of citizens to support enhanced and perhaps extra-constitutional presidential power increases. The political institutions that are supposed to constrain executive power tend to be overwhelmed by such a public mood; at the extreme, executive power can come nearly full circle, back to the original model of unconstrained prerogatives—the untamed prince, but this time, a prince whose power is legitimized by his democratic claim and verified by election results so that he represents the voice and the will of the people.

The most obvious risk associated with this possibility is that highly personalized leadership in which substantial power, formal and informal, comes to reside in the hands of the president can lead to an authoritarian political system. In such an environment, political decision-making becomes more centralized, and legislative voices become more marginalized; civil society in the form of interest groups, non-governmental organizations, and the media become intimidated, and dissent, along with other basic civil liberties, are put at risk or restricted. Presidents who believe that they represent the will of the people, that they have widespread popular support, and that the destiny of their nation is in their hands may be less tolerant of those in the mass media or among their political opponents who disagree with them. Inevitably, it is argued, such presidents will seek to control the judiciary and the media, harass their political opponents, deploy the financial and law enforcement resources of the state to their political and electoral advantage, and, if they think it is necessary, exceed existing constitutional limitations on their power.

In 1973, in the wake of Vietnam and Watergate, the historian Arthur Schlesinger, Jr. wrote of "the imperial presidency."[7] He worried that the increasing concentration of power in the hands of the American president had transformed the energetic but constrained executive that the framers had created into something akin to an elected emperor. These virtually

unlimited powers seemed to Schlesinger to be most apparen
cially dangerous in the area of foreign and defense policy, and
potentially be used to expand the president's power in the don
beyond the limited role anticipated in the Constitution. Befo~~re the peo~~-
ple decide to accept expanded presidential power in order to deal with
a crisis or to accomplish needed systemic change as rapidly as possible,
they would do well to consider the possibility that this power will remain
with the presidency, even after short-term policy goals are achieved. As
we noted, the emergency powers that Lincoln discovered during the Civil
War and used to emancipate the slaves remained to be used by Franklin
Roosevelt during World War II to imprison Japanese Americans.

Schlesinger's prophecy seemed to be verified in the wake of the September 11th attacks. At the time, President Bush said that in the war on
terror "one of the most critical battlefields is the home front."[8] That view
provided the White House with justification for a number of intrusions
on the civil liberties of Americans, as well as for his decisions, reflected
in his signing statements, to ignore various congressional actions that he
asserted would impede his efforts to fight terrorism. Bush proceeded on
the assumption that the president was utilizing his constitutional authority as commander in chief to protect the nation, and therefore, whatever
he did in this respect was by definition within his constitutional powers, and congressional or even judicial attempts to limit his actions were
therefore unconstitutional. Vice President Dick Cheney suggested that
these domestic manifestations of the president's commander in chief role
would likely become a permanent part of American life—what he called
"the new normalcy."[9]

The threat of presidential unilateralism is further enhanced by the rise
of the bureaucratic state under the formal control of presidents and the
exponential increase in the volume and reach of government rules and
regulations that emanate from the executive. Because neither legislatures nor courts have the expertise, time, or inclination to review each
of the decisions made under the statutes from which these rules derive,
there is a legitimate concern that excessive power is now in the hands of
the bureaucracy and, by extension, the president. In the United States, the
predominantly procedural approach that the judiciary has taken to the
task of reviewing the application of federal statutes and regulations suggests that the courts will intervene only when formal administrative procedures have been violated or if the decisions in question can be viewed
as contrary to the Constitution. If neither of these conditions apply, the
general rule has been to defer to the substantive content of agency decisions and, therefore, to the president.[10]

Conclusion

The growth in the size and power of the federal government and the
increasing importance of the international arena has created a much

stronger presidency than the Founders had imagined. This transformed presidency is legitimized not by constitutional adjustments and only in part by legislation, but primarily by a fully democratized selection process that enables presidents to claim that their exercise of broad powers represents the will of the people. The centrality of the presidency to the consciousness of the American public and the democratized selection process have combined to inflate the expectations that citizens have for the presidency. The charismatic candidates, the demagogues, the populists, and the celebrities that the democratized system encourages make extravagant promises that raise the hopes and expectations of those who vote for them.

But despite their enhanced powers, what presidents can actually accomplish will and must disappoint these expectations. That is because the campaigns that candidates now run, with their emphasis on their own special qualities and their mostly unachievable plans to change the lives of their followers, elevate expectations beyond the capacity of any president, no matter how gifted he might be, to meet. It is also because the constraints on presidential power have not disappeared and the political window in which they can achieve real change is small. There are two possible results from this state of affairs, each as unappetizing as the other. The one that we have the most experience with is compromise or deadlock, resulting in disillusionment and alienation on the part of citizens who are continually disappointed by the gap between what they were promised and what they have received.

The other is presidential authoritarianism. A president, frustrated by his inability to deliver on what he promised, or simply by his inability to do what he wishes to do, can resort to extra-constitutional or unconstitutional steps that weaken the political system and have the potential to lead to a more authoritarian approach to governing. In that context, it is well to recall Hamilton's warning about those politicians who "pay an obsequious court to the people, commencing demagogues and ending tyrants." Hamilton voiced his fear of a tyrant with a democratic mandate when very few people were allowed to vote and when the presidency that he created was highly constrained. His warning is much more compelling in the contemporary context of universal suffrage, a democratized mass media that provides politicians with instant access to voters, and a presidency with much greater power than Hamilton or his colleagues could have imagined.

Notes

1 See Michael L. Mezey, *Presidentialism: Power in Comparative Perspective* (Boulder, CO: Lynne Rienner, 2013), chapter 1.
2 Guillermo O'Donnell, "Delegative Democracy." *Journal of Democracy* 5:1 (1994, January): 59–60.

3 Adam Nagourney and Marjorie Connelly, "Polls Find Faith in Obama, Mixed With Patience." *New York Times*, January 18, 2009. www.gallup.com/poll/113824/Obama-Wins-83-Approval-Rating-Transition.aspx; This and the following paragraph are from Mezey, *Presidentialism*, 1–2, with permission from Lynne Rienner Publishers, Inc.

4 Andrew Tangel, "Companies Plow Ahead With Moves to Mexico, Despite Trump's Pressure." *Wall Street Journal*, February 8, 2017.

5 Jeffrey K. Tulis, *The Rhetorical Presidency* (Princeton: Princeton University Press, 1987), 18.

6 William G. Howell, *Power Without Persuasion: The Politics of Direct Presidential Action.* (Princeton: Princeton University Press, 2003), 17.

7 Arthur Schlesinger, Jr., *The Imperial Presidency* (Boston: Houghton Mifflin, 1974).

8 Quoted in Benjamin A. Kleinerman, *The Discretionary President: The Promise and Peril of Executive Power* (Lawrence: University Press of Kansas, 2009), 2.

9 Ibid., 3.

10 See Mezey, *Presidentialism*, 108–9.

9   The Perils of Democracy

Democratic political systems are predicated on the assumption that the people are capable of ruling themselves either directly or by selecting office holders who are capable of governing in the name of the people. The central concern of this book goes to the heart of that assumption as it relates to the American presidency. Simply put, is our now fully democratized process for selecting presidents compatible with the need for a president who is well prepared for the position by virtue of intelligence, education, experience, and temperament? Can democratic elections be depended on to produce a president who is up to the challenge of leading a nation as large, complex, powerful, and diverse as the United States, or is there an inherent tension, or even inverse relationship, between democratic selection and candidate merit?

This is not a new question. Plato, who was at best skeptical about democracy's capacity to produce good government and virtuous leaders, suggested that the whole business of governing might be turned over to philosopher-kings. Max Weber thought that elected politicians would not have the necessary expertise to understand and deal with the problems and challenges of the modern nation-state.[1] Tocqueville condemned American democracy's "depraved taste for equality" that discouraged its citizens from accepting the authority of experts and instead created a bias toward mediocrity.

This tension between democratic procedures and governing competency was central to the Founders' decisions about presidential selection. They wanted to ensure that the presidency would be held by a person highly qualified by virtue of experience, intellect, and stature, someone who would be able to stand above partisan politics, who would be immune to the influence of public opinion, and who would advocate and act for the public interest. They believed that to the extent that ordinary citizens were involved in the selection process, there would be less likelihood that a candidate who measured up to these standards would be selected.

To reduce the influence of voters, the Founders designed a complicated presidential selection system that placed the decision in the hands of electors who would have, at most, an indirect connection with a very restricted electorate. The electors themselves would be selected by state legislatures and were therefore likely to be men of stature. As noted in Chapter 3, with the electors choosing the president, Hamilton thought that the office "will never fall to the lot of any man who is not in an eminent degree endowed with the requisite qualifications." Although a person with "talents for low intrigue, and the little arts of popularity" might win a local or statewide election, "it will require other talents, and a different kind of merit, to establish him in the esteem and confidence of the whole Union . . . to make him a successful candidate for the distinguished office of president of the United States."[2] When the Electoral College ceased to be an independent body, the selection of the president moved, in effect, to Congress through the congressional caucus system. That too was an elite body, so a disposition toward the selection of someone with stature, experience, and intellectual ability could be assumed.

Initially, the system seemed to work as the Founders had hoped. The first six presidents, each selected by either the independent Electoral College or Congress, all met Hamilton's requirements. Washington, Adams, Jefferson, and Madison were themselves prominent Founders and men of national stature. Washington, in the view of the men who wrote the Constitution, was the presidential prototype—the man who had won the Revolutionary War and presided over the Constitutional Convention, and a person of demonstrated leadership abilities who was esteemed throughout the country and admired for his moderate nonpartisan temperament. His three successors were among the great thinkers of the founding period, the authors of seminal commentaries, statutes, and documents that are still read and cited today. James Monroe and John Quincy Adams, although not quite in the same league as their four predecessors, were well prepared for the office by virtue of their experience in government; both had been senators and had served terms as secretary of state.

But after these first six presidents, the British statesman James Bryce observed that the quality of America's presidents had declined. In his book *The American Commonwealth*, written toward the end of the 19th century, he offered an explanation for "Why Great Men are Not Chosen President." There were several reasons, he thought, for the elevation of mediocre talent to the presidency, but the main one was that the selection process was dominated by party leaders who privileged political considerations over the educational background and governmental experience that, in his view, characterized great men. He thought that such men might be viewed as poor candidates because they would likely have made too many enemies during their careers, or because their history, their personality, or the section of the country from which they hailed would render them unlikely to win. Bryce, like Tocqueville, saw this aversion to great men as a byproduct of America's democratic culture. The American voter, he said, "does not object to mediocrity. . . . He likes his candidates to be sensible, vigorous, and, above all, what he calls 'magnetic,' and does not value, because he sees no need for, originality or profundity, a fine culture or a wide knowledge." Those who select the candidates at the party conventions, though "expert as party tacticians, are usually commonplace men; and the choice between those selected for nomination is made by a very large body, an assembly of nearly a thousand delegates from the local party organizations over the country, who are certainly no better than ordinary citizens."[3] And, of course, under our current procedures, it is exactly these "ordinary citizens" who choose the nominee through the primary and caucus system. If Bryce was correct then, now we should be even more disposed against the selection of "great men."

The usefulness of Bryce's analysis is limited a bit by his somewhat dated concept of "great men" and by his implicit assumption that such men would make great presidents. Bryce's criteria for greatness reflected the nature of the times in which he wrote, a time of much greater social stratification than is now the case. Then, access to the type of education that would produce the intellectual skills that he valued so highly was restricted to a select few, and access to the offices that would provide the best experience for the presidency was similarly restricted. And history has taught that predicting who would be a "great" president before he ascended to the office can be difficult. When historians rank American presidents from the greatest to the worst, Lincoln is usually found at or near the top of the listings. But Lincoln's pre-presidency career consisted of only two years in the United States House of Representatives and eight years in the Illinois State Assembly. He had no formal education and became a lawyer simply by reading the law. By the standards of the Founders and Bryce, Lincoln would not have been an obvious choice for a great president. And Andrew Jackson, despite the educational, temperamental, and intellectual deficiencies that so revolted Tocqueville, usually makes the top ten in rankings of great presidents because of his role in democratizing the American political system and enhancing the power and the prominence of the presidency.

As we evaluate the qualities of presidential candidates, it is probably useful to discard the "great man" concept and speak in more modern meritocratic terms, focusing on people who are well prepared for the presidency by virtue of their personal characteristics and their experience in government, people who, in other words, have demonstrated a capacity to meet the challenges of the position. And the point of our discussion is that Bryce's view, reflecting those political thinkers from Plato to the Founders, is that the more democratic the selection system, the less likely that such a person will come to occupy the office.

Bush, Obama, and Trump

Beginning with the presidential election of 2000, we now have three instances of people ascending to the presidency who were ill prepared for the office, especially when their qualifications are compared with those of the people they bested. Although it is too early to say how the presidencies of these three men will be remembered, it is not too early to say that George W. Bush, Barack Obama, and Donald Trump are examples of the perils of the democratic selection process that the Founders feared and that Bryce assessed so negatively. Both the Obama and Trump campaigns, in different ways, reflected the dual impact of the new nomination process and the new media environment on the manner in which parties select their presidential candidates. Their campaigns underlined the heightened focus on charisma, populism, and celebrity and, in Trump's case, pure demagoguery, as a means to winning the presidency. Bush and Obama, although men of quite different temperaments and intellectual abilities, are examples of candidates with very little previous governmental experience who were able to reach the highest office in the land. And even their modest resumes were much stronger than Donald Trump's, by far the least experienced and informed candidate to ever become president.

Although the Bush candidacy is not usually thought of in terms of celebrity, his early name recognition and visibility can be attributed to the fact that he was the son of a former president. This counted for a great deal in light of his obvious lack of knowledge and experience at the national level, a deficiency that stood in marked contrast to that of his very well-prepared father. The Bush name helped him to defeat other candidates for the Republican nomination who were much better prepared than he was for the presidency, especially Senator John McCain. And in the general election, he defeated Al Gore, a candidate whose record and abilities closely fit the expectations for the office that Bryce and the Founders articulated. Ironically, Bush's older brother, Jeb, a much more knowledgeable leader than his brother George, failed in his 2016 quest for the Republican nomination, in part, because he seemed to be too cerebral, too moderate, and unable to connect with the Republican primary and caucus electorate.

In Obama's case, he exploited the celebrity status derived from his 2004 convention speech, as well as his estimable rhetorical skills to defeat several candidates for the Democratic nomination who were much better prepared for the presidency by virtue of their experience in national office. In addition to Hillary Clinton, the 2008 field included two long-serving senators, Joe Biden of Delaware and Christopher Dodd of Connecticut, as well as Bill Richardson, who had served seven terms in the House, was UN Ambassador and Secretary of Energy during the Clinton administration, and after that, a two-term governor of New Mexico.

Obviously, these three presidents constitute a small sample from which to draw generalizations, and there were certainly idiosyncratic factors involved in their victorious campaigns. But as we made clear earlier, the changes in the nomination process that enabled these three successful candidacies reach back decades, and there were indications, even then, that the new process would affect the sort of people who would become nominees. However, it wasn't until the end of the 20th century that we saw how the impact of the new media environment would combine with the new nomination process to open the door to the presidency to people from disparate backgrounds, many with extraordinarily weak claims to the credentials that the Founders and Bryce thought presidential candidates should possess. And lest we think of these credentials as outmoded ideals of previous centuries, it would seem to be a matter of simple common sense that the American presidency should not be an entry level position, that it is not a job that just anyone can do, and that educational background, policy knowledge, and demonstrated governing skills should be a requirement for those applying for the job. This argument should be even more compelling given the vast unilateral powers that the transformed presidency has come to possess. It is a perverse irony that the qualifications for becoming president have decreased as the powers and the responsibilities of the office have increased.

Although we cannot address the question of whether the opening that the new selection process provides for less prepared candidates necessarily produces poor presidents, we can ask whether the system favors those who the Founders thought might be dangerous men. Aside from their not insignificant worry about a president who had neither the experience nor the intellect to hold the office, they believed that it would be dangerous to have a president who followed public opinion rather than led it, or a president who opted for short-term solutions at the expense of the long-term national interest. Equally dangerous would be populist candidates and presidents who sought to advance themselves solely by playing to the class interests of the multitude, ingratiating themselves with the public through folksy rhetoric, or with the ability to project empathy with the problems of the common man—"paying obsequious court to the people," as Hamilton put it. And most dangerous of all were candidates, as well as presidents, who took on the role of demagogue, appealing to the passions, prejudices, and fears of the people rather than to their reason, their sense of community, and their hopes. Unfortunately, all these dangers are inherent to democratic politics, the unavoidable perils of a fully democratized selection process in which the person who gets the most votes from a very broad electorate is awarded the office.[4]

These perils can be reduced to the extent that the electorate is composed of politically aware and informed citizens who value experience and intelligence, understand that what is popular is not necessarily wise, appreciate the fact that short-term fixes may create long-term problems, know that a friendly demeanor can mask incompetence or even malevolence, and are aware of the dangers of making voting decisions based on one's passions and prejudices rather than one's reason and on one's fears rather than on one's hopes.

Unfortunately, there is little in the vast literature on public opinion and voting behavior to suggest that ideal democratic citizens of this sort constitute anywhere near a majority of the American voting public. Frankly stated, most Americans know virtually nothing about government and the public policymaking process. They focus most of their attention on their private lives—their families, their values, and their economic well-being. They live their lives in the short term, seeking to meet their immediate economic needs and gratify their psychic needs for pleasure and enjoyment. They pay relatively little attention to the long-term challenges before the nation or to the great political and policy issues of the day, most of which they do not understand and over which they believe they can exercise no control. Most are episodic citizens who, if they focus on politics at all, do so primarily during election time, or when there is an easy to understand issue that involves them directly. At best, they respond to an inchoate and not very informed sense of whether things are going well or poorly for themselves or for the country at large. And when deciding whether and for whom to cast their votes, they are more likely to be aroused by the passionate rather than the thoughtful candidate, the new and different rather than the old and familiar, and by the candidate who, for whatever reason, they have come to believe best understands them and their needs. Clearly, passion, novelty, and a capacity to empathize are qualities that can attract votes, and they also can be relevant to successful governing. But just as clearly, these are not the only or even the most important factors that voters should consider as they make their decision about who should govern.

It is therefore not surprising that many of the dangers of popular selection that the Founders worried about have become part of the modern presidential selection landscape. In addition to inexperienced candidates, there has been little evidence that we have had candidates willing to think or campaign on long-term rather than short-term issues or candidates able to lead public opinion rather than respond to what their pollsters tell them about public opinion. Telling voters what they want to hear, rather than what they need to hear, is standard operating procedure in an electoral environment where gaining the most votes is the name of the game and there is no prize for coming in second. Saying that the issues that we face are difficult and complex and that there are no easy pain-free answers is not the secret to a winning presidential campaign. As Donald Trump demonstrated, saying that the answer to the challenges of immigration are to build a wall and deport several million people is an acceptable, though fantasy-based position. As Barack Obama demonstrated, the mantra of hope and change was enough to inspire voters, especially during an unpopular war and a collapsing economy. And George W. Bush invented something called "compassionate conservatism" as a way to assure voters that his proposals to cut taxes on the rich and reduce government spending would not hurt anyone.

Candidates oversell their ability to accomplish what they say they will and emphasize what they view as their own special qualities rather than the collective policymaking processes associated with constitutional government. Taking full advantage of the absence of gatekeepers in the new media environment, candidates establish direct ties with their supporters, purveying their own version of the truth, and finding support from media sources, many of which have, at best, an ambivalent relationship with the facts. Candidates who arouse the enthusiasm of the electorate are advantaged, and it doesn't matter if they succeed in doing so by employing the tools of demagoguery, the simplistic solutions of populism, the public persona of the celebrity, or the time-honored technique of vilifying their opponents. Abetted by the insatiable hunger of cable news, social media, and websites for viewers and clicks, all these techniques, from the most to the least reprehensible, provide an avenue to success, even if they have little or nothing to do with an ability to, as the presidential oath says, "execute the office of president."

Modest Changes to the Current System

There are some problems with the current process that can be ameliorated with modest steps. Although they would be mostly at the margin, some might decrease the likelihood of poorly qualified candidates emerging and others would address other problematic features of the current system.

One possibility is to reduce the number of convention delegates selected in caucuses and primaries and increase the number of delegates who are party leaders in the manner of the current super-delegate arrangement that the Democratic Party uses. This would provide party leaders with the opportunity to assess the quality of the candidates who emerged from the primary and caucus system and eliminate those candidates who they find personally or politically unacceptable. In a sense, the primaries and caucuses might return to their original role—as vehicles for demonstrating the preferences of the voters rather than as vehicles for determining the nominee. Delegates to the convention would accord serious attention to the results of these primaries and caucuses, but they would also consider a number of additional factors as they decided on a nominee. But even this modest proposal would be viewed as contrary to democratic values, just as Bernie Sanders argued that the role that the super-delegates now play in the Democratic Party was undemocratic.

One frequently advanced proposal is to consolidate the state primaries and caucuses into four events that would take place over a shorter period of time. Several variants of that plan have been proposed, each calling for different methods of grouping the states and sequencing the primaries.[5] The advantage of such a system is that it would require aspiring candidates to appeal to a larger and more diverse electorate rather than to smaller, more homogeneous state electorates and thereby reduce the influence of the most ideological primary votes. Such an arrangement would mean four campaigns rather than fifty campaigns, and it would eliminate the outsized attention that the current system accords to Iowa and New Hampshire. It would reduce the influence of the media in terms of declaring winners, losers, and leaders after each state primary or caucus. And if the parties decided to reduce the number of debates among their candidates, perhaps to one before each primary, the media influence might be further diminished. Condensing the primary season could also shorten the length of the entire presidential campaign. No other country in the world has such a lengthy selection process for either its president or its legislative chamber, in the case of parliamentary systems. The American process, as we have observed, is essentially a two-year marathon. Highly qualified people may be discouraged from participating because the process is so long, tortured, and expensive, because they need to slight their commitment to their current positions, or because the toll that the process takes on their health and their families is too high. Because the process dominates news coverage for so long, it also contributes to the unreasonable elevation of expectations for the president.

Some have gone a step further, arguing for a nationwide primary that would determine the nominee, with all states voting on the same day. This would do away with the convention's formal decision-making role because the national primary would produce the party's nominee. It would liberate the candidates from the complexity of dealing with fifty plus state campaigns, reduce the impact of special statewide interests, and probably reduce the influence of the party's hard-core base. It might mean less voter exhaustion than the current system seems to induce with a new winner each week. And it might also reduce the impact of the media, which would focus on one election rather than on the current seemingly endless series of primaries and caucuses, each producing its own winner and loser.

The most important critique of this proposal is that it exacerbates the problem of candidate quality and approach. With a national primary, dangerous demagogues and unprepared celebrities are likely to have even more of an advantage than they have under the current system. A nationwide primary can be conducted almost entirely on television. Appeals to the emotions and prejudices of the voters will be incentivized, especially in a primary environment in which there are no real policy differences among the candidates. Such a step may well increase the cost of the nomination process, as aspiring candidates seek to raise the funds for what amounts to an all or nothing nationwide primary. And because the nationwide primary will likely result in no candidate receiving a majority of the vote, there would have to be either a runoff among the top two finishers or a second election that would eliminate the requirement that the nominee receive a majority of the votes.

The practical problem with this reform, like the regional primaries suggestion, is whether the state parties and their state legislatures would be willing to give up their individual systems and submit to a nationwide procedure. Certainly, Iowa and New Hampshire would resist, given their commitment to what they view as their first-in-the-nation entitlement. There would also have to be some agreement on whether voting would be restricted or not to registered members of the party and how such a provision could be enforced, given the control that states exercise over voter qualifications. The main problem, however, is that this change would further weaken the role of the party by making the nomination process even more democratic than it is now, with all the perils we have discussed, in terms of candidate quality and the types of campaigns that they would run.

Alternatively, a national primary could coexist with the convention. If candidates receive delegates to the convention in proportion to the vote that they receive in the national primary and no candidate receives a majority—the likely result with no incumbent in the field—then the delegates would have to negotiate at the convention to produce a consensus candidate. Such a process could weed out a candidate like Trump, who might receive a plurality in the primary, but whose delegates would be a minority at the convention. One other suggestion is to have the convention before a national primary, much as Connecticut does when it nominates candidates for statewide office. There, if a candidate does not achieve the nomination at the convention but does attain 15% of the convention vote, he or she is free to challenge the convention nominee in a primary. Such a change at the national level might make the restoration of the convention system more palatable, providing a democratic check on the possibility that party leaders might slight a candidate with at least some level of popular support.

Resurrecting the Convention

It is possible for a party to decide to abandon state primaries and caucuses entirely, and return to a convention system with attendees selected in any manner that it wishes. Minor parties in the United States, such as the Libertarian and Green parties, regularly nominate their presidential candidates in this manner. Nothing would prevent the Democratic and Republican Parties from doing the same. Attendance at the convention could be designed to afford the interest groups, donors, and activists who constitute the extended party with a voice in the decision. The result would be a restoration of the party's ability to designate its nominee, presumably one more fully vetted as to his or her credentials and capabilities than is the case with the current system. The party would actually confer the nomination on its candidate rather than having it seized by a candidate who may or may not be qualified or in concert with the party's positions on the major issues. The nomination process would be more condensed, candidates would have no reason to engage in the demagogic and populist rhetoric that the prolonged process now all but guarantees, and the party could truly decide on a candidate who could conciliate its different factions, rather than relying on the murky and uncertain mechanism of the "invisible primary" that scholars have put forth as the saving grace of the current system. The result would also be a closer connection between the president and his party, with a collective partisan responsibility for policy successes as well as failures, rather than personal presidential responsibility.

A step such as this would undoubtedly encounter strong resistance from an American public that has been told for so many years that they are the ones who should decide who will be the major party candidates. But if we are to begin to address the problems of the presidential selection process, political parties need to be viewed, at least in part, as private organizations. As such, they should be able to exercise control over their procedures, particularly those governing the selection of their leaders and their nominees. The American Association of Retired People and the National Rifle Association are, like political parties, organizations that have a great deal of influence on American public policy. But no one would suggest that the leadership of these groups should be selected by the American people in a popular vote. Yet there is an assumption that the presidential nominees of the two major political parties, but not minor parties, need to be determined by the votes of those who decide to participate in primaries and caucuses.

It is important to remember that the open procedures that the parties now utilize are for the most part the result of decisions that the parties themselves have taken. Although some of these decisions have been incorporated into state laws, this took place largely at the behest of the parties, and presumably, such laws could be modified at their request. At the national level, the only rules that have been imposed by the courts are those governing discrimination against participants based upon judicially protected factors, such as race, gender, and religion. While these restrictions certainly apply to voting in primaries, it is not entirely clear how or if they would apply to delegate selection procedures that do not involve voting.

Although it may be difficult to imagine such a step being taken, retaining the current system means accepting all the chaos and irrationalities associated with it, as well as its vulnerability to candidates who have neither the experience nor the temperament nor the intellect for the presidency. Of course, there will be resistance. Popular participation is a pervading ethos in the United States, and many will resist such a move, simply as a reflexive defense of democracy. Those voters who now exercise so much control over the nomination process are not likely to be pleased by a decision by party leaders to claw back their control. The Democratic Party's capitulation at their 2016 convention to the demand of Sanders supporters to reduce the independence of the so-called super-delegates is not a good sign for those who advocate even modest steps toward increasing party control. The success of Donald Trump's campaign for the nomination over the nearly unanimous opposition of the Republican Party leadership suggests that President Trump and his people will have little interest in reducing the role of voters in the nomination process.

The democratized media environment, especially the broadcast and cable networks, would also resist, given the advantages that the current system affords them in terms of viewers. It is important to remember that the decline in the party's control over its nomination process has coincided with the rise of the media's influence. The democratized media environment and the open nomination process means that candidates no longer need the party or its leaders to run a successful campaign. Media industry leaders and the reporters and commentators they hire, as well as the legions of bloggers selling ads for their sites, will surely attack a proposal to restore the conventions with high-minded defenses of democracy, but they may well fail to note that such a change also has the potential to do damage to their balance sheets.

Bring Back the Parties

As we have seen, Bryce was critical of the role of political parties in the nomination process, describing the party leaders who determined the nominee as ordinary men and, therefore, no better equipped than ordinary citizens, in terms of their ability to make a wise presidential selection. But that was not the case. The party leaders who assembled at the national conventions when those bodies actually designated the nominee may not have been the intellectual and social aristocrats whom Bryce would have preferred, but they were political and governmental professionals. As a group, they were certainly more informed about politics and government than the ordinary voter; therefore, they would have a better idea of the qualities and qualifications a person aspiring to the presidency should possess. Of course, their decisions were heavily affected by their desire to select a candidate who could win the presidency, but as they searched for such a winner, they tended to choose from among qualified people and ignore those who were manifestly unprepared to be president.

When the parties controlled the nomination process, there were people who were thought of as "presidential timber." This category included incumbent vice presidents and cabinet members, widely respected senators, and successful governors of large states. It would be difficult to imagine a party-dominated system producing a presidential candidate such as Donald Trump, a person with no experience in government or politics, with no apparent knowledge of how government works, and with a penchant for hurling crude insults at his opponents, even members of his own party. It would be almost as difficult to imagine a party-dominated system selecting a young African American with a very brief tenure in the Senate as its nominee, no matter how impressive his intellectual and rhetorical skills. This is not to say that the party-dominated system always picked extraordinary men as their nominees or that what was always foremost in their minds was whether or not the candidate would make a great president. But certainly, the delegates were in a position to recognize the deficiencies in experience, knowledge, and temperament that should disqualify someone from the presidency—in other words, to distinguish between the contenders and the pretenders. Our current arrangements make it very difficult for the parties to play this discriminating role.

The most important step that can be taken to improve the quality of our presidential candidates is to restore the role of the political parties in deciding who their nominees will be. Such a step could also draw the parties and their presidential candidates closer together. When Obama and Trump are able to seize their party's nomination and win the general election with their own campaign organizations, their own rhetorical styles, and with their own funds (in the case of Trump) or with their own fund-raising prowess (in the case of Obama), they are likely to view their victory in personal rather than partisan terms. This will lead to a personal presidency run largely by the people who got him elected, with weak connections and coordination with the party under whose banner the president ran. The president and his people will be more concerned with the president's level of popular support and his record of success and failure than with the party's reputation and future prospects.[6]

Barack Obama left the presidency with a relatively high level of public approval, but with a Democratic Party in a much weaker position than it was when he came into office. Entering 2017, Democrats are a minority in Congress, for the last six years in the case of the House and the last four years in the Senate. They hold the governorship and majorities in both houses of the legislature in only six states (for the Republicans, the figure is twenty-five). Six of the states where power is divided between the parties have Republican governors. As Donald Trump moves through his presidency, it doesn't take much imagination to predict that he and his advisors will be more focused on his reputation and his accomplishments than on the fortunes and future of the Republican Party.

Aside from a return to a convention system, none of the more modest changes in the nomination process—regional primaries, a national primary, adding more super-delegates—really go to the heart of the problem, and, if the argument of this book is to be taken seriously, many of those reforms amount to rearranging the deck chairs on the Titanic. Tinkering with the nomination process still means that issues of candidate competency and policy differences would be relegated to a minor role compared with the personality and campaign style of the candidates. The tools of populism and demagoguery would still be available, the quality of the campaign discussion is not likely to be elevated, and it is unlikely that any new procedures would produce a more informed electorate. Although the role of the media might change with some of these proposals, the ability to do well in the new media environment would still be a critical factor, if not in the nomination phase of the selection process, then certainly in the general election phase. The media's vulnerability to manipulation by the most provocative candidate, and its disposition to focus on the sensational rather than the substantive and on personalities rather than capabilities, would remain.

This returns us to the conundrum at the heart of the popular selection process. No matter how one tinkers with the selection process, if we operate on the premise that the broader public needs to decide who their presidential candidates will be, then the problem of citizen information and their vulnerability to the "vicious arts" by which elections are contested remains, a situation that the media environment will continue to contribute to rather than mitigate. It is difficult to increase citizen information when the media message is that all facts are in dispute. It is difficult to talk about candidate qualifications when the media coverage will, like the moth to the flame, be drawn to personalities and celebrities. When the bottom line for cable and network news programs is the number of viewers they attract, celebrity candidates, as well as candidates with outsized personalities, will receive more than their fair share of attention. An entertainment media environment that encourages crass behavior, crude language, and no-holds-barred sporting events will continue to provide a fertile ground for populist and demagogic candidates who tailor their appeal to the lowest common denominator among the potential electorate.

In the race to the bottom for votes, the modern mass media is a willing and enthusiastic participant and we are eager consumers. And the peril of our democratic selection system is that the qualities of our presidential candidates and our presidents will, to an increasing degree, come to reflect this race to the bottom. Donald Trump's selection as the Republican Party nominee and his electoral vote victory in the general election suggests that we have arrived at the bottom. The question is whether or not we are destined to stay there.

Notes

1 Reinhard Bendix, *Max Weber: An Intellectual Portrait* (Garden City, NY: Doubleday, 1962), 423–430.
2 *The Federalist Papers* (New American Library edition, 1961), Number 68:414.
3 James Bryce, *The American Commonwealth* (London, 1888), http://oll.liberty fund.org/titles/bryce-the-american-commonwealth-vol-1.
4 Again, the capacity of the Electoral College to frustrate the will of the voters, as exhibited in 2000 and 2016, is noted, as is the caution that although the Founders intended the Electoral College as a means to frustrate the wishes of

the people, the examples of 2000 and 2016 were not the way in which they planned for that to happen.

5 Elaine C. Kamarck, *Primary Politics: Everything You Need to Know About How America Nominates Its Presidential Candidates*. 2nd ed. (Washington, DC: Brookings Institution, 2016), chapter 7. In a recent paper, Kamarck argues for enhanced "peer review" for presidential candidates which could take the form of introducing super delegates to the Republican process, a pre-primary endorsing convention, or a pre-primary "vote of confidence" from party leaders. See Elaine C. Kamarck, "Re-inserting peer review in the American presidential nomination process." Washington, DC.: The Brookings Institution, April, 2017.

6 See Theodore J. Lowi, *The Personal President* (Ithaca, NY: Cornell University Press, 1985).

Bibliography

Abramowitz, Alan I. and Steven Webster (2016) "The Rise of Negative Partisanship and the Nationalization of US Elections in the 21st Century." *Electoral Studies* 41: 12–22.

Achen, Christopher H. and Larry M. Bartels (2016) *Democracy for Realists: Why Elections Do Not Produce Responsive Government.* Princeton: Princeton University Press.

Aldrich, John H. (2011) *Why Parties: A Second Look.* Chicago: University of Chicago Press.

American Enterprise Political Report (2016) *Assessing the 2016 Candidates* 12:10, November.

Arendt, Hannah (1965) *On Revolution.* New York: Viking Press.

Atkeson, Lonna Rae and Cherie D. Maestes (2016) "Presidential Primary Turnout, 1972–2016." *Political Science & Politics* 49(4): 755–760.

Baker, Peter (2016) "Rise of Donald Trump Tracks Growing Debate Over Global Fascism." *New York Times,* 5/28/16.

Barber, Benjamin R. (1984) *Strong Democracy: Participatory Politics for a New Age.* Berkeley: University of California Press.

Baumgartner, Jody C. and Jonathan Morris (2011) "Stoned Slackers or Super-Citizens: *The Daily Show* Viewing and Political Engagement of Young Adults." In Amarnath Amarasingam, ed. *The Stewart/Colbert Effect: Essays on the Real Impact of Fake News.* Jefferson, NC: McFarland and Co., Inc.

Bendix, Reinhard (1962) *Max Weber: An Intellectual Portrait.* Garden City, NY: Doubleday.

Binkley, Wilfred E. (1962) *American Political Parties: Their Natural History.* 4th. Ed. New York: Alfred A. Knopf.

Brennan, Jason (2016) *Against Democracy.* Princeton: Princeton University Press.

Brown, Campbell (2016) "Why I Blame TV For Trump." *Politico Magazine,* May/June.

Bryce, James (1888) *The American Commonwealth.* London: McMillan and Co.

Caplan, Bryan (2007) *The Myth of the Rational Voter: Why Democracies Choose Bad Policies.* Princeton: Princeton University Press.

Ceaser, James W. (1979) *Presidential Selection: Theory and Development.* Princeton: Princeton University Press.

Cillizza, Chris (2016) "Early Leads in '20 Race, But No Clear Democratic Heir." *The Washington Post,* 11/28/16.

Cohen, Marty, David Karol, Hans Noel and John Zaller (2008) *The Party Decides: Presidential Nominations Before and After Reform.* Chicago: University of Chicago Press.

Converse, Philip E. (1964) "The Nature of Belief Systems in Mass Publics." In David Apter, ed. *Ideology and Discontents.* Glencoe, IL: Free Press.

Deery, June (2014) "Mapping Commercialization in Reality Television." In Laurie Ouellette, ed. *A Companion to Reality Television.* Sussex, UK: John Wiley and Sons.

DeSilver, Drew (2016) "Turnout Was High in the Primary Season, But Just Short of the 2008 Record." *Pew Research Center,* 6/10/16. www.pewresearch.org/fact-tank/2016/06/10/turnout-was-high-in-the-2016-primary-season-but-just-short-of-2008-record/

De Tocqueville, Alexis (1981) *Democracy in America.* New York: The Modern Library.

Edelman, Murray (1985) *The Symbolic Uses of Politics.* Urbana: University of Illinois Press.

Emrich, Cynthia, Holly H. Brower, Jack M. Feldman, and Howard Garland (2001) "Images in Words: Presidential Rhetoric, Charisma and Greatness." *Administrative Science Quarterly* 46(3): 527–557.

Enten, Harry (2016) "Trump May Have More to Gain From the First Debate than Clinton." http://fivethirtyeight.com/features/trump-may-have-more-to-gain-from-the-first-debate-than-clinton/

Farrand, Max, ed. (1966) *The Records of the Federal Convention of 1787.* Volumes 1 and 2. New Haven: Yale University Press.

Fenno, Richard (1976) *Home Style: House Members in Their Districts.* Boston: Little, Brown.

Frank, Reuven (1988) "1948: Live . . . From Philadelphia . . . It's the National Conventions." *New York Times,* 4/17/88.

Fromm, Erich (1941) *Escape From Freedom.* New York: Holt, Reinhart, and Winston.

Gayo-Avello, Daniel (2015) "Social Media, Democracy, and Democratization." *IEEE Multimedia* 22:2, April–June: 10–16.

Graber, Doris (2001) "Adapting Political News Top the Needs of Twenty-First Century Americans." In W. Lance Bennett and Robert M. Entman, eds. *Mediated Politics: Communication in the Future of Democracy.* Cambridge: Cambridge University Press.

Hamilton, Alexander, James Madison, and John Jay (1961) *The Federalist Papers.* With an introduction by Clinton Rossiter. New York: Mentor Books.

Hofstadter, Richard (1948) *The American Political Tradition.* New York: Vintage Books.

Hofstadter, Richard (1965) *The Paranoid Style in American Politics and Other Essays.* New York: Alfred A. Knopf.

Howell, William G. (2003) *Power Without Persuasion: The Politics of Direct Presidential Action.* Princeton: Princeton University Press.

Isaac, Max Isaac (2016) "Facebook in the Cross Hairs after Election, Is Said to Question Its Influence." *New York Times,* 6/12/16.

Iyengar, Shanto, Helmut Norpoth, and Kyu S. Hahn (2004) "Consumer Demand for Election News: The Horserace Sells." *Journal of Politics* (February) 66(1): 157–175.

Kagan, Robert (2016) "This Is How Fascism Comes to America." *Washington Post*, 5/18/16.

Kamarck, Elaine C. (2016) *Primary Politics: Everything You Need to Know About How America Nominates Its Presidential Candidates*. 2nd. Ed. Washington, DC: Brookings Institution.

Kellner, Douglas (2009) "Barack Obama and Celebrity Spectacle." *International Journal of Communication* 3: 715–741.

Kleinerman, Benjamin A. (2009) *The Discretionary President: The Promise and Peril of Executive Power*. Lawrence: University Press of Kansas.

Kondik, Kyle and Geoffrey Skelley (2015) "A Brief History of Presidential Primary Clashes." www.centerforpolitics.org/crystalball/articles/eight-decades-of-debate/

Kornhauser, William (1959) *The Politics of Mass Society*. New York: The Free Press.

Kurland, Philip B. and Ralph Lerner, eds. (1987) *The Founders' Constitution*. Chicago: University of Chicago Press.

LeDuc, Lawrence (2015) "Referendums and Deliberative Democracy." *Electoral Studies* 38: 139–148.

Lippman, Walter (1946) *Public Opinion*. New York: Penguin.

Loss, Richard (1982) "Alexander Hamilton and the Modern Presidency: Continuity or Discontinuity?" *Presidential Studies Quarterly* (Winter) 12(1): 6–25.

Lowi, Theodore J. (1979) *The End of Liberalism: The Second Republic of the United States*. 2nd Ed. New York: W.W. Norton.

Luo, Michael (2008) "Small Online Contributions Add Up to Huge Fund Raising Edge for Obama." *New York Times*, 2/20/08.

McDonald, Forrest (1985) *Novos Ordo Seclorum: The Secular Origins of the Constitution*. Lawrence, Kansas: The University of Kansas Press.

McFadden, Robert D. (2009) "Paul Harvey, Homespun Radio Voice of Middle America, Is Dead at 90." *New York Times*, 3/2/09.

McGinniss, Joe (1969) *The Selling of the President, 1968*. New York: Trident.

Madison, James (1793) *Helvidius Papers*, #4. http://oll.libertyfund.org/titles/hamilton-the-pacificus-helvidius-debates-of-1793-1794, 84–89.

Mair, Peter (2006) "Ruling the Void? The Hollowing of Western Democracy." *New Left Review*, 42. 25–51. (November–December).

Manjoo, Farhad (2016) "How the Internet Is Loosening Our Grip on the Truth." *New York Times*, 11/2/16.

Mansfield, Harvey G., Jr. (1993) *Taming the Prince: The Ambivalence of Modern Executive Power*. Baltimore: Johns Hopkins University Press.

Martin, Jonathan (2016) "Anything-Goes Campaign an Alarming Precedent." *New York Times*, 9/18/16.

Meacham, Jon (2008) *American Lion: Andrew Jackson in the White House*. New York: Random House.

Meyer, Theodore (2012) "How Much Did Sheldon Adelson Really Spend on Campaign 2012?" *Pro Publica*, 12/20/12.

Mezey, Michael L. (1989) *Congress, the President, and Public Policy*. Boulder: Westview Press.

Mezey, Michael L. (2013) *Presidentialism: Power in Comparative Perspective*. Boulder: Lynne Rienner.

Michels, Robert (1968) *Political Parties: A Sociological Study of the Oligarchical Tendencies of Modern Democracy.* New York: Simon and Schuster.

Morris, Richard, ed. (1956) *The Basic Ideas of Alexander Hamilton.* New York: Washington Square Press.

Mudde, Cas (2015) "Conclusion: Some Further Thoughts on Populism." In Carlos de la Torre, ed. *The Promise and Perils of Populism: Global Perspectives.* Lexington: University Press of Kentucky.

Nagourney, Adam and Marjorie Connelly (2009) "Polls Find Faith in Obama, Mixed With Patience." *New York Times*, 1/18/09.

Neustadt, Richard (1980) *Presidential Power.* 2nd Ed. New York: John Wiley.

Nyhan, Brendan (2016) "Relatively Few People Are Partisan News Consumers, but They're Influential." *New York Times*, 9/7/16.

O'Connell, Michael (2016) "Political Ad Spending to Hit $11.7 Billion in 2016: Trump's Free Coverage Unprecedented." *The Hollywood Reporter*, 3/31/16 www.hollywoodreporter.com/news/political-ad-spending-hit-117-879699

O'Donnell, Guillermo (1994) "Delegative Democracy." *Journal of Democracy* (January) 5(1): 55–69.

Pitkin, Hanna Fenichel (2004) "Representation and Democracy: Uneasy Alliance." *Scandinavian Political Studies* 27(3): 335–342.

Polsby, Nelson (1983) *Consequences of Party Reform.* New York: Oxford University Press.

Poniewozik, James (2016) "Roger Ailes Fused TV With Politics, Changing Both." *New York Times*, 7/21/16.

Postman, Neil (1985) *Amusing Ourselves to Death.* New York: Viking.

Read, Max (2016) "Donald Trump Won Because of Facebook." http://nymag.com/selectall/2016/11/donald-trump-won-because-of-facebook.html

Remnick, David (2016) "Introducing a New Series: Trump and the Truth." *The New Yorker*, 9/2/16.

Roller, Emma (2016) "Everything I Learned from Professor Trump." *Washington Post*, 7/10/16.

Rousseau, J. J. (1968) *The Social Contract.* London: Penguin.

Saunders, George (2016) "Trump Days." *The New Yorker*, 7/11/16 and 7/18/16.

Schattschneider, E. E. (1960) *The Semisovereign People.* New York: Holt Reinhart.

Schumpeter, Joseph A. (1942) *Capitalism, Socialism, and Democracy.* New York: Harper and Bros.

Searles, Kathleen, Martha Humphries Ginn, and Jonathan Nickens (2016) "Here's Another Reason Not to Trust TV News Reports About Election Polls." *Washington Post*, 8/23/16.

Shklar, Judith N. (1987) *Montesquieu.* New York: Oxford University Press.

Sides, John (2016) "Here are 5 keys to Watching Monday Night's Debate Between Clinton and Trump." John Sides, *Washington Post*, 9/26/16. www.washingtonpost.com/news/monkey-cage/wp/2016/09/26/here-are-the-5-keys-to-watching-monday-nights-debate-between-clinton-and-trump/

Somin, Ilya (2013) *Democracy and Political Ignorance.* Stanford, CA: Stanford University Press.

Street, John (2004) "Celebrity Politicians: Popular Culture and Political Representation." *British Journal of Political and International Relations* 6: 435–452.

Taub, Amanda and Max Fisher (2016) "Why Referendums Aren't as Democratic as they Seem." *New York Times*, 10/4/16.

Trippi, Joe (2004) *The Revolution Will Not Be Televised*. New York: Harper Collins.

Truman, David (1951) *The Governmental Process*. New York: Alfred Knopf.

Tulis, Jeffrey K. (1987) *The Rhetorical Presidency*. Princeton: Princeton University Press.

Turner, Graeme (2014) "Reality Television and the Demotic Turn." In Laurie Ouellette, ed. *A Companion to Reality Television*. Sussex, UK: John Wiley and Sons.

Urbinati, Nadia (2006) *Representative Democracy: Principles and Genealogy*. Chicago: University of Chicago Press.

Urbinati, Nadia (2014) *Democracy Disfigured*. Cambridge: Harvard University Press.

Ward, Janelle (2013) "Exploring How Young People Use the Internet for Political Participation." In Richard Scullion, Ronan Gerodimas, Daniel Jackson, and Darren Lilleki, eds. *The Media, Political Participation, and Empowerment*. New York: Routledge.

Wayne, Stephen J. (2016) *Road to the White House 2016*. 10th Edition. Boston: Cengage Learning.

Weigel, David (2016) "Democrats Vote to Bind Most Superdelegates to State Primary Results." *Washington Post*, 7/23/16.

Wheeler, Mark (2013) *Celebrity Politics*. Cambridge, UK: Polity Press.

Williams, David Lay (2016) "Shadow Boxing and Pizzerias: Plato's Cave and Fake News." *Washington Post*, 12/13/16.

Wodak, Ruth (2015) *The Politics of Fear: What Right Wing Populist Discourse Means*. London: Sage.

Wood, Gordon (1969) *The Creation of the American Republic, 1776–1787*. Chapel Hill: University of North Carolina Press.

Zelizer, Julian (2016) "Why Donald Trump is the Next Walter White." www.cnn.com/2016/05/30/opinions/trump-as-tv-anti-hero-julian-zelizer/.

Index